Anne Hooper i
editor of *Forum*
specializing in
to a wide range
magazines. She
Clinic, a couns
of the London
women. The mother of two school-age children,
she is also involved in setting up a co-operative
housing association which builds homes
incorporating after-school and holiday care for
children living within the scheme.
As an international editor of *Forum*, Anne Hooper
has made many television appearances and has
broadcast across the United States and in England.

Also available in Mayflower Books

Edited by
Anne Hooper

More Sex Life Letters

Mayflower

Granada Publishing Limited
First published in 1977 by Mayflower Books Ltd
Frogmore, St Albans, Herts AL2 2NF

A Mayflower Original
Copyright © Forum Press Ltd 1973, 1974
Made and printed in Great Britain by
Cox & Wyman Ltd, London, Reading and Fakenham
Set in 9 on 10 pt. Times

INTRODUCTION

'Are the letters real?' As an editor of *Forum*, that is a question I am constantly asked. 'Do you write them yourself?' 'Are they complete fantasy?' An American television presenter even went so far as to accuse the magazine of employing three Hungarian midgets, whose job it was to sit all day composing erotic fiction.

The truth is that there is absolutely no need for midgets, since there is never any shortage of the most marvellous, poignant and factual readers' accounts that come flooding through the letter box every day.

We estimate that *Forum* receives at least 200 letters a week, some recounting erotic adventures, others plainly asking for help.

It's the letters that have always been the backbone of *Forum*, and to which we owe our existence.

Thirteen years ago, our parent magazine *Penthouse* was publishing, as it still does today, an Open Forum column. This section was so deluged with mail, much of it agonized and confused, that it was decided to found a second magazine based on these letters. Hence the genesis of *Forum* ten years ago.

Today, at least 50 per cent of *Forum* consists still of readers' letters, all of them 'genuine'. We have become adept at spotting the fakes. And of course, there have been many attempts to deceive us over the years.

For instance, we are in possession of 17 letters all purporting to be by different authors, from different addresses, but all written on the same notepaper in identical hand-writing with identical postmarks. They're pinned to the editorial noticeboard as a reminder of what shall not get past us.

'What about the fakes that aren't so easy to spot?'

Practice makes you familiar with the too easily turned phrase, the small slips that men sometimes make when pretending to be female correspondents, the experience recounted so outrageously that by no stretch of the imagination could it be true.

7

As, for example, the American letter from a reader with a brilliant streak of fantasy. He wrote about his escapades, driving around town with three naked girls in a car, which of course can, and occasionally does, happen. But when he went on to discuss his meeting with a police officer and his subsequent departure from the scene, complete with nude ladies, scot free, the police apparently refusing to bat an eyelid, we began to have our doubts – and doubts don't get published.

There are times when we suspect that a letter may be 'fantastic' but decide to publish it just the same. Our reason is that fantasy is a perfectly natural, indeed vital aspect of human sexuality. Hence our publishing a letter such as Cosmic Sex, where a male reader goes into raptures about 'fucking the universe'. It was a satire on the sort of erotic letter that can appear in our columns. But it was so funny and original that we were very happy to share the joke with our readers.

I had my doubts, too, about a letter where a husband was so hung-up on music that he could only perform sexually with some kind of melody sounding in his ears. Fair enough! But to the point where he employs a three-piece band to play inside the bedroom? We gave the enterprising husband the benefit of the doubt and printed (the rich can do strange things and there are a lot of swinging bands around).

Even the Adviser section, where we attempt to help readers with their problems, comes in for its share of amusing queries. Hence the case of a reader from Cornwall who asked the question. What happens to a man's sperm if he doesn't ejaculate?

'My query is: what happens to a man's sperm if he doesn't have orgasms or wet dreams? What happens to a good monk's sperm who doesn't masturbate or have wet dreams? Does the sperm go on being produced at the same rate? If it does and there is no release of this sperm, is it re-absorbed by the body, why doesn't the man just blow up with spermatozoa? Puzzled. Bodmin.'

The answer, incidentally, is that the body does re-absorb the sperm.

The Adviser section has probably done more to help people with sex problems, during the last ten years, than most members of the English medical profession.

The volume of cries for help increased so rapidly after the birth of *Forum*, that it became apparent that something more was needed than the anonymity of the printed column.

Hence the conception of the *Forum* Personal Adviser Clinic

five years ago, to carry through the counselling service that the magazine was already providing.

I myself read *Forum* five years ago when a friend gave me a pile of back copies. When I saw articles on such practical problems as 'women who can't climax' and 'marital infidelity' I was interested. But it was when I scanned the Open Forum and Adviser pages, meeting with such titles as 'a guide to oral love', 'she needs other men', 'how do lesbians do it?', 'smacking routine' and 'threesomes – can the male really cope?' (all in the same issue) that I was absorbed to the point of being re-educated.

It is the readers' revelations that have made the magazine a vehicle of this informational progress. It has been through the opportunity to learn about other people's problems that every reader has gained an insight into what makes his own emotional ups and downs.

Mrs S.D. of London, for example, has learnt to live with her husband's penchant for dressing in women's clothes. Hundreds of English wives, reading this, realize that they are not alone. It is here that the value of the letters becomes apparent.

Of course, there are limits. There was only one Hitler and one Moors Murderer; both were abnormal and both were horrible. The rule at *Forum* is that nobody has a right to interfere with what takes place between consenting adults which does not cause demonstrable harm to others.

It is not easy to be a pioneer. There are many conservative elements in English society that dislike and disapprove of us. Because we dare to publish the personal stories of our readers' sex lives, we come in for our share of persecution.

The following facts about *Forum* speak for themselves. The readers' letters are genuine (in our offices we have files full of them). When we published a *Forum* Sex Life Survey 10,000 asked for the questionnaire. When we called for volunteers to test a new serum designed to aid impotence, over 3000 males applied to take part.

G.P.s telephone us to ask our advice on what to do with patients who have sexual problems. Doctors use us as one of the best available methods of giving themselves a detailed sex education. (They write to us with queries about their nearest training facilities in problems of sexual dysfunction, and their patients are referred to the *Forum* Clinic.) The magazine is used as a means of therapy for people who have visited doctors, psychologists and the Samaritans for sex counselling.

I quote the remark of one G.P. from the Bristol area who

telephoned our office to ask where his nearest training hospital was so that he could bone up on sex therapy. 'I want to carry on where *Forum* leaves off.'

It has become fashionable for television channels to feature sex problems. Recently, in the space of two months, *Forum* has advised five projected programmes, and members of the staff have appeared on a further three.

Authors, whose books range from serious treatises on sexual dysfunction to film scripts on lesbians in love, telephone us when they need specific information about their subject.

The Times, in a full-page review of our work, concluded that *Forum* was 'a social service' from which everybody would benefit by subscribing.

Forum has become a clearing-house for sexual information, sensual case histories, erotic problems. It has lived up to its apt title.

In this book we are publishing an exclusive index of *Forum* letters. Certain sections are included because they are erotic and fun, others because they are informative, with medically detailed replies.

All these letters have been published in past issues of *Forum*. One of the most recent missives to come to our eyes, has *not* yet appeared in the magazine. It reads as follows:

FRIENDLY ANTS

When I was a boy of twelve, my mother bought me one of those science-fair-type ant farms. I found it only mildly interesting until one night something happened that wasn't in the instruction book. I went to bed thinking that the ant farm at the foot of my bed was locked and secure. But little did I know that my younger brother had been fooling with it earlier that evening.

During my sleep I dreamed that I was having my penis sucked by the most beautiful girl in the world. As I came in her mouth, I woke up realizing that I had come all over my sheets. As I lay there, awake, I could still feel a tingling sensation in my throbbing pecker. I reached up to turn on the light. Pulling back the sheets, I was horrified to see that my cock was almost completely covered with tiny crawling ants. I was frightened until I realized that it was the ants who were obviously responsible for making me come.

Since that time I have always had a supply of ant friends

10

close at hand. They come in quite handy on cold lonely nights, I just lie naked on my bed and pour the horny little critters all over my cock and let them do their act. They start off slowly but end up running up and down the entire length of my organ, throwing me into ecstatic fits of pleasure. I love to watch the little buggers shoot up into the air as 'Old Faithful' erupts. Sometimes I swear I can see them shaking with excitement as they reach their individual miniature climaxes.

I've made love to a lot of nice girls in my life, but nothing compares to my ant friends. Now, whenever someone asks me if I have ants in my pants, I just tell them, 'Don't knock it till you've tried it!'

C.A.,
New York

Genuine or fantasy? It goes without saying that if we publish it in the Open Forum it will be with a warning. *If* we publish it, that is!

ANNE HOOPER
Associate Editor
Forum

THE OPEN FORUM

The Open Forum exists to express our readers'
genuine opinions, experiences, criticisms and
interests on any aspect of human relations.

NUDIE MODEL'S FASHION HINTS

When I came to London five years ago, at 17, I tried to get a start at modelling. I soon discovered that the only way I could make a decent living at it was to go nudie. I was very shy and didn't know how to pose, but luckily most of the photographers had at least one lady assistant. In any case most of them were too busy taking pictures to have much time for sex and some of the best were female anyway.

Because I have very fair fuzz I didn't have so much shaving to do, but at first I always had to pose so that one hand cast a shadow there – a thing which always annoyed me. Then a change took place; I suddenly was asked to dye it so it would show up more! The days of the pubis had arrived.

More recently, I was again asked to shave it and adopt a one leg up pose more often – the day of the clit had arrived. Now I just shave near my labia and leave my fair tuft, so the photographers get the best of both worlds.

Some years ago another model remarked in the changing room, 'Do you still wear a bra? How do you get any sex life dressed up like that?'

She was right. Because I wasn't a fashion model, I hadn't noticed that nobody who was anybody fashion-wise wore bras. Certainly they turned men off three years ago just as do knickers today. I've given them both up now.

I am often asked to parties and because I have been featured in just about all the girlie magazines by now I'm quite an attraction. I usually wear a simple long dress, high-necked but flimsy enough to outline my nipples and crotch and slit. I usually can have my choice of man as this really gets them guessing. On the other hand, now that I can afford to go to work by taxi or in my MG, I usually go dressed only in my long fur coat. If I decide to get some clobber on my way home no one turns a hair in Kings Road when I step starkers from my coat. It does give the girls a start in the changing rooms in Oxford Street, and the straighter parts of London.

I haven't worn underwear for two years now and am still waiting for my tits to sag. (They get bigger and bouncier all the time.) I must say I go through a hell of a lot of paper tissues which I stick up when I get a bit creamy in case I spoil a dress, and have to use a bloody big matron's model tampon every few hours on the second day of my period.

The trouble nowadays is that you can go on a bus, sit sexily on a park seat, and (especially if your fuzz is the same colour as your sun-tan) even wearing a micro mini hardly anyone notices. Since so many girls wear minis and tights no one bothers to look nowadays.

Two things really seem to work at parties now – when wearing a long skirt wear a bolero with buttons open to swing aside to show a nipple or two when dancing, or wear a prim high-necked mini dress very short to show the pubic fuzz when one dances with one's hands above the head.

Lately, everyone seems to be letting underarm hair grow Continental-style.

Miss S.S.,
London

BRAS ARE ... POINTLESS

I am, I think, a normal fairly sexy schoolgirl. My tits didn't start to grow much before I was about 12 but when they did it was sudden and spectacular, and at 13 they were big enough to be quite proud of for a skinny girl like me.

My sensible parents never even suggested getting a bra, but by 14 my girlfriends were all commenting that I needed one, so rather than be odd girl out I got one. I didn't really enjoy being all pulled up, and only wore it to school. Like smoking and drinking and going on the Pill, I assumed it was part of the grown-up feeling and would be more pleasant as I got used to it. By the time I was 16 I had several bras, either very flimsy or rather loose ones, for my boobs still didn't take to being hauled up and out like an ice cream tray. I hadn't got used to it or got to like it at all.

Then I went to London for a holiday and noticed how few girls wore bras, while in Chelsea no one did, no matter how big their boobs or how see-through their blouses. So I said what the hell and back home dumped them at the back of my drawer with a sense of relief.

But I now had a 36″ bust with down pointing boobs sporting big dark aureoles and the trouble started. No school blouses were see-through-proof if my seat at school was at the window. Although strictly segregated for PE, the mistress stated it was indecent the way they bobbed about at basketball, and the points my nipples made on my singlet offended her, poor thing.

The Medical Officer at inspection told me I was ruining my figure for the future, and was annoyed when I pointed out they were bigger and firmer than ever. When sent for an X-ray, I was given a lecture by the radiographer lady about going topless, while they hunted around for one of those old X-ray bras it seems they used to use.

But every one of my boyfriends has insisted they very much prefer me braless, especially when dancing, as I really can move to the music.

When in my room swotting, or any time there is no one other than family in the house, I usually go topless with my jeans. My family think I am eccentric, but support me loyally. Elsewhere, when not in school uniform, I wear a singlet or clingy sweater, according to the temperature. For dancing I wear a backless halterneck or a low cut wrapover top.

So in spite of school troubles, at least my parents back me up. I will never willingly go back to bra-wearing and its discomfort. Most are now so flimsy they are useless for uplift on a girl of my shape anyway. All they do is make both boobs move together when one walks rather than bobbing alternately as is natural and more comfortable (less of a jolt).

Bras are probably the silliest of all girls' fashions ever to catch on. I notice that halternecks are all the fashion with my pals now who go braless at least when they go out on dates or dancing, even if their ruined breasts feel sore all the time after being bra'd-up all week. But I see that halterneck bras are now in the shops so the 'Mafia' is catching on quick!

I see you can even buy sleep bras – how stupid.

Miss T.Z.,
Cardiff

DRESSING DOWN THE YEARS

A bunch of us got to talking the other night about the new 'look' in dress and how we all think nothing of the near-nudity that would have been strictly verboten in public a few years back. It is really amazing, when you put it all together, how much change there has been in lifestyle as well as fashionstyle in the past several years. My own case is an example.

I'm now in my early 30s, have been married twice, divorced once, and am separated from my second husband and do not expect to go back to him or even to bother to divorce him. Instead I will continue as a contented single.

I started dating when I was 17 and virginal. I dressed in the conventional modest 1959 pattern. That is, I 'protected' my body from prying eyes with all of the following: a full slip with

16

a shadow panel for opaqueness in bright sun, a heavy cotton utterly unglamorous cover-up bra, droopy cotton underpants for everyday or opaque nylon panties for dates, a garter belt like a small girdle, and of course sensible semi-sheer nylons.

When I was dating my first fiancé I began to dress a little sexier. My slips were sheerer and my panties briefer and lacier. I am fairly heavy in the bust so I continued to wear quite matronly bras. I progressed to tinier and more beribboned garter belts and darker sheer hose. I felt very naughty flashing a length of bare thigh getting in and out of a car. My nights in bed with my man got me out of the habit of wearing a nightie or liking to wear one and I never wore one after we were married and haven't since. My husband bought me sexier bras from a mail-order house and persuaded me to eliminate panties altogether around the house.

Then came miniskirts, pantyhose and my divorce. I was 22 and dating once again and as my hemlines went up my half-slips got briefer and finally vanished altogether. I got a bang from showing off my buttocks and a nylon-sheathed crotch as often as I could. My pantyhose were always as sheer-to-the-waist as I could buy for dates, and later this became standard operating procedure for daytime wear too. I moved into underwired, front plunge bras, and for work I would wear dark bras that showed through a light dress or white blouse to 'advertise' a bit.

Eventually hemlines came down, but I have damn good legs and still love minis in the summer. I also went in for the slits and button-front skirts that left a lot of me peeking through. During my second marriage I began the 'daring' experiment of leaving my bra off, at first for evening wear then for informal occasions, and finally, four years ago, I gave up bras entirely. I hate having to wear a bra on the *extremely* rare occasions when I think I have to, and I admit I thoroughly enjoy the freedom and the *look* I have with my goodies joggling along in front. It is certainly the only way to fly.

During the past two years, I have been single and my necklines have plunged so that I am more than adequately exposed. The summer before last I had a gorgeous holiday in the Caribbean, was able to get a wonderful overall tan, and began dispensing with pantyhose when I returned to work. It felt delightful to feel the breezes frisking playfully up my skirts and around my thighs again, and I abandoned pantyhose almost altogether in favour, again, of sexy garter belts. I suppose my lingerie now weighs all of two ounces.

Meanwhile, of course, my swimsuits went the same route, from a one-piece knit with a half-skirt in 1958 to maillots to two-piecers to bikinis, smaller bikinis, smallest bikinis, monokinis and finally to strings this past summer. This has prompted a closer and closer trim of my pubic hair, so that I am now *quite* bare of that natural adornment.

With all this, I have never felt immodest or indecent. The normal list of paraphernalia required only 15 or 16 years ago — four items of underwear in two layers that every 'nice' girl wore — just isn't necessary any more. What a change in a few short years, and all for the better!

I'm sure the world will never go back to its former cover-up complex and false modesty and that the trend towards less clothing will continue and probably accelerate. I only wish men would hurry up and follow the trend a little faster.

Mrs J.B.,
Address withheld by request

MISSES EX-WIFE

I am 36 and divorced after 13 years of marriage. Though I have been divorced for nearly three years now, up until my moving to Germany from the United States some nine months ago, I 'dated' my ex-wife off and on even though I was going out with other women at the same time. These encounters with my ex were for the most part purely sexual, as we do not get along at all in any other respect.

Now I am living with a beautiful and shapely German girl of 25 with whom I am very much in love, and we plan to marry in the future. My problem is I cannot get these sexual encounters with my ex out of my mind. When I was married to her, our sex relationship was rather dull. It was only after our separation that things got hot and heavy. We both acted out all our sexual fantasies. I bought her a dildo and took delight in watching her use it in every possible way. She would sit across from me in a long dress or négligée, wearing high heels and stockings, and expose her upper thighs. Eventually, her legs would spread to reveal her bare vagina, which was especially beautiful because of the shape of her pubic hair. This naturally turned me and her on. She would masturbate with the dildo as well as using anything else that came to our minds. We would then switch the voyeur roles and she would watch me perform and delight in having me do whatever turned her on. I bought a Polaroid

18

camera and we took pictures of each other and, in general, had a real fling at just plain sex.

I have a very good sex relationship with the German girl I now live with, but it must be called average compared to sex with my ex. At first, this girl appeared to take a rather passive role, but with my experience I have been able to really turn her on. We both enjoy oral sex and both have no difficulty in reaching orgasm.

However, when I am away from home for some period of time (which occurs frequently in my work) I think about those times with my ex-wife and end up masturbating while imagining having her all over again.

This is disturbing to me since I have no intention of getting together again with my ex, and I'm afraid it may eventually affect my new relationship or any other I may try, for that matter.

What advice can you give me? Anything would be appreciated.

R.G.,
Germany

Of course you miss sex with your wife. In that respect, she was most men's dream – highly sexed and completely uninhibited.

But, as you found out, sex alone does not make a marriage. Having experienced the heights, however, it is unlikely that you will ever be entirely satisfied with a merely average sex life, however good the emotional aspects of the relationship.

Clearly, you have two choices. Teach your girlfriend, gradually and patiently, to express herself sexually as freely as your wife did; or accept that most people have to compromise to some extent in their relationships. In the long run, the emotional aspects of a relationship are often more important than the purely sexual; but people have different needs and before considering remarriage you should be sure that you have sorted out your priorities in this area. If you do have to settle for less than your sexual ideal, there's nothing wrong with masturbation and fantasy as an outlet for your more uninhibited desires.

It would obviously be a mistake for you to link up with a woman who is markedly repressed or has a low sex drive, however you felt about her, but I see no reason why you could not be happy with a woman a little less forthcoming than your wife, if you loved her.

I LIKE WOMEN

Ever since I can remember I have had a pre-occupation with the female body. This appears to be growing worse and I have a constant desire to make love to any desirable or semi-desirable female I see.

I am 43 and had an authoritarian, relatively sheltered upbringing. I went to boarding school. I am married, with three children, and holding down good, well-paid work.

Until I was about 17, I don't think I knew there was any difference between girls and boys and was baffled by the word 'fucking'. I had no idea of the physical anatomy of females until I was 19 and knowledge of the 'curse' came several years later.

I was initiated into the mysteries of lovemaking and sex by a girl while doing National Service. I then had a breast fixation. Since then I have had a number of serious relationships – intense too – with women. All ended in a hateful way – as though I was rejecting them. I slept with three women before marriage and some after.

I was married about 20 years ago to someone as inhibited as I am. During this time I have had two affairs, one of short duration, one of 12 months or so which nearly wrecked my marriage, cost me my job and almost led to a nervous breakdown. The sex though was wonderful and completely uninhibited but it did not quell the desire to see other women's bodies. I hated myself most of the time.

Running through all my adult life since about 18 has been the almost overwhelming compulsion – obsession is probably the right word – to look at and be with women. This has taken several forms but mainly involves buying magazines to study the nude girls. The interest seems to be centred on the pubic/vaginal regions and breasts. Sometimes masturbation occurs and prostitutes have been visited for this reason.

There is a definite cycle to these activities which I would identify thus: pressure or stress, at home or work, leads to nudes/prostitutes. This goes on to masturbation/sex and then I get a revulsion then regret, followed by calmness; then the cycle begins again. I also suffer from depression and this, too, leads to nudes and prostitutes.

The problem seems to be getting worse and I fear that my work may suffer.

I feel if I could understand what lies behind all this I might be able to live with it more easily or perhaps alleviate or ease the situation.

Name withheld by request,
Edinburgh

It seems to me that there are two major factors making the situation which you describe into a problem. The first is that after masturbating to pictures of nudes or visiting prostitutes you become revulsed and depressed. In order to alleviate this revulsion and depression you go back to your nude fantasy or prostitutes and masturbate again. Every time you go back to your nudes and fantasy to alleviate depression a powerful re-inforcing situation arises whereby because of the relief of depression and revulsion brought on by your sexual arousal the method by which you do it – ie fixation on nude bodies – becomes more and more entrenched.

I feel that it is necessary for you to do two things here: first to begin to accept that fantasies such as the ones which you use are not at all uncommon and that your response of revulsion and later depression should be and can be avoided by accepting the masturbation when it occurs rather than trying to fight against it.

Secondly, and possibly more usefully from your point of view, you can start to re-shape the sort of imagery which you use while masturbating. This very powerful approach to re-learning sexual responses may be useful in two ways. First you can start to introduce imagery concerning your wife and your sex life with her. Secondly you can at least start to diminish the amount of imagery and fixation on other women in the nude.

The way to do this is to allow yourself to become aroused using your usual nude fantasy. When you are approaching orgasm, switch your fantasy to a scene in which you are having intercourse with your wife and enjoying it very much. When you have your orgasm make sure that you are using this imagery as your orgasm will act as a powerful reinforcer of this new imagery concerning your wife. Then gradually, when you are able to do this easily, start to introduce your wife in the imagery earlier and earlier during the masturbatory fantasy. Eventually you may well find that you can use the image of your wife entirely in masturbation. When you have developed this skill to some degree, I would advise that you actually bring your wife into your treatment programme and have her physically stimulate you to orgasm. Then gradually increase the repertoire of sexual behaviour together with your wife.

This brings me to my second important point. I feel that, if at all possible, you should discuss this problem with your wife and enlist her help. With this sort of problem one of the things which almost paradoxically keeps it going is often found to be the secretive, possibly at times exciting, conditions which surround it. Furtively buying a nudey mag or going off in solitude to masturbate wondering if you will be caught may well be introducing factors into the situation which help in such things as removing depression. Thus, to bring the thing into the open and rid it of its secretive nature may be helpful in getting rid of some of these factors.

PS. We all experience 'pressure' at work which leads to a sense of lust or desire which in turn causes most of us to want sex. This is a normal description of the sequence of human sexuality! What you have to do is break the link between your sex urge and guilt.

I MIGHT BE TEMPTED ...

I am likely to visit Denmark this year and while there I might be tempted to purchase porno films, magazines etc to bring back home.

Would I be committing an offence by bringing back this sort of thing? If I didn't declare it, could the Customs confiscate any of the material?

Quite naturally I wouldn't want to spend a considerable sum of money on anything for the benefit of a Customs Official's private collection. And I'd hate the embarrassment of being found out.

A.T.,
Manchester

Customs Acts dating back nearly a century forbid the importation of indecent or obscene articles into Great Britain. If you try to sneak through the type of hard core stuff I think you have in mind, A.T., you would certainly be committing an offence. 'Indecent or obscene' covers a pretty wide range, particularly as the courts now define these words to mean anything which offends the recognized standards of propriety.

The Customs men have fairly daunting powers when it comes to search and seizure. They don't need a definition of obscenity because the authorities supply a 'black list' (not available to the public, I'm afraid) of works considered to go beyond the pale. And even this doesn't limit their discretion.

The law can hit hard at the citizen who tries to smuggle in forbidden fruit. If they nab you with real hard porn you could end up (in theory anyway) with two years' imprisonment plus a money penalty of either £100 fine or three times the value of the goods, whichever is the greater.

Incidentally, the value of smuggled goods for the purpose of a fine is based on the price they might reasonably be expected to fetch on the open market!

In fairness to the courts, the law aims to quash traffickers in porn rather than the randy individual who stashes a few creased magazines at the bottom of his suitcase to regale the lads back at the local.

I don't have any statistics of sentences handed out for these offences over the past few years, but I can't believe for a moment that you'd get anything like the maximum. Indeed, I would not expect you to go to prison unless you'd already had hassles with the law or get caught with so large a cargo that the judge has to assume you're running a porn shop.

As for your suggestion about not declaring what you've got, Customs officers can ask any relevant questions about your luggage. And if you lie you risk a fine of up to £500 and/or two years' imprisonment.

They catch you either way . . .

I think you do our Customs men an injustice when you refer to their 'private collections', for if the authorities confiscate your treasure trove you yourself can have the dispute brought before a court. You must object within one month to the Commissioners of Customs and Excise alleging they've wrongfully seized your property. They must then ask the court to have the goods condemned. To succeed, you'd have to show good reason why your hoard should not be forfeited. No mean task, I assure you.

If you don't object within the month or if the court condemns your erotica the commissioners may order it to be destroyed.

SECOND HONEYMOON

About 12 months ago I had my first orgasm after 20 years of marriage. It was so wonderful, I have had one with my husband at least once a day ever since. I can't wait for the evening to

23

come when we can go to bed and have sex sessions which last for an hour or so.

My husband never fails to have an erection, or maintain it even after having intercourse a few times in 24 hours, which we can manage while on holidays or weekends away.

Do you think all this extra lovemaking will turn him off it? Perhaps he feels it is a chore because he was unable to bring me to orgasm for 20 years, and now feels he must make up to me for lost time. I have not said anything to make him feel this way.

He says he is much happier with the new interest we have in each other and certainly seems to get as much pleasure out of it as I do.

When we married at 20 neither of us knew anything about sex and we muddled through the years blindly enjoying sex but never getting the full indescribable feeling we get now. My orgasm gets better all the time.

My husband has never had anyone else nor does he want to, so you can see I don't want to drive him away from me with my insatiable appetite for sex. We have read – within the last 12 months – numerous sex books, and to my surprise we have – again during the last 12 months – tried most of the things written in them, and again to my surprise I'm getting to enjoy everything we do more and more.

Another thing, my husband looks much better, comes home earlier and wants to spend as much time with me as he can. He tries to get me away for weekends without the children as much as possible. He has also put on half a stone in weight, which he could well do with. I feel marvellous – as though I'm on an extended honeymoon. My only concern is that I will wear him out.

Mrs L.T.,
Australia

I feel you have no worries about 'turning your husband off'. On the contrary, I am sure you will find your blossoming interest in sex will greatly enhance your husband's feelings for you and will ensure you a perpetual extended honeymoon.

Your obvious concern for your husband's feelings indicate a depth of understanding sufficient to overcome any difficulties he might have in adjusting to the new situation.

SEX DURING MENSTRUATION

This letter is directed to those men who 'turn up their noses' at having sexual relations with a woman during her monthly period. Several times during my 21 years I've had the pleasure of experiencing intercourse with women in this state.

I started having sexual relations when I was 12 years old and it usually takes me from 20 to 30 minutes to come for the first time, unless I'm really turned on. The first time I had relations with a woman having her monthly, I had to be coaxed before I would enter her. After succumbing to her insistence, I experienced something I will never forget. Upon entering her, I found her vaginal temperature so hot that I came in about 10 seconds. I was so overwhelmed, I found myself hard again in minutes. The next time I penetrated her, I came in even less time. My stamina amazed me! Not to mention that she went wild because I was so excited.

Usually, after I come, it takes me about 45 minutes to get really hard again so believe me, there must have been something pretty wonderful about her hot vagina. This has happened to me a number of times since then, much to my delight. I urge all men to try intercourse with a woman in this state at least once. There's nothing like it!

L.M.,
Address withheld by request

Many of the women you meet must be delighted by your enthusiasm, for women often feel sexiest before, during or just after their period. Orgasm also helps relieve menstrual congestion and cramps.

Very occasionally, a man may be sensitive to menstrual blood and risk urethritis from having intercourse during the woman's period.

Some women find it uncomfortable to engage in intercourse during their periods, so do be considerate.

SEX ADDICT

I know this sounds silly, but I am serious and would like your adviser to help me. Is it possible to turn your sex drive off about half-way or put it on the back burner half the time? I am 19 years old, and am now separated from my second husband and don't even know or care where he is. I live alone and I work as a typist for the Government. I would like to get more education and improve myself, and think I am smart enough to even get a college degree if I had the chance and then get a much better job somewhere. I mean this very sincerely and have enrolled in courses three or four times trying to make a start in that way. But I always drop out very soon, and must face up to the fact that my problem is that I also like to have sex all the time and in spite of my good resolutions I wind up spending more time making love than attending night school or studying.

I do not think I am a nympho; I have been known occasionally to turn fellows down. But I have to accept the fact that I enjoy 'casual sex' with a good many different friends and that I can't imagine missing a chance to make love with any new fellows I meet socially if they are cute and if I turn them on as much as they do me. The thing is, the kids I run with have this same lifestyle too, and it really isn't casual sex because I love it every time. I can't see myself sleeping with someone less than four or five times a week. If I don't have a real date or meet a fellow after work I start feeling itchy and empty and lonely by seven or eight o'clock and either call a friend up, drop in on someone, take off to the neighbourhood tavern alone or propose to a girlfriend that we go prowling together. I couldn't take money or dream of asking a stranger to make love to me in so many words, but having sex night after night is the most important damn thing in the world to me. I love it. If I don't get it I am miserable, I don't sleep well, can't get satisfactory relief by masturbation, and I am a wreck the next day.

I also want to say I am not ashamed of liking sex so much and often, and I am not ashamed or embarrassed about it at all. I am not sure one man will ever be enough for me.

I was brought up in a West Virginia city, which *isn't* hill-billy country at all. I had an older brother and a younger sister and brother. I started screwing in school, and fell in love with a neighbour when he came home on leave from the Army. When he went back to his North Carolina base I followed him and lived with him for three months. We got married so he could get home more often and we lived together for four months before he was sent to Korea. I couldn't go. In the meantime, both before and after the ceremony, we had attended some huge drinking sessions lasting all weekend and joined the others (married and single) in making it with other partners. I have never experienced such wild times as those were, where everyone was high and everything went on. By the time my husband shipped out we both knew this had just been a phase we were both going through, so we agreed to a divorce. I stayed in the same town until it was final and got a job typing on the base and finished school there too. But I also got in the habit of 'casual' sex with a lot of other kids on an almost-every-night basis, plus those weekend marathons.

Two years ago I came to Washington with my mind made up to de-emphasize sex a little and think of my career. I fell in love, I thought, a month or so after arriving, and loved being married again and making love all night and all weekend too with the same great stud. For seven months we tried to break all records for quantity and probably did so. Then we had a big fight because he wanted other girls, one especially, but wanted me to be true to him. I rebelled and told him I would agree to anything, such as partying where we all might trade off or whatever, but I sure as hell would not stay home alone while he went out with others. The next thing I knew he took off for California with another woman. Her ex-husband and I consoled each other in bed for a while, but then each of us found other partners. I deliberately chose many guys, not one.

So that's my problem. I feel I am drifting in my career prospects and everything concerned with the future and really ought to do something. But I am 'hooked' on sex and really need it practically every night to be comfortable. I do *not* want to stop screwing altogether, and am not sure I am really ready for marriage or that I am prepared emotionally to settle down with one man, no matter who he might be or how good he is in bed. So I am confused, and get upset, because of these two kinds of desires. I want to train myself for something better but can't because I do so much screwing around and feel bad about missing that boat. But I also love making love more than anything, and it won't stop being my greatest interest. What advice is there you can give?

> Mrs J.A.,
> Washington, DC

I understand full well how much you enjoy sex. But if any activity, whether it be eating, drinking or having sex, is engaged in as compulsively as you are doing it, one can generally find an underlying cause which would be best treated by psychotherapy.

There are many reasons for enjoying sex outside its physical pleasures. In your particular case I feel you are using sex to raise your self-esteem to eliminate loneliness and to provide yourself with the affection you so obviously need.

Because your two marriages did not work out, you cannot even bring yourself to invest your emotions in one relationship for fear of being rejected again, but security and self-esteem cannot be found in multiple sexual encounters.

It can possibly be found by going back to college, which I'm sure you can do. It's your low self-esteem, not your sexual activity that prevents you from doing so. But if you managed to finish school and learn typing you can do it again.

Loneliness is a very painful feeling, but busy people rarely find the time to be lonely. Your present sexual activity is not only failing to meet your emotional needs, but could one day even prove dangerous, as you appear quite indiscriminate about who and how many men you go to bed with.

You know 19 is really a very young age to be living totally alone. Let me suggest that you go back to college, find a female friend with whom to share your flat, and restrict your sexual activity to close friends at weekends. With homework and a friend to listen to your confidences, you won't have time to be lonely, and the closer you get to your BA the greater your self-esteem will increase.

HOW TO CLASS A CALL GIRL

Recently a national newspaper pronounced the opinion that there was no such person as a high class call girl. I couldn't disagree more. Recently, at the age of 50, I visited a call girl for the first time and she was in a class of her own for enjoyable physical experience, honesty, cleanliness and sympathy.

I had had a painful examination of the scrotum which the hospital specialist admitted had bruised the area around the prostate gland, and which left me frightened that I might be impotent.

As my wife is very cold about sex, I took a day's holiday and travelled to a nearby city. I had first obtained a telephone number from a contact magazine. When I rang around noon, the lady could not accommodate me, but when I explained my desperate need she rang a friend and put me in touch with her after explaining that this lady was not a regular at this sort of service and would need careful handling. Margot, the second lady, instructed me to be waiting at a particular crossroad at a certain time.

I must have been waiting about 10 minutes when a pretty blonde woman appeared at the entrance to some flats and smiled a welcome to me. She introduced herself and led me into a tastefully furnished lounge with her new stereo record player playing soft background music. She waved me to a seat by her side on the settee, and I nervously explained my need. I was encouraged to relax and listen to the music for several minutes before being invited to follow her upstairs to a fine boudoir. I enjoyed a fine display of black stockings, white thigh and suspenders as I followed.

In the bedroom she explained that her usual clients needed flagellation, and showed me all the apparatus of whips and canes which made me slightly shudder. These were not for me and were quickly locked away. Margot stripped to bra and panties and invited me to undress. As I nervously removed my trousers she laughingly said, 'Now you may as well admit this is your first time, for any professional call girl would take care to receive the £5.00 fee *before* undressing!' I groped in my pockets and paid.

Then I was gently pushed on to the bed and massaged by hand and with a vibrator but after 20 minutes my penis was still only partially hard. I apologized, for Margot whom I had stripped and fondled by this time had a lovely compact figure. I judged her to be in her early 30s.

'Look, you idiot,' said Margot, 'your trouble is that you aren't relaxed and concentrating on the pleasure. I really like you and time is immaterial as I have no other clients today, so just relax.' With this she lay beside me and we began petting and cuddling each other like true lovers. Strangely, this brought me to a full erection.

Margot surveyed my penis and remarked that it was a pity to waste it now and pulled a rubber from a nearby drawer. Pushing me on my back she mounted me, jockey fashion, and we rode to a fantastic orgasm. I was shown how to remove the rubber with a tissue and wipe myself with a tissue in the other hand to cut down the risk of a VD contact.

After washing in the bathroom Margot explained that all this and even the use of a sheath was only to allay my fears, as she had regular medical checks and had never had VD herself. She also told me over coffee that she had never walked the streets and warned me strongly against picking up this type of girl.

We parted great friends and I consider this lady gave me very good service and value. She was a credit to what I consider a much-needed calling.

L.M.,
Sheffield

How lucky you were! What your professional lady gave you was just what the doctor ordered – a speeded-up version of the Masters and Johnson treatment for impotence. The massage, the emphasis on relaxation, the petting and cuddling with no demand for performance (not 'strange' at all that you got an erection – it happened as soon as you forgot to worry whether it would!); even the woman-above position, are all important components of modern sex therapy.

For various reasons (the General Medical Council and the News of the World *prominent among them) surrogate partner therapy for impotence and premature ejaculation is virtually if not entirely unobtainable in this country. The result is that it is difficult to help the man whose wife will not co-operate in treatment. Sex therapy is consequently wide open to the intelligent prostitute and I'm surprised that not one of them – to my knowledge – specifically offers it!*

A GENEROUS COUPLE

My wife and I married in 1949 and moved to a small village in Berkshire. The second summer we were there my wife's sister Ruby came to stay for a short holiday. I usually went every evening down to the pub, about a mile away, for a drink.

Ruby had been with us about a week when, almost at the end of my usual walk down to the pub, I suddenly realized it would have been kinder to ask the girls to come with me. So I retraced my steps to ask them. I went in by the kitchen door and caught them both almost starkers, obviously enjoying themselves!

It would take too long to tell about the row that followed, but when my wife and I got to bed she started to tell me about when they were young. Her two sisters and she had slept in the same room, two in one bed and one in a single. They used to change around from time to time and all three had played with each other. To cut a long story short, on the Saturday morning Ruby joined us in our bed after I had just fucked my wife, and she laughingly suggested getting her sister to show me how to please a woman.

As I lay and watched them kissing and fondling and feeling

round I became roused in a very short time. While Ruby was kissing my wife, it was suggested that I take Ruby from behind and I needed no second asking. With my hands on her hips I enjoyed one of the most enjoyable and exhausting experiences I have ever had, and afterwards I lay beside them and watched a show of love for almost three hours.

Ruby eventually married and emigrated to Canada. A cousin of my wife's was our next companion – she was just 20 and came to stay with us. It was a beautiful hot summer afternoon, and the two girls were in bikinis in the garden. I whispered to my wife to take hers off and get her cousin to do the same; after a lot of giggling and a bit of horseplay we were all starkers and it didn't take long to get cracking.

The list of our amours since would take a long time in detail, but both my brothers have had my wife, and so have a cousin of mine, two milkmen, one postman, a gasfitter (several visits) and a local greengrocer who used to call weekly – and others.

I have enjoyed my wife's two sisters, two of her cousins, a hairdresser who used to do my wife's hair and the mother-in-law of one of my brothers (older but very worthwhile) and one or two others.

The reason that prompts me to write all this is to tell couples to talk to each other. If only husbands and wives would forget all the old taboos and openly discuss their feelings and desires they would be able to cooperate with each other and lead a happier, fuller life.

I realize in our case we were lucky; I found out by accident. But the same result could come from more open discussions between couples.

If either my wife or I fancy someone, we tell each other and try to help each other realize their desire. I love my wife and love to see her enjoying herself. I wouldn't leave her (but even if love was not there I would still stay with her – because she helps me to get what I want). So it does bind you together more.

It might not suit everybody, but it suits me.

R.J.,
Essex

It almost seems that you and your wife have had conquests enough to rival the celebrated list of amours in Mozart's opera Don Juan ('. . . and, in Spain, one thousand and three!') – and made some tradespeople and relatives pretty happy in the process. As you say, it wouldn't be right for everybody – but it works in your particular marriage, and that's the important thing – for anyone inclined to criticize – to remember. (Consultant)

LOVE-BITES

You may think that this problem of mine is trivial compared to others, but it is worrying us both 'scatty'! It all started after we had had our first son who's now four. When he was just a few days old I used to kiss his hair and progressed to licking it and pulling it gently with my lips. At the time I didn't realize I was doing it; it was, and still is, a form of showing my affection towards him.

One weekend my mother noticed me doing this while we were watching TV and she told me, mockingly, that I ought to get my head read! I laughed it off.

Months went by and I still found myself doing it. I was only expressing my love for him. When his hair grew longer and more coarse, I naturally stopped. Not long after, my husband and I started reading *Forum* and for the first time enjoyed oral lovemaking. I naturally took to licking his pubic hair among other things; I like to lick and pull it with my teeth and lips. My second son was born when my first was two and, just as with my first son, I had this habit of licking his hair. For some reason I grew embarrassed whenever I caught myself doing this and finally stopped when he was six months old.

My husband and I still enjoy our sex life and I still lick his pubic hair occasionally – but I have developed a terrible urge to bite him hard on any part that I am in contact with at the time (except when I'm making oral love to him and then I go for his legs). It's an urge I can't control.

Recently I bit him hard on the shoulder when I climaxed, but wasn't aware at the time that I'd done it. Now he's afraid to come too close to me when we make love. I do not want to hurt him and I have never wanted to beat him or tie him up, so I am not sadistic, am I?

Even when I think about sex during the day, I get this urge to bite, but it has got to be human, not raw meat which I hate. I did try it to see if it would cure me!

I've tried masturbating several times, but gave up without any satisfaction; my husband has always managed to bring me to orgasm. I love him dearly and try very hard to please him, but feel I could give more somehow – perhaps it's because of my annoyance with myself that I can't express the love that I have for him and so I resort to this biting.

To you it may seem just a laughing matter, but to me it's a real problem and if I can't find a way to cure this urge of biting him I'm afraid he will leave me alone altogether and I'll go crazy if that happens.

I daren't ask our own doctor as I once went to him before on a sexual problem and he made me feel quite embarrassed and foolish when I mentioned it.

*Mrs J.S.,
Carmarthenshire*

The mouth is a very important focus of sexual sensations and experienced lovers gain as much excitement as they give by all-over body kisses. You have evidently become more aware of oral sensations in recent years than formerly, and have become a connoisseur of textures in your licking of hair.

Individuals often differ in the proportion of excitement which they get through stimulation of one part of the body rather than another. For you, oral sensations are highly important. The urge to bite is in part an extension of this interest in oral sensations. It is heightened by the muscular tension (myotonus) normally caused by sexual excitement and approaching orgasm, which also shows itself in spasms of the limbs, writhing, gasping etc. Your wish to bite, in other words, is increased by the tension felt in the muscles which close the jaws. It may be that you are also a little sadistic, as are many lovers who like to bite, scratch and mark each other.

I am sure that you will not do your husband any serious damage and that the fear of losing control of the biting is unfounded. But if your anxieties continue I suggest a trial of these remedies. (1) Get your husband to shout loudly, immediately the pain of your biting is more than slight. (2) Equip yourself with a piece of soft chewing gum, secrete it in your mouth and chew it when the urge to bite becomes insistent. (3) Make love beside a large, body size mirror, and watch a reflection of your facial expressions whenever you feel like biting hard. The mirror may also enrich lovemaking for you both, by giving you a new range of visual stimuli.

FOUR-LETTER ORIGINS

Having read Miss Greer's article on the 'Vaginal revolution',

33

I am prompted to ask something I have wanted to know for many years.

She uses the word 'cunt' many times and I should like to know where this word comes from.

'Fuck', we are told, is an Anglo Saxon word, but in that tongue was it regarded as obscene, as it is now?

'Prick' and 'balls' are self-explanatory, but 'fuck' and 'cunt' have always left me puzzled, at least wordwise!

Perhaps one of your consultants could explain?

G.S.,
address withheld by request

These taboo twins 'fuck' and 'cunt', owing to their powerful overtones, have not, until recently, been discussed in standard dictionaries. Our ancestors were less prissy about language – as early as 1235 a street in the City of London was named Grope-cuntelane, later to become Lover's Lane.

'Cunt' was found in related forms throughout medieval Europe – Norse 'kunta', Old French 'kunte', German 'kuntun'. All these forms, it is thought, spring from Latin 'cunnus', itself related to 'cuneus', a wedge.

'Fuck' appears about 200 years later. Its etymology is still a source of controversy amongst word-watchers. One rather endearing explanation is that it is imitative of the sound of the penis in the vagina. It is generally thought to derive from Middle English 'fucken', a Germanic verb originally meaning to strike, to move quickly, to penetrate. (There were no obscene overtones during this period.) In the sense of strike, one can compare it to the later terms 'bang' and 'knock'.

Its colloquial use as in 'couldn't give a fuck', 'for fuck's sake' and 'how the fuck' has rather weakened its force and magic. Certainly the word has more romance than such ephemera as 'ball', 'screw', 'have it away', 'make it', 'lay', etc. 'Cunt' is certainly more basic, 'quim' being as old and probably more fitting.

When using these words it is worth bearing in mind the judgement of a famous lexicographer (Brophy) who calls them 'utterly unvoluptuous, their use will coarsen and degrade, but it will not soften or seduce.'

FOUR-LETTER WORDS

I am not very happy about your definitions of the words

'Fuck' and 'Cunt' and the comparisons made do not make very much sense at all.

In 1932 I bought a 'A New English Dictionary' by Ernest A. Baker, MA, and from this I arrived at the definitions of these two words because I am never happy about the general use of words I do not understand. Incidentally I never use them except to explain them and I very rarely swear – it is so needless. To hundreds of people over all these years I have shown that these two words are quite innocent and their definitions show clean and unabusive functions.

To take them in the order you place them: 'cunt'. Ernest A. Baker gives: cont-line = The space between casks stowed side by side; the external space between the strands in a rope.

Dr James A. H. Murray gives the same definition in 'A New English Dictionary on Historical Principles' in 1893. Webster's 'Third New International Dictionary of the English Language' gives the same definition and adds: cont-line as being pronounced 'cunt-line by folk etymology (Influence of cunt)'.

So you see, Cunt refers to a shape: the twin beautiful curves of those parts of the anatomy situated side by side: but specifically 'by folk etymology' the woman's external genital shape.

Now to take 'Fuck'. Ernest A. Baker gives: fyke (From Dutch fuick) = A bag net open at one end so as to allow fish to enter; but opposing their exit.

Dr James A. H. Murray gives the same definition. Webster also gives the same definition.

So now we see the bag net as the cervix and womb and the fish as the sperm and in conception their exit has been opposed so the woman has been fyked or fucked.

I do not know how the Dutch pronounce their fuick but it looks to me the same as our fuck or another popular word frick.

Many a chap is amazed when he is told he cannot fuck a woman if he uses an effective contraceptive. Really a woman can only be fucked if she conceives and in these days of the Pill and Vasectomy fucking is going to be non-existent.

Incidentally, as a matter of interest, to bring in another word 'shag'. If a man says he will 'shag' a woman he could really mean 'shad' because the bag net (fyke) was mainly for catching shad fish. On the other hand the dictionaries give two definitions of shag: (1) The refuse of barley, corn, oats, etc. (2) Roughness; brutality of manner.

So we can derive the origin of 'wild oats'; or we can take it as

35

giving a rough treatment (your terms 'bang' and 'knock'). Or referring back to shad he would fill her with sperm; much nicer.

I hope G.S. who asked for the derivations of two words will be interested in the probable relationship of the additional words I have mentioned.

A.M.,
Hampshire

Our consultant writes:

Your derivations are not given in Partridge or the Oxford English Dictionary and are certainly too early to be definitive (a case of swallowing an attractive theory hook line and sinker), but I'd be delighted to hear from other readers, C/O Forum, who may disagree or possess further knowledge.

AUTO-FELLATIO

I am 17 years old and I have been masturbating since I was 14. I enjoy masturbating very much and feel great while performing it. Recently I read about 'auto-fellatio' and it has caught my fancy. I do not feel that I am a homosexual, but I certainly enjoy fellating myself. I could not even think about sucking another guy's penis, but I have great orgasms when I do it to myself. I also come in my mouth and I like the taste of my semen. What I am asking you is, how unnatural is auto-fellatio and am I crazy?

M.B.,
London

No, you are not crazy. Auto-fellatio is one more way for you to pleasure yourself, and all self-pleasuring is a form of self-love. Loving yourself physically is natural for all of us. What is unnatural is for you to feel guilty about loving yourself in a way that makes you, as you say, 'feel great'. Not everyone can perform auto-fellatio, but for those that can, the experience can be a very exciting and satisfying one.

SHOULD I TELL?

I am a young married woman of 24. During the past six years my husband has well and truly initiated me into the exciting arts of sex as a result of which I have become a highly-sexed girl and look forward to my sexual encounters with him.

However, recently his work has started to take him away from home and I get terribly frustrated and find it hard to control my sexual urges. First I tried masturbating and then I used a vibrator. This went on until six weeks ago, when we took in a lodger called Jim. My husband liked him and asked him if he would take me out sometimes during the week. He did this and I enjoyed his company.

At first we used to go to our respective bedrooms when we got home. But one night I was lying on my bed working myself up with my vibrator and moaning, when Jim came in to see if I was all right. He seemed embarrassed when he saw what was going on, but I asked him to sit on the bed while I explained how difficult it was for me to go through the week without sex. He began to get very aroused and before long we were making love. Now he sleeps with me during the week and says if I want to tell my husband he won't mind. Sex with my husband has also improved immensely since.

I would like to tell my husband what has happened but don't know whether I should. Am I right in getting what I can from both of them, or should I go back to my frustrating ordeals?

Mrs. L.P.,
Oxfordshire

'Rightness', in the moral sense, doesn't really come into it. It would be more practical to look into your reasons for wanting to tell your husband and the possible results if you did.

You may feel rather guilty, at some level, and want to tell your husband to relieve your mind. This is hardly fair on him. If the knowledge of what you are doing is likely to distress him, then you must bear the burden of it alone and give serious thought to giving up your relationship with the lodger. Sooner or later, if it continues, your husband is bound to find out and the damage to your marriage could be irreparable.

But this is supposing that your husband takes the conventional view of your adultery. However, he is clearly a highly-sexed man and it is possible that he could get pleasure either out of knowing about your affair, and perhaps hearing the details of your lovemaking, or from joining in a threesome. The fact that he happily leaves you alone with an attractive lodger, and encourages you to go out together, lends support to this – though it could also mean he has a total trust in your loyalty to him.

I think your best bet is to bring the subject up hypothetically.

37

Mention casually that although you love him you sometimes feel it could be fun to sleep with someone else, especially in a threesome with your husband. Or say jokingly that you find your lodger quite attractive and sometimes feel tempted. His reaction should make it clear whether your affair would hurt him or please him. If he gives you 'permission' to make love to Jim, I feel it would be wise to pretend that you have not already done so. 'Open marriages', in which the spouses take lovers outside the marriage, depend on honesty and openness between the partners; secret affairs are out.

Of course, if your husband is upset and worried by the mere idea that you fancy other men – then, I'm afraid, you must decide between Jim and your marriage. If you opt for the latter, a change of lodger would be a good idea.

INSATIABLE HUSBAND

I'm 30 and my husband is 49. Although I agree with Marion Meade's article 'How to love a liberated woman' to the letter, I must take exception to her statement that a man's teen years mark the height of his virility. I've met many men in their 40s and 50s who were still active at swinging parties long after the younger men had fallen asleep or gone home. My own man has grown progressively hornier over the years, I'm happy to say.

We recently became involved in the swinging scene. While I've always known my husband has a great capacity for sex, I never realized how insatiable he really is. Our last session was a 16-couple encounter and he screwed every woman there. On the way home he pulled the car into a rest area and wanted me to give him more!

All of the wives enjoy him very much, but the men always tease him about his incredible appetite. He is not an aggressive man, and in most instances women make the first advances when they see he still has a hard-on and all the other men have gone flat. Every other man I have ever known has gone limp immediately after orgasm. Some can be brought back to full arousal only after 10 or 15 minutes. But, even after very intense orgasms, my husband stays as hard as ever and keeps right on functioning as if nothing happened. I asked him his secret but he says he doesn't know! He insists his penis has a mind of its own.

His capacity is inconsistent with everything I've ever experienced or read. He has had workouts at these swinging parties which would kill a horse. He can come off four or five times and still be ready for more. Most of the women who encounter my husband feel (as I do) that they must be sexual failures because they can't give him enough. He denies that he isn't satisfied even though he still has a hard-on.

What I want to know is whether or not there is something organically wrong with my husband? And if so, how can I keep him from getting 'well'?

Mrs D.P.,
Address withheld by request

I certainly would not say that there was anything organically 'wrong' with your husband. There is certainly something right about his enormous and startling abilities – though don't forget the possibility that he is not actually ejaculating every time he screws. I do not think, however, that you must feel responsible to cater to his sexual appetite. It is obviously too much to expect of any woman; and whatever his activities elsewhere, there will clearly always be enough left for you. (Consultant)

FINDING THE KEY

I had an unhappy romance soon after leaving school and married on the rebound. He was much older. I was scared of the honeymoon. I went up first each night and lay without a stitch on trying to look seductive. We kissed passionately but his rise failed whenever he entered me and left us in mid-air. We talked and smoked dozens of cigarettes, but by the time we got home, we took separate rooms to catch up with lost sleep.

This became a habit and we went our own way and avoided emotional scenes. Deep down, I was hurt. Pride kept me from walking out for my parents had made a fuss about the marriage. Besides, I had no training to earn a decent living and when I looked round for something to do, I was lucky to find a job part-time in a curio shop.

It gradually dawned on me I was better off than a lot of my friends. I had every comfort and the use of a car of my own. My husband was easy-going and seemed quite content as long as he could go shooting at weekends and follow the football on the telly. I was suspicious about his business trips once or twice a month and felt sure he had women then, but we never spoke of it.

But, almost five years ago now, our deadly routine was broken by a cousin of his coming to stay for a few weeks. Within a few days, it was obvious even to my husband that the boy was gone on me with that infatuation women seldom resist.

I expected one hell of a row and a quick end to the visit. But no. My husband seemed fascinated by the situation. I caught a new interest in his eye and he paid me one or two compliments for the first time for years. He almost threw us together by suggesting places to visit, some of them over 50 miles away.

This all went to my head and I felt recklessly happy. I had a new hair-do and went shopping for some trendy clothes. I tarted myself up with heavier lipstick and mascara and looked and felt a different woman.

In little, mischievous ways, I played one against the other. I could do no wrong, of course, in the boy's eyes. But when my husband jumped out of his chair to open the door for me or fetch a table for the coffee, it thrilled me more than all the wolf-whistles that now came my way.

I could not resist trying myself out on our guest. I could have seduced him any time but waited till we had had lunch one day at a hotel in a remote village before suggesting we took a room for the night. His hand shook and he looked so pale as he signed the register. I thought for a moment he would faint.

His nerves made me feel icy calm and in control. I undressed at once and as he gazed at me, the colour came back to his cheeks and made me feel beautiful. I made him undress too and he looked less boyish with his dark, body hair. I stroked his balls and under his prick. It reared in my hand and to make it easy for him I sat on the edge of the bed with my legs spread wide. Just as he stooped over me, he gasped and his fluid spurted over my thighs. He cursed and murmured apologies but we collapsed on the bed together laughing helplessly. I was secretly flattered by such a quick emission, but he grew solemn all of a sudden and kissed me wildly and flung himself against me in desperation till he came again and proved his manhood.

We lay for hours. I was amazed at all the dirty stories that poured from my lips and he bent close to an ear and murmured all sorts of indecent compliments about me. He forced me to lie still and went over my whole body showing me all its charms. He paused to open my cunt wide and run his finger round the rim. I helped him to find my clit and he watched me shudder and gasp helplessly as he made me come more than once.

We had sex every day and often more than once. He

sometimes undressed me and took me in the lounge and once or twice in the shower just before my husband was due home. We had so much of each other that when his visit was over, we could part without too much of a pang and arrange to meet in a few weeks.

I felt about 10 years older. I saw now what I'd been afraid to admit before; that my husband's sex had been with prostitutes and my baby-doll image had merely embarrassed him. I cooled off for a few days, however, keeping him guessing about just what had happened. He was still too proud to make any approach himself so I let him simmer and was in no hurry, till the boy was out of my system.

I waited till his next wrestling night, when he always came home late and a bit high. I laid out his coffee in the lounge as usual but instead of going off to bed, I tarted myself up and even put on a dark wig I'd bought and was surprised at the difference. I'm still sure he didn't know who it was that came in wearing only a robe and a belt and stockings!

He never spoke a word. He kissed me only once and then with his eyes shut tight fucked me. I lay where I was when he went upstairs, not exactly happy about it but with a little glow of triumph. It was at least a start.

We're not an ideal couple. We go our own ways often and have different interests. But he's a better lover now and can take more time and open his eyes when he's doing it. I know now I'll never be in love with him but I've learnt a lot about men. It just needs a little courage to be able to satisfy a man and even if we do split up eventually, I feel I could make my own way now quite easily.

I sometimes think about that lover that jilted me and wish I'd known then all that I know now. But meanwhile, I'm sure I'm much happier than most women. And I would advise any 'nice' wife with a bored husband to turn herself into a tart for him. My husband can't be the only man who just doesn't know what to do with a 'good woman'.

Mrs L.E.,
Edinburgh

GROUP MASSAGE

My wife and I recently had our first experience with group sex. We were both surprised at how pleasant and exciting it was and thought your readers might be interested in hearing how we got on.

It came about during a recent visit by my sister and brother-in-law. He and I had never had the time to get to know each other, so the day after they arrived, the two of us went out for a long afternoon beer. We got along well and soon found ourselves involved in a very frank discussion about our sex lives. This turned me on greatly because it was my sister that he was talking about, and I never had any idea she was as sexy as he said she was.

When we got home, we found that our wives had been having a similar discussion and everybody was feeling pretty horny by the time we had dinner. Before sitting down at the table, my brother-in-law and I amused ourselves by leafing through back issues of *Forum* a publication that my wife and I have been reading regularly for about a year.

After dinner we went to the cinema and ran into old friends. This couple quickly accepted our invitation for drinks at our home.

We were all drinking wine and talking about the film which was rather sexy, so the conversation naturally returned to sex. As the evening developed, the talk kept getting franker while everybody seemed to grow friendlier. Somebody raised the subject of vibrators, and my wife went upstairs and brought hers down for a demonstration.

Shortly after this, my sister suggested everybody give me a group massage. I lay down on the rug to receive a mass of prodding fingers and palms. My sister, I discovered, has the most skilful hands. She ran them through my hair with a devastating lightness.

Well, after this, we all did the same thing for my brother-in-law who started to unhitch his pants for better access. Next came my wife, and by this time I had a strong urge to undress her in front of everybody else – so I decided, 'why not, these are all my friends anyway'. In what seemed like no time, everybody was taking off their clothes or helping somebody else undress.

I felt a little self-conscious at first, but this soon gave way to surprisingly pleasant feelings about being naked in the company of other people. There was something very human, very animal and very erotic about it all at once. Ironically, my wife had been telling my sister just that afternoon that she never thought she'd like to indulge in group sex. Yet, when the stripping began, she went right for my brother-in-law's balls. In fact, her

42

eagerness surprised me a bit, but it made me desire her tremendously.

The massage atmosphere carried into the actual lovemaking. That is, people were touching each other without special regard for who the person was or what sex he or she was.

My sister and I more or less agreed on the spot not to fuck each other, though in retrospect I'm pressed to find a rational reason. When it was finally over, nobody got dressed right away. We just kept on drinking wine and talking and dancing until about 5 a.m. It was a great night.

P.M.,
Canada

A GIGOLO'S STORY

I have recently spent a year in Germany and am not at all ashamed to say that I was a gigolo there. Out of a job and with nowhere to live, I answered an advertisement last July for a manservant to live in. Although I had not had any experience, I thought I could bluff it out, and went after the job, which was in a luxury block of flats in a very expensive suburb. A lady who looked 35 (I later discovered she was nearly 50) opened the door – I had made the appointment by telephone – and invited me in, looking me up and down all the while.

We sat and chatted and she was extremely pleasant and very friendly, and I thought it odd that she hardly asked what experience I had had, or for references. She kept saying she found my English accent fascinating (my German was quite poor then).

Eventually she said I could have the job, and named a very high salary, but added that, as she was an artist, she would expect me to pose for her as part of my duties. I agreed to this, which I thought might be quite fun, and thereupon she told me to take off my clothes, so that she could see what sort of model I would be.

Perhaps I should add that I'm 25, have a good body and am tall, and have never been ashamed of showing my body, especially to a woman, so I stood up and started to take off my shirt. Madame (which is what I had to call her invariably) told me not to hurry, as she wished to watch me in movement. When I had got down to my underpants she told me to turn round, came up behind me and pulled them slowly down. It was such a sensuous thing that I immediately had an erection, and when I turned round this evidently pleased her. She made me assume

43

various poses, sitting, standing and lying down, and each time she touched me my erection semed to enlarge. After about half an hour of this we fairly naturally found our way to bed, and she was a wonderful and enthusiastic lover.

I moved in next day, and there began our employer-employee relationship. I knew perfectly well that I was a gigolo, that I was taking money for going to bed with Madame – yet this was a situation that pleased us both, so what the hell? I worked hard, kept the place spick and span, drove her around, collected parcels for her and went on errands, and in between would pose for hours naked on a stool as she drew extremely poor pictures of me.

She never struck me as being a nympho, we rarely made love more than twice a day, but she did get great delight in seeing me around the place naked, and after a week or two I took to spending all my time in the nude, as she obviously liked it, and we didn't have to do so much of the posing lark, which got rather boring.

I tried to earn my money by giving her more and more thrills in bed, and think I succeeded. When she started getting tired of me there was no hard feeling, and we parted amicably.

The money I earned I saved, as there was nothing to spend it on, Madame used to buy me expensive presents of clothing too, and I had a super holiday afterwards with the proceeds. I suppose I would be condemned as a layabout by most, but I've no regrets and would do it again. I'm sure Madame is happier, and she didn't need that money for anything else. I'm sure, too, she has another naked young man hanging around the flat now, and good luck to them both.

There are many women who allow themselves to be kept by men – and these days no one thinks much of it. So why does society think it so wrong if the situation is reversed? There are plenty of older women who need sex – and plenty of younger men who need money – why shouldn't they get together for mutual benefit?

M.P.,
London

IDEALLY BORING

When I was a child I thought how unfair it was that successful men were able to have pretty, young, supportive girlfriends, while successful women still had to look around for men superior to – and probably uglier than – themselves. This being the age of women's lib and all, I finally went out and got myself a young pretty lover. It was lovely for a little while, but that was it. I don't understand how otherwise self-respecting men can be content living with someone they consider inferior their whole lives.

My ex-boyfriend Allen was absolutely gorgeous – half Argentine and half Swedish! He was two years younger than me, but we look about the same age, so I didn't get any 'dirty old lady' looks (why is it men with girls 10 years younger don't get those looks?). Allen was the ideal – well, 'wife'. He was very loving and affectionate and a generous and undemanding lover. He's a carpenter and loves to work with his hands. He was always fixing up the house, which I never had time to do, and liked experimenting with gourmet recipes, making leather clothes and that sort of thing. He was very emotionally supportive, always willing to listen to my complaints when I got home from the office.

I make quite a bit more money than Allen, so I paid most of the bills. I didn't mind that at all, nor was Allen a social 'embarrassment' or anything like that. Even though he wasn't successful or powerful, he's charming socially and very good looking. He was a good escort.

But after a while, an 'ideal wife' isn't a very ideal thing. Besides being affectionate, sweet, loyal and supportive, Allen was – well, a little boring. He's charming, but not nearly as intelligent as I am, and not very educated or even well read. He would be very sympathetic when I told him about office politics, or emotional problems at work, but when I talked about ideas or projects that excited me intellectually, I got no feedback, no stimulation. He just listened dutifully. When I had the kind of depression where you want someone to love you, he was great. But when I had the kind of depression that has to do with re-examining values, he wasn't much help. Fond as I was of him, I reached the point where I wanted a man who was my real equal – maybe less supportive, but at least more challenging.

Every woman, and man, should have an Allen once in their lives. But when I meet men who have contentedly passed 15, 20, 25 years with a woman considerably duller than themselves, I marvel at what a frail thing a male ego is.

Ms N.S.,
Los Angeles

SELF-DEFENCE

For the past year I have studied Akido, a Japanese self-defence art. I have found that knowing I can defend myself physically has made me much freer sexually. Perhaps my experience can benefit other women.

When I was a young woman I was 'semi-raped' twice. I found myself alone in a flat with a man I didn't want to sleep with, who wanted to sleep with me. There was a struggle. Both times I gave in – the first time because I was really afraid of being hurt, the second because I felt I had 'asked for it' somehow and giving in seemed easier and less embarrassing than struggling. One result of this was that I became very shy of picking up men, and never let myself be alone with a man I wasn't sure I wanted to sleep with. Even with a man I did want to sleep with, I was always a little nervous the first time.

I realized how timid I was last year when I lived in France. My French is adequate, but I wasn't fluent for five or six months. During this time I met several marvellous Frenchmen, but I didn't ball any of them. I was afraid to let myself be alone with a man when I couldn't understand his language well enough to be sure I had judged his character properly.

As a result of this, I decided to take Akido. It made even more of a difference in my feeling about men than I expected. For the first time in my life I knew the strength of my own body – what it could and couldn't do. When I had studied long enough so I felt I could defend myself I was able for the first time even to go up to a man I wanted to meet at a party, and aggressively seduce him. Besides the emotional freedom it gave me, knowing how my body was put together and where my muscles were made the physical side of sex better too.

It takes at least six months of bi-weekly lessons in a self-defence art for a person to be able to use it effectively, and at least two years of study to be really good. For me it has certainly been worth it. I'm sure my fear and distrust of men was exaggerated and somewhat neurotic, but I'm also sure many women must experience a milder version of my feelings. It might be worth it for them, too, to spend some time learning to defend themselves.

Miss M.R.,
Address withheld by request

DEPRIVED CHAUVINIST

I'm 25, and for years I have been considered the most highly-sexed man in my crowd. Other fellows always poked fun about how I could seduce women at the drop of a hint, and my former college room-mates even used to keep score of my conquests. I could always get it up, and when a girl was hard to satisfy, I could keep from climaxing for hours. I think this success with women comes from a real security about my masculinity, as I have never suffered from 'fear of rejection or refusal' from a woman. A healthy man is turned on by resistance from a girl!

But I have a problem. Lately, girls have been too willing, too direct and too brash to turn me on. It used to be that when I made a pass at a girl in a bar or a party, she always looked shocked and rebuked my advances. I could always get to her, but she insisted on the usual preliminaries of dinner in a restaurant, a few drinks to loosen her morals, and maybe some flowers. I never minded that type of courtship and enjoyed seducing females into bed.

Nowadays, the chicks I meet take one look at me and ask me to fuck them. They have no shame about it any more! The most recent shocker came when an 18-year-old girl from a good family walked right up to me and said, 'I think you are very handsome, and I'd like to taste your come'. She is not a whore or a cheap girl from the street, and I must admit I was so horrified, I almost slapped her. I don't consider myself a prude – far from it – but when I take a girl to bed, I don't expect her to make the moves and ask me to suck her off or to sodomize her, and that is the very thing which keeps happening to me!

My reaction to this type of behaviour on the part of the girls I pick up is my problem. My formerly stiff and obedient penis will not perform for this kind of chick. I go limp. I guess you call it impotence. Whatever it is, I have it!

Am I going crazy? Is it old-fashioned to expect a bit of decency from girls? Please don't tell me to go for younger girls because they are the worst offenders – they act like they invented sex! Have you any suggestions? I am truly perplexed.

L.K.,
Address withheld by request

I think you're going to have to change a lot of your attitudes. Begging your pardon, I would suggest you have a very real 'insecurity about your masculinity' and that this has been demonstrated by the impotence you experience when 'modern' girls

47

*offer you sex without crawling and without the guilt you seem
to require from them! Why do you have to 'make the moves'?
Why should girls feel ashamed of their sexuality? Why are
street girls 'cheap'?*

*No, you are not going mad. Girls are more aware of their
own bodies' longings than ever before, while you are caught up
in what we might term the 'conquest myth' about sex.*

*Some of the behaviour you describe women performing does
not comprise the most dignified or elegant approach to a man's
heart. But you need to be indulgent about it. Girls are only just
learning about their own rights to possess any object they find
attractive. They are not perhaps practised in the art of seduction and they may sometimes be too openly blunt about their
desire for sexual contact.*

*You now have to unlearn some of the things you once knew
about women because women themselves are changing. They
want men as much as men want them.*

*Your temporary impotence is due only to the fact that you
feel your 'masculinity' is threatened. All you've got to do now is
to learn to respect women as people who have a right, if they
like, to treat fucking as no more than fucking, just as you have
done. You've got to stop being so arrogant about your male
sex-role – men are no more marvellous than women! 'Get to
know the people you fuck' – learn a little sexual democracy and
perhaps then, when you can condescend to respect the rights of
others to behave contrary to the ways in which you think they
should behave, your limpness will wear off and your penis will
work again!*

A HAPPY MARRIAGE

I am a woman of 60 and should like to add my comments on
some topics discussed in *Forum*.

I married at 20 as a shy virgin. My husband had had the
foresight to openly discuss sex with me and I soon overcame my
shyness and did everything he wanted. I quickly found out
what really turned him on, and was surprised at all the things I
started to enjoy. There was nothing like *Forum* in my young
days, but there were those certain books you could get if you
tried and I obtained some very useful information which I put
into practice. My husband never refused me and I never refused
him; communication was really open between us.

I surprised him by shaving completely and he joined me, the

coming of the electric razor meant I only had to shave once or twice every three weeks as the hair softened considerably.

We overcame the problem of him coming off too soon by a method that may help other readers. I would sit him down once or twice a week and stimulate his penis manually and orally until he told me he was about to come. Then I would stop, let him cool down, then start again, doing this about four or five times and bringing him off the last time. This meant he became used to a great deal of stimulation and our lovemaking lasted a lot longer.

One day when we were out on a picnic he took a photograph of me climbing over a style showing a lot of leg and undies. As this pleased him I posed some more without undies and since then we have taken a lot of pictures of each other doing all sorts of things, both indoors and out.

We always made the utmost use of any time when the children were out of the way, from a quick fondle under our clothes to a quickie on the table.

Our greatest wish was to be photographed together, and this came about when we were entertaining a couple of very close friends who asked us if we would photograph them. That evening we all photographed each other and I experienced sex with another man for the first time, something most women must think about sometime.

A happy marriage and a healthy sex life show when a woman looks in the mirror of a morning. She is conscious of a glow from being deeply loved and well fucked! I am often thought to be about 40 and women ask me how I maintain my figure and looks.

But how can one explain it's in the mind and way of life. If you live like my husband and I you stay young together. It is very sad when one hears a woman say it's too late to change her ways or her husbands or when women start dressing old, thinking old. They very soon look and feel a lot older than they are and wonder why their husbands start looking around or have affairs.

Three years ago my husband was killed in an accident, and our photos have been of great consolation to me, reminding me of all the wonderful times we had together. I would recommend any couple to do this; apart from the pleasure gained in taking them and looking back at them, there comes a time when their worth is beyond price.

Name and address withheld by request

CAN'T MAKE LOVE TWICE IN AN HOUR!

I have been having sexual relations with my fiancée for four months. We are very much in love and enjoy our sex life.

My problem is that I find it easy to make love once, but when it comes to doing it again within an hour I find it almost impossible. I have managed to make love again quickly once or twice but never so much as I would wish. My fiancée says she does not mind but I would dearly love to be able to do this. I have read about psychological reasons for not being able to make love but often I am relaxed and calm, yet I am rarely aroused. Sometimes I can get a partial erection yet cannot maintain it.

We make love fairly regularly, sometimes two or three times a day, but only after going a couple of days without making love.

I am 21, in good health and very fit, please, please help.

M.C.,
Birmingham

I think your letter illustrates one of the difficulties which arise in connection with sexual prowess. Since we don't have sexual olympics where all can see for themselves the performance of which the best are capable, the subject is shrouded in myth and doubt. Thus a perfectly normal and adequate performer such as yourself can develop totally unwarranted feelings of inferiority.

Stories about huge penes, prolonged and repeated acts of intercourse, and of men who can seduce women more or less on sight abound and are the subject of many sex jokes. They are rarely confirmed by the women who are in the best position to know – namely prostitutes. A very large penis is a rarity and similarly men capable of repeated acts of intercourse are rare. Prostitutes who sell time rather than an act of intercourse are quite scathing about male sexual ability. They compare men with children whose eyes are bigger than their bellies!

Interest in sex and responsiveness to it is quickly lost in most males after orgasm. The commonest desire is to sleep and this is true also of animals. (Rats, in fact emit a special sound which warns the females that they must not disturb his post-orgasmic sleep in an attempt to seduce him.) Biologically speaking the reason for this is obvious; it allows the semen-producing organs to recuperate. Females, on the other hand, have no such problem and are therefore, other things being equal, 'always ready'.

Since everyone is different, there are obviously differences between males in their capacity to undertake repeated intercourse just as there are differences in athletic and intellectual capacities. Kinsey looked into the matter and reported that a few males can perform a number of times over short periods of time. Male prostitutes, he says, usually have orgasms and ejaculate (a small quantity) during their contacts and do so up to five or six or even more times in a day. Between the ages of 16 and 20 something like one per cent of boys claim to be able to manage three to four orgasms in one prolonged sex act, perhaps not even losing their erection between ejaculations. In the 36 to 40 years age group the proportion is less than one-half per cent – one in 200! When it is remembered that the individuals giving the information to Kinsey may have been boasting a bit it is possible that these figures are over-estimates. It not uncommonly happens in practice that the female often fails to substantiate her partner's performance claims, especially if they are interviewed separately!

Turning to my own cases, as opposed to Kinsey's, I find, as he did, that during adolescence most males can and do, at least occasionally, ejaculate three to six times in a day. A fair number of young adult males may have intercourse up to three times in a day when circumstances are favourable. However, even adding intercourse and masturbation together, an ejaculation rate of between two to three times daily to once weekly is the general norm. One West Indian sought and managed intercourse between six and eight times in a day but his reactions, when he was refused, suggested that his motives were not purely sexual! Other similar cases make me think that many of these men are 'in trouble'. Because they have a poor male self-image, or because they are latently homosexual, or because they are so inhibited they can't 'let go' and have one solid, satisfying orgasm, they are neurotically obsessed with their ability to give repeated performances. It is their main preoccupation in life. When sex is such a labour it can't be a pleasure.

You're doing more than fine! Forget it!

DON'T TELL

I feel I must write in defence of Robert Chartham, who has been taken to task for saying that one should not necessarily tell one's spouse if one has been unfaithful.

My wife and I had been married (I thought reasonably happily) for 16 years when out of the blue she confessed that she had had a love affair. It had started two years after we married and continued for seven years.

She confessed, she said, to ease her conscience. But she also put the burden of her guilt on my shoulders. I was shattered. I would have staked everything I had on my wife; I loved her very dearly.

For some months life between us was pitiful and it was only because I could not let our children know that I stayed at home. Whether this was a good decision I am unable to say.

However for some three or four years we continued together, though we did not have sex for this period. Nagging doubts in my mind gave way to curiosity and very, very slowly I have persuaded her to talk to me about her affair. (Eventually I found out there had been more than just one.)

Our children have now married and left home. My wife and I are far more free; she will often give long intimate details of the fucks she has had and I thoroughly enjoy this. We have patched things up. She will very occasionally allow me to bring a friend in and sometimes lets me watch while she enjoys him.

But the whole point of this letter is to say to anyone who thinks of confessing their illicit love affair: 'DON'T!' If your partner is blissfully unaware – keep quiet and leave him or her in peace. From my personal experience even the (innocent?) partner feels somehow tarnished or degraded – it seems as though one is fucking another man's woman.

Only if you have already confessed, and your partner shows some interest, then I recommend giving all the sexiest details you can – and answering his/her questions quite frankly and fully. In other words allow him/her to join in and get some enjoyment from it. It cannot do you any harm, but it will please your partner, and will gradually wear itself out so that you may both settle down to a reasonably happy relationship.

I devoutly wish my wife had never told me. My previous love for her has disappeared and I no longer worry so much about her. We have however a reasonably happy life together, in view of all that's gone before. And as I am now allowed to join in her past experiences I admit I thoroughly enjoy listening to the most intimate details and get real pleasure in imagining the situations she describes.

Please don't think I am blameless. But I never knew about the sexual desires she had – she wanted to do slightly unusual things and didn't know how I would react. So when the opportunity occurred to have an affair with a man with a reputation as a womanizer, who knew most sexual variations, she jumped at it.

Finally, I believe Dr Chartham to be correct. If your partner doesn't know, keep quiet – if he does and wants details, share them with him.

M.M.,
Essex

LIFE IN THE SILENT MAJORITY

There are so many people with problems that we thought it might cheer some of your readers up to hear how one typical, middle-aged, monogamous couple passes a typical week, sex-wise. I'm 53 and keep a shop; my wife is 49, helps in it part time and keeps the house.

Sunday morning usually begins with a long, long mutual masturbation. A favourite way is with her face upwards on top so that we have four arms like one of those Eastern goddesses, my two caressing nipples, hers gently using my penis as a vibrator on herself – but all hands seem interchangeable. There'll be a long walk in the Welsh hills in the afternoon, and at night I'll fall asleep curled round her with my penis in situ; a marvellous way to start a night of lovely dreams.

Probably Tuesday, at lunchtime (and how sorry I feel for those people who have no chance to play in the middle of the day) either one of us may get a spanking interspersed with some delicate, prolonged but (all in the game) apparently quite unintended digital manipulation of the culprit's genitals, ending up at about a quarter to two with a wonderful 69. That night looking to see if there are any marks will be bound to lead to a fuck.

By Thursday or Friday morning something is bound to be started that there isn't time to finish before it's time to get up, so lunchtime finds us wandering naked round the flat. Getting a meal or trying to do some chores while being, as they say, orally stimulated anywhere, any time, is an incredible way to spend an hour and by night it takes at least another one to clear the blockage.

About four climaxes a week is par for me, but she gets three or more to my one and as each one averages an hour and a half of foreplay I suppose we are at it six or seven hours a week.

We also have some silly clothes like my track suit with an elastic ringed hole for my prick and balls to protrude through and her absolutely respectable and fashionable dress – at the front – without any back of any kind whatsoever, except the belts at the waist and neck which keeps it on.

Apart from this we read and walk, do some yoga exercises, spend a time meditating every day and go to Church sometimes. We both love food and wine (she is a dream of a cook). Several times a year we drive 150 miles to London to go to a film, or a concert or a play or exhibition. It is almost certainly illegal to drive at night with your trousers off and your wife with her knickers round her ankles, talking over what one has been doing, concentrating every necessary faculty on driving one handed, seriously, safely, and well, but at the same time having this quite separate and interesting sensation.

So after 27 years and some lovely grandchildren we are a typical middle-aged couple. Typical of that silent majority that our dear Muggeridge, Whitehouse and Longford say they speak for and understand so well.

W.D.,
Wales

FAINTING IN BED

I am 18 and my girlfriend 17. We have had sex about a dozen times but recently we had the chance to spend the night together. We had never been able to be in a bed naked together and we had a lot of foreplay before we had sex. When we had finished we lay holding each other and after about 15 minutes I started caressing her again. I used my mouth on her nipples for a while and was using my finger on her clitoris. After a time I started using my tongue on her clitoris and she got very worked up fondling my penis and balls. She was soon squirming all over the bed and pulled me off and guided my penis into her. I had no sooner gone in when she came and after a couple of minutes she came again. I was feeling very much in control and she was moving with me. I kept on and she started to come without pause and this went on for at least 10 minutes with her groaning and gasping.

Suddenly she gave a terrific shudder and jerked even harder. I could feel the movements of her around my penis and I came too. As I did, she went limp. I lay there for a minute. And then I saw that she had fainted!

I was very worried and got a cloth for her forehead. She came round, then we went to sleep. In the morning she got me hard again and I had her again.

I read something Dr Robert Chartham wrote about women

fainting sometimes and would like to know if there is any danger in it or if it could happen again?

D.G.,
Gloucestershire

I am delighted to hear that you both enjoyed such a fulfilling night together! The fainting attack which your girlfriend experienced is not particularly unusual in an instance like the one you so well describe where the emotional and sexual build-up and anticipation of a whole night in bed together has caused immense excitement. Obviously, your previous sexual experiments must have been very successful, so that when you were able to realize so many of your previous fantasies, then the result was just too much for her to take, all in one fell swoop. No doubt there will be occasions again when you will reach such a sexual peak as to cause her actually to faint, but as opportunity will become kinder to you, then so you will find that your lovemaking will more usually adopt a more moderate pace. Her fainting may then occur only after periods of separation, or other intense build-up.

I ought to express a word or two of caution, I think. Firstly, it would be reassuring to know if she has ever had a full medical check-up. If she faints on other occasions, or too often after a more relaxed sexual binge, then she really ought to tell her doctor of this tendency to faint. There is the vague possibility of anaemia, or a heart defect which could cause this. But that is extremely unlikely. A girl of 17 tends to faint more readily than at other ages.

Also, when she does appear unconscious, please remember to treat her so; keep her lying down on one side, and with her head to one side, propped to face downwards.

This is to avoid the inhalation of vomit, or her tongue, in the unconscious state.

Please don't let me alarm you; it is my inborn doctor's caution! Do ask her if she remembers fainting. If not, I feel that is another good reason to seek her doctor's advice.

But there is a 99·9% chance that she is just a lucky, highly sexually-attuned young woman!

ELECTRIC BANANA

Until quite recently, I always thought fellatio to be disgustingly abnormal. The very idea of accepting a male penis

55

into my mouth really turned me up. However, I have changed my mind completely all because of a simple little thing that happened one evening when copulating.

Jim and I were in that position – for which I'm sure there is an 'official' number but which I wouldn't know – whereby I was sitting astride his lap on a chair facing him. It was all going a bit flat on us and thinking it just wasn't going to work I suggested we broke off and had something to eat.

In fun, Jim reached out and took a banana from the fruit dish and began feeding me with it. The feel of the banana in my mouth did things to me and I realized that I was actually making love to the silly thing and almost immediately found myself and Jim galloping to orgasm. It was absolutely extraordinary. We did it on several subsequent occasions until Jim brought in an artificial whatsit which we used instead whenever I fancied it. It's like having your cake and eating it too!

It seemed quite natural after a while for me to try the real thing, although I confess that I have yet to brave it without a sheath.

I've heard of foods being aphrodisiacs, but not of the actual act of eating turning one on.

Mrs S.W.,
Essex

Remember that famous eating scene in 'Tom Jones'? It was sexier – to my mind – than practically anything in 'Last Tango'.

The first sensuous pleasure any of us received was through our mouths; no one who has watched a baby at the breast can be in doubt of that.

This oral sensitivity becomes overshadowed by genital sensation in later life, but its erotic potential is never lost. Hence our pleasure in deep kissing – hence also the tendency of fashion to emphasize women's lips with make-up, both for their own sake and because (it has been said) they are unconsciously seen as analogues or symbols of the vulva.

The act of sucking itself, whatever its object, can be deeply relaxing – as though it recalls the warmth, security, and tenderness experienced in the suckling situation in infancy. And it's well known that relaxation is highly conducive to sexual arousal. Part of women's pleasure in fellatio obviously arises from the genital contact, but this mainly affects the 'adult' in us. The rhythmic, repetitive motion of lips, tongue, even throat *involved go deeper still; they reach the sensuous, uninhibited 'child' who is buried within each of us.*

TAKE HEART

I am six foot tall, slim, pleasantly shaped and with 'acceptable' looks. My penis when flaccid is small enough to embarrass *me* – but not anyone else! When erect and at its most excited, it is a slim five and a half inches.

These very few ounces of erectile tissue have given me and my lovers of both sexes and all races some 12,700 minutes of intense pleasure: over 2,000 hours of sexual intimacy. (Not counting almost half as much time spent in pleasing myself with the sin of Onan!)

The diaries I have kept since I was 15 tell me that my insignificant weapon has successfully given many hundreds of orgasms to many hundreds of lovers – including my wife, to whom I have been very happily married for 15 years and with whom I still enjoy a sufficient variety of sexual intimacies to make sure that 'custom does not stale' our intercourse two, three or four times a week.

No one, out of all those hundreds and in all those years has ever complained about the size of my penis, or even remarked upon it – except to assure me that it gave them as much pleasure as any other that they had enjoyed: whenever possible, *all* my lovers have come back for more 'of the same, please!'

Moreover, I and my penis have very often followed or preceded a magnificent whopper ... without suffering from any comparison.

Of course, I am a very expert and experienced lover and do not solely rely on my tool to get results. But the point remains: my below-average cock *works*, giving and taking pleasure; and it is often far more efficient, long-lasting in its efforts to please, more effective and better remembered than the bigger – and better? – organs I have so often wished that I possessed!

So take heart, all ye with the little peckers! Make merry and sacrifice to Eros with what you have – *make the best of it*: you *could* be the envy of millions of handsome, virile, stalwart, and *lonely* well-hung studs – who just haven't a clue, don't know where it's at, can't get it, and don't know what to do with it when they have got it!

I am 50 – and look forward to quite a few more years giving and taking pleasure; making the fullest use of that which in retrospect now appears a far more formidable friend than it does at first sight, or did when first I compared it to the proud brutes my teenage friends displayed with such (unwarranted, as I know now) superiority.

Name and address withheld
by request

HELPFUL NURSE

My husband and I enjoy Forum and discuss the letters which interest us the most in each issue. Our sex life is still active and exciting, although we have been married 17 years and have three children. We try to make each sex event mutually thrilling and satisfying. The letter from Miss M.W., a nurse, in a recent issue makes us believe that we might contribute to your readers' understanding of another aspect of hospital life.

A few months ago, I was hospitalized for 23 days. At no time was I 'ill' in the sense of incapacitation. After the first few days, my husband and I were horny and spent the most of each of his nightly visits sneaking feels. With nurses and others coming and going, it was very frustrating. My husband would go home and masturbate, while I required mild sedation in order to get to sleep. My attempts at masturbation invariably were interrupted until I gave up trying.

One night, when I was particularly aroused, a nurses' aide, a cute young woman of 29, came in after my husband's departure to give me my nightly back-rub. I am sure that she sensed my condition and, in fact, brought the subject up in an off-hand way. Lying on my tummy, with my gown pushed up to my armpits, she applied the lotion and her hands with what I thought was unusual enthusiasm. Instead of stopping just below the small of my back, which was the usual terminal, she applied more lotion to my buttocks and proceeded to knead and stroke them in a most skilful way. Then she said, in so many words, that what I needed was a good relaxing orgasm and that if I had no objection she would take care of it for me. I threw caution to the wind and told her to do whatever she wished.

She raised my rump, pushed my legs apart and went to work. She knew her business. She pushed both thumbs into my cunt and while she thrust her right thumb in and out, her right palm and fingers caressed my mound and clitoris in circular motions. I came quickly, but intensely.

My nurses' aide took care of my sex tensions every night during the remainder of my stay. She was truly an expert. She told me that she did this for several patients when she saw evidence of sexual frustration. She also said that she was bisexual and enjoyed rendering this service for both men and women.

I said nothing about this to my husband until I had been home a couple of weeks. At an opportune moment, I told him how the nurses' aide had taken care of me. To my relief, he thought it a great idea and was truly glad that I was able to assuage my sex-hunger in such a logical and harmless manner. We often talk about it in moments of passion and he teases me about my 'lesbian' experiences.

I have no idea, of course, how prevalent such practices are in hospitals, but I certainly do not see anything wrong with anyone getting their sex needs taken care of in such a pleasant and harmless way.

Mrs A.I.,
Address withheld by request

LOVE BY LETTER

I am a salesman, and I have to spend a lot of time away from my wife. It is a lonely life and the hours you spend alone in your room are often those of reflection. The temptation to find company is great, but I've always had strong scruples about that sort of thing because I love my wife.

However, about two years ago, I decided to write and tell her exactly how I felt when I was away from her. My letters became highly erotic and, whereas I had always been so careful to use 'correct' language even when making love (we've been married for 25 years) I tried to explain my thoughts in as vivid and stimulating a manner as my imagination could produce.

She was surprised because the letters revealed a different person than she thought she knew. As the letters got sexier, my returns home got more and more beautiful. She started giving my cock a lot more attention, especially by kissing it and sucking me off. I think I taught her how through my letters. She looks forward to receiving them more than ever now.

My wife writes to *me* now as I write to her. She explores the depth of her own sensuality. We are both surprised and turned on, and our marriage is better than ever.

I think one reason this worked so well for us is that it is often easier to write things than say them. Perhaps other couples who have difficulty communicating what they really want from each other sexually should try letter-writing rather than talking.

Name and address withheld
by request

JOB SATISFACTION

I have been a prostitute for several years and I am a little bewildered by the fact that very few people really understand or appreciate the world's oldest profession. Whenever I meet a new person who isn't in my business world and I want to be honest with them, I come across the problem of explaining my profession. For some reason men don't believe me, but women seem to understand how I can have sexual relations with a man who pays me for that purpose. I don't feel that I am detrimental to society, to the men who pay me, or to myself. The only thing I find wrong with prostitution is that it is illegal and thus may lead a prostitute to fall into the wrong crowd and settle into a destructive life.

I have never had a romantic or sexual interest in the men who pay me. I meet many nice men but for some reason if they have been a customer of mine, I cannot get interested in them. When I meet a man I can love and enjoy sexually it is usually someone who knows nothing about prostitution and that's the hard part of my work. A man cannot understand how I can perform my job and still consider him to be the one in my life. A few years ago I married a pimp because I couldn't find a man with whom I could have an honest open relationship. That helped me to understand that I was pretty desperate just to have a man. I don't know why pimps ever came into existence and I feel they are becoming extinct because a woman doesn't have to make so many excuses for even becoming a prostitute these days. The profession is more openly accepted around the world and in some societies it is even respected.

I became a prostitute because I had two children, no education, no husband, two jobs and bad health because I was working 16 hours a day and trying to be a good mother at the same time. I didn't like living at welfare standards and I didn't want to go on welfare because I felt that I didn't want to exist on that. I could have married someone who was willing to help raise my children but I didn't find a man with whom I felt I wanted to spend the rest of my life. So I started seeing a man

60

for money and he introduced me to more people and soon I was in business making a good living.

During the years I have been a prostitute, I have learned many things and got to know many people. Outside of trying to justify myself for being a whore to the few men I really cared for, it has been a good experience for me. I feel that prostitution should be legalized so I can pay my taxes and feel like an ordinary woman raising her children and giving them and myself a good comfortable life.

I would like to know what other people think of prostitution. Is the body any more sacred than the mind? Do I have to be ostracized because I use my body to make a living? Do I have to lie to the man I care for because I am afraid that he will be unable to accept what I do for a living, thinking I am decadent and not worthy of his affection and love? I want to be honest with myself and with the man I love.

Maybe your magazine is going to do away with prostitution by informing people about the beautiful and natural side of sexual union and love. There is a need for prostitutes now because there are so many wives who still won't or can't satisfy their loved ones. There are still people who don't know how to express their needs or desires because they are ashamed or ignorant of the fact that we were born with physical needs that we must satisfy. If sex were just meant for procreation then women would come on heat like most animals. Frankly I feel that men pay prostitutes for their favours just to have a physical partner to satisfy their needs. I have hardly met a married man who doesn't care for his wife. Most men don't want to fall in love just to satisfy their sexual appetites or maybe they are too shy or too busy to find a partner. Mainly they see a prostitute because they just can't communicate. I don't feel bad because I can bring a few moments of happiness and pleasure into someone's life and get paid for it all at the same time. However, it's not the answer to fulfilment and happiness.

Sex is a very important part of my life and one of my greatest pleasures is making love, sharing, giving, pleasing and receiving the intense feeling you get from a lover. It's just another form of communicating with the person you love.

(*Miss*) *Name and address withheld*
by request

NEEDS APHRODISIAC

As an avid reader of your publication and knowing how you are able to help other people with their problems, I wonder if you could help me?

I am courting a girl and we plan to get engaged later in the year. My problem is that, while she allows some very heavy necking, she will not go the full distance, so I wondered if you could recommend some place where I could purchase an aphrodisiac of some sort which I could administer to her?

It would require to be of a tasteless nature, as she does not drink alchohol and does not take either milk or sugar in tea or coffee.

I feel that once she gets over her initial coyness everything would be O.K. with us.

Trusting you may be able to come up with some 'solution'.

J.S.,
Scotland

I think you're probably copping out. If you want to go to bed with your girlfriend, why don't you own up and tell her, so that she can decide if she wants to go to bed with you?

Are you afraid she's been turning you down because she doesn't actually fancy you? It might be so. Can't you be brave enough to find out?

If your girlfriend doesn't want to have pre-marital or pre-engagement sex at all, the decision is hers. We might suggest she's missing out on a lot. But you've no right to go around removing her liberty to do what she likes with her own property (namely, her own body) by 'administering' things to her without her knowledge.

On the other hand, if she's just being coy then she deserves whatever sly tricks you can play on her – provided you don't bully or coerce. Because life's short, according to the poet, coyness is a crime and seduction's fair in love and war if only you get your foot in the door.

What to use? First, drugs are out because they're dangerous. The best-known aphrodisiac is Spanish Fly, also known as Russian Fly or Spanish Blister, obtained from the dried bodies of insects (mylabris cichorii, campharis vesicatoria and marcobasis albida). The active ingredient is cantharidin, which gives rise to the group of substances known as the cantharides. The effect of the cantharides is to increase the blood-flow to the area in question; then to produce a warm itching sensation; then to dilate the surrounding blood vessels so extremely that their walls collapse and fluid escapes into the tissue spaces under the skin (hence the term Russian Blister). If taken orally, they are absorbed from the gut and excreted through the kidneys with a burning pain in the mouth, vomiting, diarrhoea, abdominal pain, blood-stained urine, the desired condition of sexual frenzy shortly followed by circulatory collapse, shock and death! This seems a rather high price to pay. Drug treatments such as hormone therapy, would not be made available by doctors for purely aphrodisiac purposes. Others such as pot or opium are illegal.

The remaining aphrodisiacs can be divided into 'mental' aphrodisiacs, and 'food-and-drink'. Mental aphrodisiacs include everything from perfumes to pornography to money. Try introducing your girlfriend to erotic literature, buy her perfume, make her feel rich by spending a lot of money in one evening.

Then during dinner, contemplate all the different items of food and drink that might work: Walter, the Victorian 'Casanova', recommends a full spicy meal with plenty of wines and spirits to 'heat up her lower regions. Wait until the food is travelling downward and success is assured.' Other recipes have included mackerel, asparagus, ginseng, celery, truffles, strawberries, caviar, raw eggs, calf's foot, pigs' trotters, capers, caraway seed, wheatgerm, cumin seed, jellied consommé, foie gras, snails, garlic, gherkins, aniseed, jasmine, pansies, radishes, frog's legs, artichokes, oysters, larks, tripe, carp, escallops, figs, langoustines, marrons glacés, camel's hump, bat's blood, rhino's horn and tigers' testicles if you can get close enough to see them.

Of course, none of these 'works' on its own. The only true aphrodisiacs are negative ones like good health, lots of sleep and self-confidence. But if you follow Walter's advice and make your friend just a little tipsy on a well-fed stomach, make her feel desirable and lead the conversation round towards sex; make no sudden fast moves – perhaps even appear less interested than usual – you will stand a better-than-average chance of success.

You'd do even better if you could really fall in love: that turns everyone on.

POPPET ON A STRING

My husband is 6ft 1in and I am 5ft 4in and he can lift me

with one hand, so sometimes I have to 'boss' him a bit. A week or two ago we were having some sex fun, and as he is too strong for me I had tied his hands behind his back. I then tied a piece of thin string under the glans penis and as he had a good erection this was tight on him so he could not pull it off. I then tied the other end of the string on to a hook we have in the ceiling of our kitchen. I tied the string taut so that he could just, and only just, keep his heels on the floor. Then to tease him I said I would go to town and do the shopping, and would see him later. He protested that he didn't want to be left like that but I told him this was my turn to be the 'boss'.

I didn't intend to be more than half an hour, but I met an old friend just in from England, and time went by so quickly I suddenly realized I had been nearly an hour and a half. I rushed back home, and he was so glad to see me he didn't even tell me off, but said, 'Get this stuff off quickly I've had this erection for nearly two hours and I'm not going to waste it.' We just got together on the floor and I didn't even lock the kitchen door. We had a fantastic session.

What happened after I left is interesting. My husband got on to his toes to ease the tautness on his penis, but as soon as his penis started to wilt the string pulled tight and he had nothing to rub against as he was in the middle of the kitchen, and his hands were tied behind his back, so he was really helpless. He said he had the erection practically the whole time I was away; it must have been getting on for two hours!

We have some fantastic beaches here, miles long, where you can swim in the nude, and sometimes I tie him up in the same way and lead him along the beach, but of course not near the ordinary beaches. I use fairly thin string as, if he is awkward, I give it a little tug and he soon comes 'to heel'.

Well, a girl has to be 'top dog' sometimes and on the quiet I know he enjoys it.

Mrs J.M.,
Bahamas

FLAVOUR OF THE NIGHT

I love going down on my boyfriend or giving him 'a trip' as we call it. Our nickname comes from the first time that I ever went down on him. After he came, he told me that it was like 'a trip around the world'.

I particularly enjoy it when he comes in my mouth since I

like the taste and feel of his semen. In the past few issues of *Forum* I have read a few letters commenting on the taste of semen.

Since I give my boyfriend 'a trip' almost every night (in addition to our regular lovemaking) I have had a chance to compare the many variations in the taste of his semen. After eating certain types of foods, I noticed that his semen has distinctly different tastes. In particular, after he has eaten spicy kinds of things like pizza, spaghetti, chilli etc, his semen tastes quite sweet and after he has drunk even a little beer, his semen has quite a sourish, beer taste.

I have no explanation for the differences in the taste of my boyfriend's semen, but I always have something to look forward to, wondering what the 'flavour of the night' will be.

Miss K.B.,
Kent

SEX AND THE BIBLE?

One morning I found a copy of your magazine on my front lawn. Since then I have read it from cover to cover. Being a fundamentalist, one who believes God created our earth in six literal days, my sincere belief is that there should not be so much flak between religious people and the sexual community. Let me explain.

Following initial events in the first chapter of Genesis, it is quite repetitious in recording after each day's creative activity, '. . . and God saw that it was good'. This statement was repeated for six days, and God rested the seventh day.

What I am getting at is our Creator derived intense satisfaction from the act of creating life, and he wanted mankind to enjoy the identical, continuous joys of creating new life. So *He* put thrills in the sex act.

That a personal God blessed our coitus with thrills is missed by religionists who relegate God to a nonpersonal, puppet role of following modernistic evolutionary processes. Being a God with feeling, he made sex the highest pleasurable, emotional function known to man and woman.

Victorianism did not come from the Bible. Nothing could be further from the truth, and we'll cite one biblical story. On his deathbed when King David had about finished his days of life, and to be sure he had no manly bedroom action left in him, something very un-Victorian was done. Following customs of their times, a call went out to bring the kingdom's most attractive virgin to King David's bedside. We'll read from the Living Bible translation of I Kings 1; 1 to 4: '. . . In his old age King David was confined to his bed; but no matter how many blankets were heaped upon him, he was always cold. "The cure for this," his aides told him, "is to find a young virgin to be your concubine and nurse. She will lie in your arms and keep you warm." So they searched the country from one end to the other to find the most beautiful girl in the land. Abishag, from Shunan, was finally selected. They brought her to the king and she lay in his arms to warm him (but he had no sexual relations with her).'

So when the warm, nude body of a virgin could not fan life in the old patriarch, one of his sons ascended the throne. Of course that was before stethoscopes and ECGs, but no modern method could surpass that ancient custom for detecting manly action.

Read another Bible book, The Song of Solomon, which is a literary parable depicting God's love for his church, told as a lover extolling soft and beautiful attributes of his betrothed. It is an inspired gem of writing, but truly not for Victorian minds.

Sex is beautiful as a natural function, the way God made it.

H.J.,
Scotland

SEX LIFE OF A GENIUS

I have a query, not a problem. Might it not be the case that an individual who attained complete satisfaction in his sexual life would have little motive and inclination for great, or even considerable attainment in other directions?

Is it not probable that the majority of major contributions to art, literature and music have been made by men – usually of strong sexual drive and sensual imagination who have been largely, sometimes nearly entirely (eg Beethoven) thwarted in their sexual desires and whose libido finds an alternative expression?

If the accumulated biographical evidence points this way, is Forum always quite right in wishing full sexual satisfaction to everyone as often as possible? Is this your answer: 'We wish it, but – alas – in the best of worlds they won't get it – or get it enough all the time. There'll always be some frustration for them all – including artists?'

F.J.,
Surrey

The Professor of Medicine at Oxford University has just said that all great scientists are neurotics, from Freud to Einstein and back again. The same has often been said of great painters.

We take the view that what counts is freedom. If people great or small want to avoid compulsory sexual neurosis, then they should be helped. But this doesn't mean that avoiding sexual neurosis should become compulsory!

It is probably true that many great works of art 'result' from the pain, suffering and sexual tortures of their artist. But if the artist had been sexually happy, who's to say he wouldn't have written or painted some other great masterpieces 'resulting' from his sexual fulfilment?

Professor Richard Wollheim who writes about art and society believes that no great artist is really neurotic. He couldn't be. Because the very process of translating pain into a picture or novel demands work and craftsmanship and a kind of careful sanity. But he has to stop being neurotic when he works to split his personality and look at himself objectively.

In general, our view is that sex problems prevent a person from expressing his personality to the full and are always counter-productive.

TOOTHLESS WIFE

Shortly before our marriage 20 years ago, my wife, who was 19 at the time, lost all her teeth due to a severe illness. A few months before we married we began sexual activities which were slightly disappointing for both of us. However, they held sufficient promise for us to continue to work at our sexual relationship. We've tried numerous ways to please each other – all sorts of positions, cunnilingus, fellatio, anilingus, and intercourse. While they were each enjoyable and worth repeating, none felt quite as good to me as the first time my wife removed her false teeth and performed fellatio on me. When she takes my penis into that warm, totally engulfing mouth I see stars. She can't perform 'deep throat' acrobatics but given her other wonderful abilities who needs that? Not only does she know how to do an expert job of fellating me, she also enjoys it almost as much as I do. When she starts from my rectum and works past my testicles and the length of my penis finishing by engulfing it in that wonderful mouth, it's all I can do to keep myself from climaxing immediately.

While I don't recommend anyone insisting that his partner

have all her teeth removed, I do recommend a toothless wife as a definite asset.

Name and address withheld
by request

WHITE NIGHT KNIGHT

I've been having an affair with a successful designer for the past month. We were introduced by a mutual friend and we liked each other immediately. On our first date he pulled up in a wonderful white Jaguar and drove me all around Chicago showing me the buildings he liked and then we had dinner at a very quiet and lovely French restaurant. During the course of the meal he was telling me about things he was planning to do and I interrupted and said 'And tell me when are you planning to make love to me?'

He was at first startled but then he settled down and all the tension that had been circulating between us faded.

He took me back to his totally white flat and I felt strange enveloped in such a stark environment. I undressed and he was turned on seeing me naked in his place since I have very white skin, large dark nipples and raven hair. He asked me to stand in the light, then he sat back and admired my body from almost every angle. I didn't say a word, just remained silent and motionless like a statue while he looked on. After about 10 minutes I moved my hand to one of my breasts and began to circle the nipple with my index finger. Both nipples immediately became erect.

He sat there amazed and I held the same pose for a few minutes longer while he looked on.

All of a sudden he stood up and undressed very quickly. He had such a lovely delicate body and the wonderful way the white environment set his body off allowed me to understand why he had asked me to stand for so long while he watched me. He had those exquisite tiny features that make a man seem almost too perfect to be real. He was tan and his dark thick hair made him look fantastically sexy.

He began to touch his penis ever so slowly and I in turn, in almost a mirror imitation of his movements, began to fondle my clitoris. We moved in unison and I felt myself drowning in deep intense contractions. He climaxed at the same time shooting his glistening white sperm in soft spurts on the alabaster tile floor. I knelt down and licked all the semen from the floor and then we made love on the spot where his sperm had fallen.

The whole evening was so intensely erotic that it still takes my breath away when I think back on it. It was the most exciting night of my life.

L.R.,
Chicago

SEXY METRO

During my visit to Denver, Colorado, I was placed in a situation where I had to use mass transit (The Denver Metro Lines). I have travelled by bus before but none could compare to these buses.

Every day while my husband worked I took the Metro into Denver and every day I got these funny vibrations while riding the bus. First, after boarding the bus I would take any vacant seat then I would sit in an upright position with my back straight and relax while I rode into town. From nowhere the seats began to act like vibrators sending millions of vibes through my hips into my vagina and out through my clitoris. What a feeling! Sometimes the urge to climax built up and then suddenly the bus stopped and I was left hanging. As soon as the driver started back up, presto, I was gone again. Now I'm not the type who's turned on easily and I don't even masturbate, but for the first time in my life a machine got the best of me. I thought only a man could stimulate me sexually but that proved to be untrue.

I was shocked by all this so I told my husband. He found it hard to believe because I am not easily stimulated. He decided to ride in on the Metro Lines with me one day and now he's a believer.

My husband requested that I take a taxi into town and get the bus for the ride back home. I refused since I thought that was going a little too far, however, I did write to the Denver Metro Lines to thank the drivers for such wonderful services.

Name withheld by request,
California

INITIATION BY AN OLDER WOMAN

When I look back on my own youth, it often occurs to me that if all young people over the age of 16 were handed over to

69

an older, more experienced member of the opposite sex to be initiated into sexual intercourse, there would be a lot more sexually happy marriages.

When I was 16 I was lucky to meet just such an older woman who did more for me sexually than anyone. Brenda was an old friend of my mother who used to visit us every Thursday afternoon. She always made a fuss of me when I was a child and as I grew older she would often run her hands down my back and remark how big I was getting. Even then, I had a kind of sexual admiration for her, and when I reached puberty I often fantasized thinking of Brenda's naked body.

One Thursday I came home from school to find Brenda in the living room with her blouse half-way undone. I couldn't take my eyes off her. She asked me to come over and give her a kiss, and when I offered my cheek, she grabbed my neck and kissed me passionately on the mouth, with her tongue protruding into my mouth. We remained in this position for what seemed like an eternity. She slipped her hand up my leg and I could feel it getting higher and higher. Then, she squeezed me and I had a tremendous climax which I don't think has been equalled to this day.

This was the beginning of our 'affair'. I would go round to Brenda's house on the pretext of helping her with the garden. Gardening, my foot! We did just about everything possible in the field of sex. The nearest I got to gardening was trimming her pubic hair! I visited Brenda for about a year during which time we experimented in every imaginable way. She would often make me kneel on the floor with my legs apart, and she would start probing her tongue under my balls and round my anus, gradually working, biting, sucking and tongueing me until I came. I must have fucked Brenda in every possible position and she would never miss any chance to caress me, even in public.

My visits to Brenda came to an end when I moved to another school but I still see her now and we often talk about our time together. She told me once that although she felt guilty about seducing me, she couldn't resist me. I am certainly glad she didn't!

I am 40 now and unmarried, but I have numerous girl-friends although I have never allowed myself to get involved. About five years ago, I met a young girl of 16. My affair with Sally lasted six months and ended because she wanted it to. I went to bed with her about twice a week and we covered everything in the book. In a way I suppose I did for her what Brenda did for me. Sally became my 'Lolita' and finished up with virtually no inhibitions and a great deal of sexual confidence. When I first met Sally, she was like a lot of young girls who have a great deal of sexual knowledge but who are afraid to put it into practice.

Sally is now engaged to a lovely boy and when she gets married, I am sure that she will have none of the sexual problems that a lot of young newly married inexperienced couples have.

My advice to any young person is to get your experience with an older person while you have the chance and don't wait until you are married to make mistakes.

R.W.,
Essex

TWIN SET

I am having such a fantastic sex life at the moment that I can't stop myself from telling you about it. Unfortunately it is not anything that (unless she's as lucky as I have been) any of your readers could copy, since by the greatest chance, my boy-friend is a twin.

I met him at a party and nearly swooned when he looked at me, he's so fantastic. Tall and slim with a lovely small bottom and broad shoulders and lovely long slim legs, I'll never forget he was wearing skin tight white trousers and a shirt open to the waist when I met him. I couldn't keep my eyes off him and he was quite taken with me!

Before long we were back in my room locked naked in each other's arms, and after a fabulous session he told me he had a twin brother! The very idea of TWO men exactly like this one was so wonderful I nearly lost my breath at the idea, and sure enough he asked me if I'd be interested in a threesome! Was I!

I just don't know how I lived through the next day at work. At last I got home and made myself look as stunning as possible. I couldn't eat I was so excited, and kept looking out of the window to see if they were arriving. Finally there was a ring at the door and there they were – Tim was an exact replica of Paul, two such marvellous looking men standing on my door-step, and I didn't even know which one was which!

The best part of course was that neither of them was in the least bit embarrassed or self-conscious with the other, as they'd obviously done this many times before. We didn't have to in-dulge in stupid and time-wasting small talk either, as we all knew what we were there for and wanted to start enjoying it to the full.

They undressed me together. One unzipped my dress, the other started to pull down my panties, then the first one unhooked my (very saucy) bra. I was soon naked and lay on the bed and watched them strip. They were wearing different clothes on top, but underneath they had identical tiny red briefs and as they came off, out came two perfect penises. They stood one each side of me to start with, and I held one in each hand as their four hands explored my body. Within 10 minutes I was gasping and Paul obliged by mounting me in the missionary position which I really enjoy in spite of it being so mundane. As soon as he was in place, Tim squatted over my head, facing towards the top of my head, and lowered himself towards my mouth.

I came almost at once, then again when Paul came, and again when Tim came. It was the most fantastic session I had ever had (and I've had plenty!).

After we recovered, we tried another position. This time Tim lay down and I mounted him. Paul stood astride Tim so that he was level with my mouth, and we did the whole thing again, this time the other way round, so that each could taste my mouth. Of course it took longer, but was even better, as we all came at more or less the same time, and literally collapsed together in a heap. Later, we all crowded into my little shower and washed each other with soapy hands.

Things have been going on this way for a few weeks now, and they get better all the time. I have no illusions about it continuing – but at the moment I am more than fulfilled!

Miss J.B.,
London

OVER-ENDOWED

I have often read in your magazine letters from men complaining about their lack of length or girth of penis. I have the opposite problem: have any of your readers ever thought of the difficulties besetting the man with too much?

From the age of 11, people have wanted to look at my dimensions. First, one of my brothers noticed how much longer my penis was than his and he was then about 18 years old. We had to sleep together and he could never resist playing with my penis in bed, so masturbation started early for me, long before I could ejaculate.

Naturally he told some of his friends about my size and also some of his girlfriends who couldn't resist wanting to look at it. I was therefore often caught up with men and women wanting to look at and fondle me, but no actual intercourse took place until I was older.

My brother then introduced me to a captain's wife while her husband was away and she couldn't wait to invite me home. When she saw what I had she went wild and literally raped me twice. I finished up after her rough treatment with my frenum badly broken and I bled like a pig. My first intercourse was not at all satisfactory!

From then on my penis really started to grow. I could by now ejaculate properly and I masturbated regularly. At 16 I had just over $10\frac{1}{2}$ inches and was still growing.

At work women who had heard of my size used to come up and ask could they just have one look, so I started to oblige, but apart from just holding it, nothing happened.

By the time I was 21, I had grown to $12\frac{1}{2}$ inches which I still am, but my life has always been the same. I have tried intercourse many times but never get the satisfaction of the deep intercourse other people get. Most women I have tried can get the first few inches in, but then they give up. I get masturbated, sucked and licked: dozens of women just want to hold and masturbate themselves with me, but really deep, full intercourse they can't provide.

I would give anything to just be normal and I envy all those men who only have five or six inches. Tell them to be satisfied with what they have; wives and girlfriends can take them in normal straightforward intercourse!

R.M.,
Lancashire

LESS SEX

Is it possible to have one's sexual desires reduced? Is there a gland which produces masculine hormones and hence masculine sexual desires, which could be cut out?

T.S.,
Wales

This is not so uncommon a wish as one might think. There are

[73]

many situations in which even a strong 'normal' heterosexual drive can be a nuisance; for instance, the elderly widower who finds it near impossible to keep his hands off any women within range. And a man whose sex drive is deviant or antisocial may well prefer to damp it down rather than risk losing control of himself with possibly serious consequences.

Castration is still the commonest method of lowering sex drive and is frequently offered to sex offenders in, for example, Germany and parts of Scandinavia. It is permanent and mutilating, and it is doubtful if any surgeon in Britain could be persuaded to perform such an operation.

A new and infinitely preferable alternative is cyproterone acetate. This is an anti-androgen; that is, it counteracts the effects of the male hormone. The effect is temporary, so that normal levels of desire return when the drug is stopped.

It is only available on prescription.

SOME LIKE IT FAT

I have just finished reading with equal parts of amusement and annoyance an article by Dr Paul Jeffrey entitled 'Fat Men Make Poor Lovers'. My husband weighs over 300 pounds and a better, more erotic, longer lasting, more considerate lover couldn't be found. He always gives me at least three orgasms.

Moreover, he never fails to come. In the eight years we've been married he has always been able to get and retain an erection when needed and many times when I'm too satisfied to do it justice.

I am not a small woman, and I can honestly say that while small to average sized men are sometimes nice to look over, I prefer a large man. After eight years our sex life gets better all the time.

Mrs G.S.,
Address withheld by request

Happily, quite a number of obese men and women, and even obese couples, can make a satisfactory and satisfying sexual connection. It depends a good deal on the encouragement which a couple receive from their sex drives, and on whether, despite their obesity, they have a happy outgoing disposition.

But in general, what Dr Paul Jeffrey said in his article applies to most fat men (and women). Their whole sexual situation is fraught with difficulties. They haven't the stamina of slimmer

74

men and women, because the load which the heart has to carry during intercourse quickly tires them. The men have erection difficulties, because for every excess pound of fat the blood has to circulate an extra 22 miles, which often makes it difficult for sufficient blood to flow into the penis to make it really stiff. And there is also difficulty, on account of protruding bellies and buttocks, in making penis – vagina contact, unless the man has a well-above-average-length penis.

I am not saying that a satisfactory sex-life can only be obtained by penis–vagina contact. If there are practical difficulties which prevent the conjunction of organs, both partners can still have a happy and completely satisfying sexual experience by way of mutual stimulation and/or oral intercourse.

In order to say anything at all about sex we have to resort to generalities, which are usually based on the experience of the many rather than of the few. As I read it, that was what Dr Jeffrey was doing in his article.

SEX POLLUTION

I'm getting tired of all this stuff about dildoes and french ticklers and special odds and ends. What's the matter with good, old-fashioned fucking?

I think the problem with lots of men and women who are impotent and frigid is that they take this business of sex aids so seriously. It's a mechanical toy, batteries and all, so what can you expect but mechanical sex? I think if we would stop depending so much on buttons and appliances, we would be much better off.

Talk about the energy crisis – how about getting back to doing it naturally?

R.L.,
Address withheld by request

OUT-OF-TOUCH DOCTORS

Since the NHS is currently undergoing a time of self-appraisal and change, I feel this is a good moment to devote more of our resources to the promotion of good health and disease prevention than hitherto.

Unfortunately, the teaching in our medical schools is still largely concerned with the diagnosis and treatment of rare and unusual diseases with which most GPs will not come into contact. Consultants tend to teach future GPs their own speciality to a level of information not required in general practice, while more important matters are neglected. All teaching must of necessity be geared to the teachers available, but most of our specialists are concerned with the origins of disease rather than the origins of good health and healthy living, particularly in these days when so much disease is self-induced – over-eating, alcoholism, smoking, eating refined foods, and driving in poor road conditions with fast vehicles.

The medical profession should now come to recognize its debts to non-medical sources:

To the chemists, for the many potent drugs we now use for the treatment of previously incurable or almost incurable conditions.

To Alcoholics Anonymous whose successes are very impressive, particularly when compared to the failure rates for costly treatment in mental homes.

To Angela Kilmartin, who from outside the profession gave us revolutionary understanding of the treatment and prevention of cystitis.

To the American insurance companies, who proved to us that obesity is a killer; and to a woman, who, through the medium of Weight Watchers, helped to combat obesity all over the country.

To group therapy – where people suffering from the same complaint get together. Many of these clubs have done excellent work.

But apart from this, we have a situation where lack of sex education for both the medical profession and laymen is contributing to the unnecessary toll of self-induced neuroses. It is simply a case of the blind leading the blind. Help can really only come from within the profession. But from where? And from whom? If one compares what one reads on such things as impotence, premature ejaculation, frigidity, homosexuality, and so on in the medical encyclopaedias with the detailed information and help available to *Forum* readers, for example, from people like Dr Robert Chartham and other sexologists, one is simply amazed by official medical ignorance.

Certainly, doctors save lives by removing an appendix or curing pneumonia, but how often do we fail to treat the real suffering of whole families simply through our lack of knowledge and time? How often do we realize that sexual frustration is the root of many depressive illnesses which can affect other members of the family? And how much of this very prevalent suffering is a festering sore which never even comes to our attention? The answer is a great deal.

Must we keep our blinkers on, or is it now time for the profession to seek outside aid to help meet the real needs of our society?

Dr Jack Fishman,
Surrey

INVERTING NIPPLES

Your expert was undoubtedly a man who unfairly dismissed the complaint of the young lady suffering from inverted nipples!

Any woman knows the erotic value of a pair of strong, well-marked teats. I corrected this trouble with my husband's help and medical know-how, this way.

Each day, after a bath or shower, I sprayed each breast with cold water. Then, with a slightly greased finger and thumb, would pull out and roll each nipple in turn, finishing with a good brushing with an old toothbrush dipped in surgical spirit. Then my husband purchased a pair of Dr Waller's breast-shields, large glass globes with a hole in the flattened side, to be placed against the breast and worn inside a bra. These I wear for an hour or two daily, usually in the evenings. If worn in conjunction with a close fitting see-through bra, they have quite a stimulating effect, making one feel very breast-conscious, and when you undress, the effects on the nipples after a few weeks are striking.

The constant pressure on the surrounding flesh forces the nipple into prominence. Care should be taken when buying the shields to get the correct size and in the case of a large mature breast, the largest size has a corresponding aperture to allow the whole aureole to project.

We have now acquired a hand breast-pump, as used by nursing mothers. This is used by my husband during lovemaking. He places it over one nipple and squeezes the rubber bulb. This has the effect of creating a vacuum and pulls the nipple, elongating it into the tube. He can then turn his attention to the other, and the exciting effect of suction on both breasts at once can be imagined. After a minute or two he moves the pump to the other side; (I imagine that to have it attached for too long might be bad for the tissues).

I can promise your correspondent this treatment will not fail, especially if she will sometimes go without a bra, allowing constant stimulation from her clothes on her nipples. If she wears a bra she should cut out the tips so that her teats will extrude. I married late in life, less than a year ago, and whereas I was quite depressed on both sides of my figure, I am now the proud possessor of nipples that are hard and prominent with a fleshy solid core they never had before.

Mrs J.L. (SRN),
London

RUNS IN THE FAMILY?

Can an event which took place when my daughter was three have left a lasting subconscious impression on her after 19 years?

Not too long ago I unexpectedly dropped in on my eldest daughter who is now 22. It took a long time for her to answer the doorbell and when she finally came to the door, she had the appearance of a woman who had just left her bed after a hot session of sex. You knew the symptoms, flushed face, uncombed hair, nervous and totally nude under a hastily donned dressing gown with her nipples jutting out through a thin robe. There was nothing wrong with that except that her husband had gone away on business the previous day. My daughter explained the delay in answering the door by explaining that she had been nursing the baby when I rang the bell. I didn't say anything but instead went to the bedroom to see my granddaughter. The baby was lying on my daughter's bed, the bedding was in complete disarray and I could tell that the baby had not been fed. I turned back the cover when my daughter left the room and I was shocked to find telltale globs of glistening semen on the sheets that confirmed my suspicions. My daughter had recently been screwed and my visit had been ill-timed. I hastily covered the evidence and looked around the room. The baby bed had not been used and I realized that my granddaughter had shared her mother's bed during the lovemaking.

I felt terrible that my daughter was cheating on her husband but I didn't say anything since I had been guilty of such an adulterous act when my daughter was three years old. I must have been the same age as my daughter is now when I took the neighbour's 16-year-old son to bed with me while my daughter napped beside me. The bouncing bed springs and our heavy breathing awakened my daughter, but I was too excited to stop

78

so my little daughter watched while her mummy spread her legs and pleasured herself with a teenager.

After thinking over the incident when I interrupted my daughter, I am wondering if she subconsciously remembers what happened when she was three and now she is following in her mother's footsteps.

Mrs L.B.,
Address withheld by request

I doubt there is any connection between what happened to you 19 years ago, and what happened to your daughter recently. Apparently, you are still carrying some guilty feelings about your own sexual experience with the teenage boy since you refer to it as an 'adulterous act'. First, let me say that there is nothing harmful in making love in the presence of a 3-year-old child. Making love is just as human and beautiful as eating a meal or brushing yor hair. What can be potentially harmful to small children is your own attitude towards what you are doing, especially if you feel you are 'cheating'.

Children spend a lot of time with their parents simply 'reading' them. That is to say, children try to comprehend the meaning of their parents' feelings about what they are doing, just as much as they notice their parents' action. So if you are feeling good about making love, whomever the partner, your child will read you and share your good feeling. However, if you feel guilty about making love because your partner is not your husband, then your child will note that feeling also. If it happened quite infrequently, as you indicate in your letter, then your daughter was probably not affected in any lasting way, so the chances that your daughter is acting out your sexual behaviour are small. I suggest either that you let the incident in which you discovered your daughter's lovemaking pass by without worrying about it; or, if you cannot stop worrying, it would be good, if possible, to bring the whole matter out into the open and have a frank discussion with your daughter about your fears.

MEN WRITING AS WOMEN

I feel I must pursue the matter of my doubts regarding the authenticity of letters published in *Forum*, allegedly written by women.

I agree that women have fantasies, but they do not write

about them in the way that they are presented in *Forum*. I am conceited enough to believe that I have been loved, over the years, by one or two women, and luckily, by women who were explicit and articulate. Nevertheless, even in the dark, and when circumstances have been most conducive, I have found it difficult to get them to express any fantasy other than in tinsel and stardust terms. Also, I find that women tend to write erotic letters, but they are not punctuated with colloquial expressions.

I am not particularly old, but my experience in matters of fantasy, viewed in a professional capacity, goes back a number of years, even before the Wolfenden Report. The groundwork for this report took place in the early 50s. It was found that in order to heighten the illusion of femininity, many male homosexuals, when writing letters, adopted a female name and style of writing. Perhaps this could be the source of many of your more unbelievable letters?

A.H.,
Essex

I hope I am not misunderstanding you in thinking that you are not questioning the source of all the Forum *letters, but only those purporting to be written by women which contain explicit down-to-earth sexual expressions! Anyhow, it is on this basis that I am replying.*

As well as my connection with Forum. *I have a private practice through which I receive roughly 4,000 letters a year from all over the word. Each deals with a sexual problem or subject, and at least 40 per cent come from heterosexual women. I can assure you that, on the basis of these letters, women are as capable of expressing themselves in as vivid sexual language as men, especially when under the stress of sexual arousal.*

This has been recognized for some centuries, and there is a term to describe it – erotolalia. In one of the erotic classics, 'The Lives of Gallant Ladies' by Pierre de Brantôme, written about 1594, the author says, 'I have heard it said by many great knights and gallant gentlemen who have lain with great ladies, that they have found them a hundred times more dissolute and lewd in speech than common women and such'. Then after giving some examples, he concludes, 'In short, wanton speech has great efficacy in the game of love, and where it is not, pleasure is not complete . . .'

Miss Nancy Friday has recently carried out the first in-depth research into women's fantasies. Her book, 'My Secret Garden' will dispel all your doubts.

I have myself completed a study of 'What Turns Women On', and the section on fantasies fully supports Miss Friday's findings. This special study is also more than confirmed by the letters I receive from many women.

In view of the suggestion in your last paragraph that these letters may be written by male homosexuals who are trying to heighten the illusion of femininity, I can assure you that this is not the case. While it is true that certain male transsexuals and homosexual transvestites do assume female names and styles of writing, besides being very few in number, they are extremely sedate in their expression of anything to do with sex, and logically so, since the use of coarse male expressions would, in their view, destroy the female illusion they are trying to create. Not only that, women's handwriting is quite distinct from men's; and when you read as many letters as I do, it becomes second nature to differentiate male from female handwriting. Even effeminate males are unable to adopt a passable women's style of handwriting.

My experience in these matters goes back 42 years. Though I would not claim to be infallible, a man would have to be very skilful to pass himself off to me as a woman. (Robert Chartham)

LOVE SUBSTITUTE

For me, and surely many others, the upsetting thing is the sacrifices one must make now in order to have things easier in the future.

My boyfriend earns a huge salary as an engineer supervising oil rig construction away out in nowhere, while I try to pass my exams so that we will be free to live where and how we like in a year and a half.

Meanwhile, we only see each other every second weekend which is no joke if you are in love and normally sexed. On these weekends, we really have a private mini-orgy; the other 11 days are pure hell.

One of the boys in the house I stay in is similarly placed and about once a week or so we make cold and vigorous 'love'. No, it's not love, it's sex, for we are both away in our private worlds and admit that we get little more out of it than masturbating ourselves. My boy is even worse off for he says the only girls available are virtually prostitutes and any relief would be minimized by the fear of VD. So, for the most part, we take a masochistic pleasure from being miserable, but faithful.

However, the weekends he is away were driving me crazy until we had an idea. We went to a Sex Shop while in Manchester at Christmas and he bought me some 'love spheres' which he had read about in a magazine. They are like two table tennis balls with a weight inside each one and they rattle when you move in a most exciting way.

Now I spend the weekend clicking away, much to the puzzlement of my friends. You see, I only wear a long loose dress and my boobs rub against the rough material as I walk. This makes my nipples tingle for much of the time and all the wobbling and bouncing keeps them just tender enough to make me aware of my breasts.

The balls are comfortable and don't pop out, but keep my vagina twitching and moist. I bring myself perhaps half a dozen times over the weekend, and on the Monday and Tuesday at classes am just about as tender and aware of my tits and vulva as if my boy had been home.

It's not at all as good as the real thing and anyway, sex is only a part of what we miss. Letters are no compensation for having him away, nor is telephoning. But many girls must be in the same situation and I offer this advice in case they wish to try it.

Miss A.M.,
Scotland

SEXUAL APARTHEID

Your consultant's answer to a letter enquiring about the sex scene in South Africa is rather misleading, if not dangerously irresponsible, for your 'consultant' neglects to warn the correspondent of the existence of a pernicious piece of legislation called 'The Immorality Act', (also ironically called 'The Sex Act').

These are the facts, then, for anyone intending to emigrate to South Africa who wants to get in on the 'sex scene'.

The Aryan ideal of Hitler's Nazi Germany finds its present-day counterpart in those of South Africa's laws which seek to legislate against 'race pollution'. White must not be tainted by black; in every respect, miscegenation is illegal. Thus, the Mixed Marriages Act forbids marriage between white and non-white, and does not recognize such marriages contracted out-side South Africa. The Immorality Act, first passed in 1927, makes it illegal for whites and non-whites to have sexual inter-course together; it is also illegal to conspire to have interracial intercourse, so that anyone found soliciting a member of another racial group for sexual purposes is committing an offence.

The Immorality Act also forbids 'any act of indecency', a suitably vague clause which is interpreted widely by the police, so that kissing and caressing are punishable offences.

The zeal of the infamous South African police has increased sharply over the past few years. Non-white women are some-times used to trap unsuspecting white men by the police, who also often peep through keyholes, hide in boots of cars, feel beds for warmth and inspect suspects for signs of intercourse in their moral fervour.

Since 1951, there have been 25,000 prosecutions under the Immorality Act although the number is now decreasing. Most people prosecuted involve white men and non-white women. White South African women have been imbued with a sense of disgust for the African or Coloured man, so they are rarely 'offenders'.

Prostitution is common among many non-whites due to the government's system of migrant labour, where African families are split up. White men with more money than non-white are frequently prosecuted for visiting prostitutes.

Should the correspondent have the misfortune to fall in love with an African or Coloured woman, he will be persecuted unceasingly by the government and fellow whites, scandalized by the thought that white and non-white can live happily together. Although, not surprisingly, non-whites are given much higher sentences than their white partners even though the charge against them is the same, the stigma against whites who 'consort' with 'inferior' non-whites is so great that some whites charged under the Immorality Act commit suicide.

Even the Church in South Africa does not protest against this sordid spying into the private relationships of individuals; the Dutch Reformed Church, in 1950, fully supported the Act.

So I say to the man enquiring about the 'sex scene' in South Africa – if you are prepared to have your personal relationships examined by the police *and* your neighbours, then you're going to the right place. Otherwise, find another country where your healthy sexual appetite is your own business. Even Mary Whitehouse seems endearingly harmless compared to the rigours of the South African immorality laws.

Miss V.K.,
London

LETTER FROM TOKYO

Housewives deplore it, police officials try to censor it and foreigners write letters to the editors putting it down, but the nude parade on Japan's late-night television shows goes merrily along. At least three shows make a point of regularly displaying strippers or nude models in the final hour of the day and with a little judicious dial-switching the horny viewer can almost always spot a nipple, a navel or – often enough – well-shaped buttocks separated only by a G-string.

Total nudity is illegal in Japan (although plenty of it takes place in the back street theatres of any city) but almost anything else goes and first-time viewers of television are invariably flabbergasted by the casually frank references to pissing, farting and other bowel movements. To say nothing about the naïvely chauvinistic attitudes towards sex objects. Bare-breasted lovelies are tied into massage chairs, asked embarrassingly frank questions about their sexual proclivities and fondled by a circle of leering males who alternate between peeking under their semi-transparent skirts and placing bottles of liquid suggestively in their crotches.

Occasionally the shows will take time out from their nude presentations to discuss social issues, for example the 'nonsense show' (in the producer's words) which had the cast gathered in front of a public toilet for 60 minutes discussing various aspects of lavatory behaviour. Or the 'wild life' tour of Izu Peninsula's Monkey Park which, needless to say, focused on the animals playing with their private parts and explicit shots of subsequent erections. To be fair, the show did eventually get away from sex – to show a snake and a live turtle whose heads were chopped off on camera to let the cast drink the piping hot blood fresh from saké glasses.

The best known of all the late-night shows is called 11 pm (it actually comes on at 11.15 pm) which specializes in artistic themes. A recent show, for example, opened with lingering soft-filter shots of a lovely nude reclining on a bearskin rug sipping tea as experts off camera discussed various aspects of sex. One participant was a young fortune teller who claimed to be able to predict personality by the shape of the breasts. As he spoke, outlined white shapes of various breast types were superimposed on the misty nude to demonstrate his thesis. In this particular show even the commercials seemed to have been chosen with care, one (advertising a Shinjuku night club) being a reproduction of the famous shot of Marilyn Monroe unsuccessfully attempting to hold down her skirt in the wind.

And the commercial breaks were all announced in English, very hip in Japanese advertising, with one being 'We'll be right back after we go to the bathroom.'

The show 11 pm is especially imaginative in its introduction of nudes who rarely come on screen as merely flesh but usually have some exotic *raison d'être* such as the New Year's calendar show which opened with film of the photographers creating the calendars ... numbered days formed by bodies bent into various figures ... portions of another calendar torn off to reveal more of the nude underneath ... nude men ('for housewives') ... a calendar of paper panties etc. Then the photographers and the nude models created some of the scenes in the studio. This particular 'double-exposure' gimmick is quite a mainstay of the show. On another occasion a celebrated nude photographer snapped merrily away as a nude couple rollicked amidst stage smoke on the studio floor, and then, later in the show, displayed large blow-ups of his nude photographs.

One night the show demonstrated how porn films are made as a couple caressed on the bed, the man stripping off a girl's bra and panties (face down, of course) while she wriggled provocatively. A tour of Japan's onsen (hot springs) gave plenty of excuses for dressing and undressing; a girl taking off her clothes in a store preparatory to buying a pair of panties; a masseur demonstrating his art on a well-oiled female back – all have a certain minimal claim to legitimacy.

Demonstrations are popular: nude yoga or slimming exercises, massages with beefsteak or seaweed, displays of prizes for various contests by bare-breasted models. A novel kind of puppet show featured a dialogue between two faces sketched on a girl's breasts with occasional interruptions from a third face whose mouth was the navel.

About a year ago Tokyo Metropolitan Police equipped themselves with video taperecorders and announced they were going to monitor the main offenders – NTV's 11 pm show, NET's 23 Hours, TBS' Night Up and Fuji's Tomorrow.

'These midnight shows often present programmes with such

titles as College Co-eds Nude Show or The Climax of Strip Tease Show', a police spokesman said, after reporting an increase in viewer complaints. 'It is not decent to send such programmes into the home.'

And a housewives' organization granted 11 pm the dubious honour of being the second most immoral show on television. (The first, an innocuous mid-evening frolic called 'It's 8-o'clock, All gather here'.)

But the TV stations counter with the claim that, 'Most of the viewers at that hour are adults. So let them decide for themselves whether or not the programmes are porn before the police brand them as too sexy.'

And 11 pm's producer Ket Katsuta thinks all the fuss is hypocritical. He recalls the night when five councillors from a town famous for its striptease theatre came on to the show to discuss nudity. All put down the theatre as an embarrassment, he says, but all were obviously well familiar with its shows personally.

On another occasion a stripper had inadvertently flashed a glimpse of pubic hair while turning around – causing Katsuta to spend five hours grovelling at the police station the following day, released only when he had signed 'apologies'.

What is this exaggerated fear of pubic hair in Japan? Katsuta can only regard it somewhat like the domino theory that once pubic hair is allowed the floodgates will collapse and licentiousness take over.

11 pm's Tokyo host (three nights a week the show is beamed from Japan's second largest city, Osaka) who has been the MC of the show for some years along with a pretty young brunette named Kikko Matsuoka, says he likes to use nudes on the show as 'an assault on the culture' – much the same argument underground papers have always given for their sexual emphasis.

True Fuji TV did refuse to transmit one movie called 'Dirty Angels' (about call girls in Yokosuka) on the grounds that shots of an actor demonstrating 'the sexual organs of a woman' with his fingers was too obscene to broadcast.

But this unusual display of morality was the first and by all accounts the only time a Japanese station has refused to show a programme because it was too dirty.

Despite the abundance of nudity on TV screens and in Japanese books and magazines there are still those who complain that in some areas the country's attitude to sex is too reserved. Such as 37-year-old Miori Watanabe, programme director for the national network, NHK, which NEVER shows nudity.

'I don't think the Japanese understand the concept of free sex as do Europeans', she says. 'When I showed a Danish book published for children there were people who called the police. A patrolman came around and asked questions. But I think things are getting better. Since April I notice that school textbooks have taken up such subjects as contraception, abortion and VD.'

John Wilcock
Forum's *Far East Correspondent*

COD PIECE

I remember reading in a previous copy of *Forum* that it is possible to obtain a false addition to the penis. Mine is of average size, but as soon as I get into the water at the beach or in the bath, everything shrinks right up. The testicles actually disappear inside me and the head of the penis is all that is left. This is, to me, a very embarrassing situation, until I am dried off and dressed again. I will be most grateful if *Forum* has the answer to my problem, especially with the present day mini swim trunks.

Name and address withheld
by request

It is of course natural, when the body is immersed in cold water, for the scrotal skin to shrivel, the testicles to be pulled up closer to the groin and the penis to be retracted. The colder the water the more marked the phenomenon.

This shrivelling is due to contraction of numerous small muscle fibres in the skin of the scrotum and in the spermatic cords in response to a cold stimulus, and the reaction in your own case seems to be somewhat more exaggerated than usual.

I don't think the artificial penile extensions which are on the market would be suitable for your purpose, namely for wearing inside your swim trunks, for they are all designed to fit over the erect penis. No. What you really want is a sort of swim trunk 'cod piece', and this should not be too difficult to make and fit yourself.

I suggest you obtain a large, finely cellular artificial sponge, and with scissors fashion from it in one piece a penis and scrotum to whatever size you prefer, starting with a large model and pruning down as required. This should then be attached to the 'jock' lining of your swim trunks by four or five deep stitches using wool rather than thread, and paying particular attention to correct positioning so that the bulge appears as natural as possible when you don your trunks. If your swim trunks are close fitting there should be little or no risk of movement of the cod piece while you swim or when you emerge from the water.

WHAT THEY DO WITH THE BALLS

As an occasional reader of *Forum* I chanced reading G.A.'s recent letter 'What do they do with the balls?' on whether one could buy bulls' testicles from butchers.

In Argentina – land of cattle – it is quite normal to obtain bulls' testicles from the family butcher (they are called creadillas at this stage), and many restaurants offer them on the menu. As many young bulls are castrated – normally at a yearly roundup, when they are also branded – the castrator will expertly operate the large cutters and with a clean sweep, slide the complete bag into the ashes of a nearby log fire. The bag is charred by the embers, but protects the balls and allows them to roast nicely in their own juice! Once removed from fire and bag they are a delicacy with bread and wine.

The Argentine barbecue (parrillada criolla) includes several tasty items: udder (ubre) a golden coloured $\frac{1}{4}$ inch thick rather spongy milky flavoured meat; rectum (tripa gorda) rather greasy with a sui generis taste; chinchulin which I think is the fallopian tube; molleja a gland; and many other parts that I for one will guarantee are available from most family butchers or most of the best restaurants there.

Our local butcher was also interested to hear about G.A.'s question over a few beers at the local and he promised to try and get some, so we may all be starting a new Kentish treat. After all, in this era of wage restraint, even if bulls' balls are removed at castration they should not be entirely wasted.

T.W.,
Kent

KEEPING IT IN THE FAMILY

I am 55, healthy, good looking and I have a good sex drive.

My paramour of some 10 years' standing has a voracious appetite for sex too.

About 5 years ago my paramour's maternal grandmother was in the hospital dying from a load of years and plain exhaustion. While I was visiting the old woman she held me to her bosom and pressed against me. She had nothing on but a flimsy négligée, a gift from one of her heirs, and I had the (morbid?) curiosity to slip my hand around and take hold of one of her breasts and nipples. I half expected her to be shocked or to simply ignore it but to my surprise she opened her kimono baring both breasts. She asked me to suck on them as a last act for a dying old lady. I did it for her both to accommodate her wish and to satisfy my curiosity. I gave her a healthy sucking on each nipple and after a bit she gave some soft moans of ecstasy. I firmly believe she had an orgasm although we did not discuss it. She died peacefully 3 days later mentioning me in her last breath to her 75-year-old daughter who is my paramour's mother.

I have no reason to suspect that the old woman divulged any of the facts but in my consolation of the bereaved heirs I also took the occasion to 'feel up' her sister, a 75-year-old lady who is a pretty well preserved specimen of womanhood. With absolutely no resistance she accepted a date for a rendezvous the following week. When I arrived to comfort her after the funeral I found her wearing nothing under her silky housecoat so I did not hesitate in waltzing her to the bedroom and screwed her as she said for the first time in 42 years.

Now my paramour's 17-year-old daughter was the only one left in a string of four generations for me to 'have special knowledge of'. Did I dare try? Not so long as she still had her cherry. But she married a no-account and within two months was calling on me for financial advice in moving away from her spouse and setting up her own flat. I helped her and I was glad to do it. I told her she didn't owe me a thing for my assistance but in her expression she said she had to repay me. I told her that I was glad to help her and that I owed that much or more to her mother for the 'take it when I wanted it' attitude she'd allowed me to have towards her. But the girl, then aged 19, insisted that she simply had to do something for me to clear her conscience. So I told her quickly 'that she had only one thing to her name that she could give me. It was located between her legs.' Without hesitation she tripped to the bath and appeared a few minutes later at the door stark naked with a drying towel held out to me and asked me to check her for squeaky cleanliness. Then she pulled me to the bed.

I did not pursue either of the ladies other than my paramour and have not touched either of them since. After all, somebody could be hurt if I did not 'walk the line'.

T.C.,
Address withheld by request

THE ELUSIVE AVERAGE

Last year a qualified nurse masseuse gave some very elucidating observations on penile dimensions, in *Forum*.

Some years ago a young female friend of mine, now herself a staff nurse, also entered into a lengthy objective study on similar lines, recruiting the aid of several friends to supply information. Included also were some interesting data on the vulva and findings concerning masturbation.

We reached the following conclusions concerning penile dimension. The minimum erectile length we encountered was approximately 5 inches, the greatest almost 9 inches, being rather longer than the optimum quoted by the previous correspondent, which, I recall, was $8\frac{1}{4}$ inches. Girths again showed variation between about $4\frac{1}{2}$ inches and over $6\frac{1}{2}$ inches.

On this basis, we found an average length to be around 6.7 inches and a girth of about 5 inches.

Penile dimension, we felt, can be misleading, since methods of measurement can vary. To a lesser degree, we found that measurement of the same organ showed slight variation from time to time. We felt the demarcation line between small, medium and large was at 6 inches and under, over 6 inches and over 7 inches respectively.

The length of the vulva opening from beneath the mons pubis to the rear was studied in four women in the 18 to 28 age group. Here we came up with a maximum difference of $1\frac{1}{2}$ inches from least to greatest.

Masturbation, even if practised frequently, is medically held to have no effect on the development of the genitals. Curiously a male with a development of almost 9 inches and a female possessing an abnormally large clitoris both had histories of very frequent masturbation from early puberty, though, as one friend interested in the survey pointed out, size is more likely to lead to the practice than be the outcome of it.

We came up with two rather interesting observations. One

concerned minor changes in the size of the labia minora, which increased noticeably several years after the end of puberty. The other was a penis which had shown an increase in erectile attainment towards the age of 30. The increase was slight, but nevertheless worth recording.

In my own case, I have always practised masturbation from an early age fairly regularly and believe that a considerable increase in the size of the prepuce by the early 30s might possibly be related to this.

We were surprised to find that only three adults in 10 and four adolescents in 10 showed any kind of regular resort to masturbation, perhaps rather fewer than is generally supposed.

One female, aged 28, is perhaps noteworthy for a detailed assessment of her masturbation over a 12-year period, totalling approximately 2,800 occasions, which rates a little high!

R.S.,
Wales

MARRIAGE

The many sexual aspects of marriage include loving relationships, orgasm, masturbation, technique, oral sex, fantasy, incest, sex therapy and anal sex.

LOVING RELATIONSHIPS

WHEN THE TALKING HAS TO STOP

I am 23, my wife 21, and we have been married for 2½ years. My parents were divorced when I was young so I knew that a good marriage didn't just 'happen'. I spent a great deal of my education on human relations and my two years of university study was in psychology. My own beliefs are competently expressed in the O'Neils' book 'Open Marriage'.

When we were first married, my wife was very quiet. I was in no hurry and had a great deal of faith that in time we would have the base of communication that I know is so important in marriage. I spent considerable time just explaining how I felt and what I believed in.

Seven months ago, my wife had an affair which she told me about two weeks later. My reaction was not to the affair but to the fact that for two weeks she was able to live a lie with me. The shock that the relationship which I assumed we had didn't exist terrified me. The depth of my feelings and my lifestyle are based on faith and trust and, when these were betrayed, I was lost. I felt that we needed to make this situation into a learning experience. In the past seven months, I have tried everything I know to get my wife to talk to me, but she just continues to act as if nothing has happened. I have tried patient reasoning, loving, coaxing, fighting, threatening, and pleading but I get only silence. At best, after a long confrontation, she will say that she will try to communicate but the next day it's the same story.

I have run out of ideas and no longer have the strength to confront her. This means that we live day to day like zombies, just pretending that everything is fine. And without communication, I don't feel there can be any hope for our marriage. We still love each other and if there is a way to save our marriage, I would certainly like to know.

S.S.,
British Columbia

Give it a rest, for heaven's sake! My immediate, feminine reaction to your letter is that if your wife is still with you after seven months of 'patient reasoning, loving, coaxing, fighting, threatening, and pleading' to 'communicate' with you about her brief affair, she must truly love you! If you accept the principles of 'Open Marriage', then you must accept that her affairs are her business. You each have a right to areas of privacy. She was honest with you in telling you that she had had an affair; your desire for (presumably) a blow-by-blow account of the emotions that led up to it and accompanied it strikes me as a sort of voyeurism.

Naturally, with your background, you feel a little insecure. But marriages are made by doing, not talking. If you follow me, you seem to have been spending your married life communicating about communicating – a sterile business, except for philosophers and Marshall McLuhan.

My recommendation (and I am sure your wife would endorse it) is that you stop continually abstracting your daily life and start living in the present. Relate to your wife with your heart, not your head. Find out that emotions are better communicated non-verbally than with words. An encounter or sensitivity group may help both of you find a more deeply rooted basis for your relationship.

MONEY MAD

I am 26, female, married and – I'm happy to say – highly-sexed; at least I think I am.

My problem is that I am married to a man who is obsessed with his business and, consequently, making money. He reckons he is normal in his sexual appetites which make him want it once or twice a week, strictly straightforward, no playing about and no gimmicks.

Very occasionally on holiday or the odd weekend when he isn't working, he's played with me or performed cunnilingus on me, but has very quickly got bored and makes no secret of the fact that he thinks a woman's sexual parts are messy and ugly.

I said earlier that I think I'm highly-sexed though sometimes I wonder whether I think about sex so much simply because I'm frustrated or whether I would be just as eager and willing if I were getting as much as I want. I rather suspect that the latter is true because I have no problem in bringing myself to orgasm by masturbating at least twice a day.

(How some women can say they prefer masturbating to the real thing is beyond me: there is nothing better to my mind than the feel of a big strong body close to my own.) Not that my interest in sex is limited to lovemaking – given the chance my whole life would be geared to the subject, in reading erotic literature, dressing or undressing in either sexy clothes or lack of underwear, in using erotic language and so on. I keep telling my husband there must be umpteen sex-starved men who would give their eye teeth for someone like me, but all he says is, 'You know what to do then, don't you?'

Sometimes I'm sorely tempted to take him up on his word but he depends on me to run the office side of the concern. If I didn't take this much interest we would have nothing in common. We have a three-and-a-half-year-old boy which complicates things further.

Twelve months ago I met a man who feels the same way as me, but whose wife is totally uninterested and ice-cold, and, like my husband, money-mad. We seem to be instinctively aware of what the other wants and we have had some truly wonderful times together. He has asked me to think about leaving my husband as he has had as much as he can take of his wife.

We have talked over and over what we should do, but his son, and my son, and my worries about feeling guilty at leaving my husband with all his business problems, have prevented us from coming to any definite decisions. We just go on seeing each other when we can.

The thing that means the most to both of us is that we feel wanted instead of useful. He works hard all day and then comes home to do the housework, very often makes his own meals, does the shopping at weekends and looks after the child. His wife has a job during the day and one four evenings a week as well.

My husband is a very dominant character who has to have all his own way and anyone who has a business will tell you that that runs your life for you. He makes love to me when he wants to, how he wants to and for as long as he wants.

What do other readers think? Should I carry on and run the risk of losing the main man in my life, or should I leave my husband for a man who is nothing like as good-looking and will never have as much money, but who is far kinder, much more considerate, nothing like as selfish and who, above all, is interested in sex?

Mrs E.H.,
Lancashire

It's not only women who can be prudish or uninterested in sex, as you have found out. There are some pretty 'frigid' men around too, and your husband is a good example.

Your husband's obsession with making money, and his rigid personality, cut him off from so much more besides sex that one cannot simply describe him as having a sexual problem. It goes deeper than that. He is out of touch with other people and, probably out of touch with his own emotional potential. He sounds more like a machine than a human being.

It is possible that a breakthrough in the sexual area will open up his whole personality; but I do not imagine that you would ever manage to get him to explore his inhibitions with a therapist. An encounter group — especially a weekend or 'marathon' session — might be more helpful but again he does not sound like the sort of man who would willingly enrol in such a group. If he has managed to retain his defences in the face of your healthy sexual attitudes, then they are obviously deep-rooted!

You and your husband are not so different as you imagine, however. Money and material things are clearly important to you as well — else why is your lover's relative lack of money worrying you? Also, you may at some level, still have some affection for your husband — you do not wish to leave him to face his business worries on his own.

I suggest you do some very deep thinking about your feelings for your husband. If you are staying with him out of guilt or pity — don't. These are poisonous bonds, and they lead to resentment and hatred. If you are genuinely happier away from him than with him, if you feel that even if there were fuller communication between you both, you still would not love him, then leave him. Your business skills will enable you to support yourself, by part-time working perhaps, until your son is old enough to go to school.

But I would advise against going straight from husband to lover. I feel that your love for him is more because he is a much-needed contrast to your husband than for any more positive reason; if you were truly in love with him as a human being and not just because he makes you feel wanted and fulfils your sexual desires, you would not want advice on whether to go to him.

I advise you to take a holiday away from the business for a few weeks and go away by yourself, with your son only if you can't find anyone to look after him in your absence. Take a breathing space to find out who you are and what your real

97

*priorities in life are. Tell your husband why you are doing this —
it may be that your absence will help him to do some re-
thinking about your relationship and stop taking you for
granted.*

NO EXIT

My husband and I are both 31 years old and we've been
married for six years. We have a young son and we plan no
other additions to our family. We are both college-educated
and we live in a lovely house in the country. We also have a
very difficult and upsetting sexual problem that is threatening
our marriage.

Prior to my marriage I enjoyed a fine sex life with many
different partners, as did my husband. We lived together for
several months before we married and everything was fine although I never achieved orgasm except through self-stimulation. Within two years of our wedding day it became evident
to me that my husband now desires intercourse once every three
to four weeks, whereas I require a much more active sex life.

For several years now I have tried everything I could think of
to interest and stimulate my husband sexually while employing
as much tact and consideration as possible. We have had long
talks on the subject and he says that while he enjoys sex, he just
isn't interested very often. He is concerned about me and he
wants me to feel happy and satisfied. We finally came to the
conclusion that although I am not a strongly orgasmic woman,
I do have a very strong sex drive. My husband has acknowledged the fact that he has a much less pronounced need for sex.

Two years ago I decided that I simply had to decide which
was more important to me – my marriage or a satisfactory sex
life. After much thought and visits to a doctor who pronounced
both of us normal and healthy, I decided to stick with the marriage.

Almost a year ago my cousin's wife had to leave our area for
three months to finish her schooling. Since we have a large
home, my husband and I invited my cousin to come and live
with us for those three months to help them save money and so
that I could help care for their two children.

One night about a week after the move, my cousin and I
stayed up late and the conversation turned to sex. Before I knew
it, I had poured out my story to him. I had never discussed our
sexual problems with anyone other than my husband and our

doctor so I was surprised that I had confided in my cousin. He was appalled because he and his wife had an active and satisfying sex life and he had more or less assumed that everyone else did too.

Several weeks later a sudden change in business made it necessary for my husband to be out of town five days a week. The second night that I was alone with my cousin, we once again discussed sex and before the night was over we were making love more passionately and with more enjoyment and pleasure than I had ever thought possible.

During the next two months we made love every evening, Monday to Friday. We did everything our combined imaginations could think of – we played out our fantasies, read books together and had fun both in and out of bed. After the first few days I began to experience orgasm occasionally and within three weeks I was able to achieve multiple orgasms without the slightest difficulty. At the same time I was able to offer my cousin more variation and more enthusiasm than he found with his wife and I provided him with a sexual outlet during his wife's absence.

That period of my life was the most joyous time I have ever known. Not only did we enjoy each other sexually, but intellectually and emotionally as well. There was never any question of continuing the relationship after my cousin's wife returned home for they are quite happy together and they have moved away from the area where my husband and I live.

In the months since then I have nearly lost my mind. After once discovering how completely satisfying an active sex life could be, it has been impossible for me to settle down again to intercourse once a month. I love my husband and do not want to leave him but I am not sure how much longer I can continue living with the frustration that is building in me. Masturbation does not provide sufficient release, nor does involvement in clubs and hobbies which was suggested by one doctor. We live in a very small town in which affairs quickly become public knowledge, so I'm afraid to try to find someone else. My husband would be very hurt and would probably leave me if he ever discovered I was having an affair. My gentle hints that we might give swinging or something of that nature a try have been firmly refused.

There is going to be a time when I can no longer endure the situation and I feel it is coming soon. Do you have any suggestions? Is there anything which would depress my sex drive or anything that would increase my husband's sex drive? Of course, leaving my husband would not guarantee that I will find the kind of relationship that I need but I'm not sure I have any alternatives. It is torture to sleep beside him each night without sex. Can you offer me any help at all?

Name and address withheld
by request

The dilemma you are experiencing is shared by many others. Differences in the amount of sexual activity desired by partners in a relationship is probably the most common sex problem among married couples. In your case, having discovered the joy of a mutually fulfilling sexual relationship, coping with the frustration of unfulfilling sex can easily stress you, your husband, your child and your relationship.

You say that you and your husband have discussed this problem in the past. Good; discuss it again. When partners have very different needs it is especially important to open up as many sexual options as possible. In order to do this it is important that both of you honestly and openly assess and discuss how well they are working for you. This requires frequent feedback.

If your husband's sex drive has been determining how often you have sex and what you do, both of you may need some time to make a change to a mutually determined sex life. It may be hard for you to ask for what you need and it may be hard for him to say yes to you, but what you have to gain is clear. Without a more satisfactory sex life, it sounds as though it will be quite difficult to maintain your present relationship.

You say that your husband wants sex less frequently than you do. Fine. Contrary to popular myth, it is really not necessary for both partners to go through a complete sexual response cycle in every sexual encounter. If you have not tried masturbating yourself while you are with your husband, I would suggest you do so. While masturbating alone may not be the sexual experience you are looking for, masturbating while in your husband's arms may well feel quite different. While most people feel somewhat anxious at the prospect of doing this, most people also report that the ability to satisfy themselves while with a partner has a profoundly positive effect on their sexual relationships. Many of us fear that our partners will feel rejected, disgusted or otherwise negatively about seeing us masturbate. In fact just the reverse seems to happen. Most people get turned on watching, or helping, their partner masturbate.

Don't expect instant results from this. It often takes some time to feel comfortable enough to give yourself an orgasm with another person present. If you have not shared your masturbation with your husband you might want to start with just having him in the house while you masturbate. Or you might feel comfortable in a dark room or with your back to him while he holds you. Even if your husband is not aroused, he may still want to participate in your enjoyment. He can stimulate you orally, manually or with a vibrator. If he doesn't feel like having an orgasm himself, he may enjoy the sensual pleasure of contact with you.

You might also try other kinds of sensual experiences with each other; massage is especially good for this purpose. Often when we say we want more sex what we really mean is that we want more opportunities to touch and be touched. Add more touch to your life; it may help enormously.

You say that you fear your husband could leave you if you have an affair. Do you know that? This is another option the two of you might discuss. Many people feel that it is easier to maintain primary relationships if one or both partners have sexual relationships outside their primary relationship. For others this option doesn't work well.

Another thing you might try is teaching yourself to have more intense orgasms than you are having now. Take more time to build up to orgasm, really noticing how your body feels along the way and take plenty of time after an orgasm to relish the relaxed feeling of resolution. When you do have sex with yourself or with your husband take time to do more of the things that turn both of you on. Take turns acting out your fantasies and let each sexual experience be as good as it can be.

From what you say about your husband's other activities, he may well be just too tired for sex most of the time. Ask him. If this is the case the two of you may need to reassess your lifestyle in order to have the time and energy for a good sex life. In order to have sexual satisfaction we must be prepared to give sex a high priority in our lives.

THANKS TO GERMAINE

A big 'thank you' to Germaine Greer, and to you for publishing that splendid article by her, Women on top. I have only recently become a reader of your magazine and I must say how much I enjoy it!

Miss Greer's article has given me a new lease of sex life. I am 45 and have been married for 25 years. My sex life, although active for most of that time, had begun to wane in recent years. I was quite content and satisfied to have sex missionary style and my husband always succeeded in giving me an orgasm. We had never thought of fucking in any other position.

After reading this article with my husband in bed, September 29 became *my* liberation day. For the first time I took the initiative and followed Germaine's advice by adopting the superior position. Trying all the positions and alternatives that she suggested gave me the biggest thrill I have ever had. Being able to move about as I wish on top of my husband with our hands free to excite each other, I had numerous orgasms, but kept wanting more. Eventually I ended up perched on him facing his feet, stroking his balls with my hands. When he came, I could feel with my hands the ejaculation starting from the roots of his prick, and I gently squeezed his balls as the semen squirted into me. The sensation made me randier and I carried on working on him until he lost his erection. Although I had had many orgasms I was far from being satisfied and still wanted more.

I raised myself off his limp penis and transferred my vagina to his mouth; then, holding his head with my hands, I made him perform cunnilingus on me. Sitting on top in this position I was able to make him take back all the sperm that he had shot into me, in addition to my own juices, giving me the feeling of having a certain superiority over my husband. Eventually his sucking brought me to my final orgasm and I just collapsed exhausted on top of him. I could still smell and taste the juices on him as we kissed and fell asleep.

The following morning reminded me of the first night we made love; but this time it was me who blushingly asked whether I had offended or hurt my partner. Surprisingly, he confessed that he had always had fantasies of being raped in this manner and that he had enjoyed every minute of it, even taking back his own juices. I also confessed that I had always wanted to do what we did but was too shy to take the initiative.

It took Miss Greer's article to arouse my passions and enable me to emancipate myself by 'raping' and dominating my husband. Whilst we were confessing to each other for the first time our innermost secrets (after 25 years of marriage!), I came on heat again and soon found myself once more on top of my husband who willingly surrendered himself to me. I refused to let him get up and go to work that morning. We just stayed in bed making love. It wasn't till the early evening that we got up, bathed and ate. In the 20 hours together in bed I succeeded in making my husband come three times. My orgasms were too numerous to recall. My wedding night was nowhere near as thrilling as this!

Since first reading the article by Germaine Greer a fortnight ago I have 'raped' my husband 10 times, whereas previously we had sex about once every 14 days.

Once again, thank you for enabling me to fulfil my wishes and desires.

Mrs J.M.,
Kent

A FEMALE EUNUCH?

I have been an avid reader of *Forum* for almost a year now, though only recently openly, for my husband, Vic, felt all such writings were filthy, perverted trash. Vic is very inhibited, he was raised in the traditions of the Roman Catholic Church and has Italian-born parents. Sex was not only not spoken of but anything concerning the genitalia or anything pertaining thereto was a mortal sin. Vic was a virgin when we married though he was 25; I had had experience and perhaps was ahead of my time. At the age of 20, 28 years ago, I saw sex as a normal, natural, enjoyable part of life.

With an experienced man I never had any trouble reaching an orgasm, multiple, from three to five depending on the man. The only way I have ever been able to attain an orgasm was when, after reasonable foreplay, the man would insert his penis fully into my vagina, holding it firmly inside with his pubis pressed tightly against my vulva. Then rolling onto my left (his right) side, I would move in a rocking or up and down motion, rubbing my clitoris and labia minora firmly against him. Every obstetrician or gynaecologist who has examined me says not only is my clitoris extremely high but unusually small, therefore the normal in and out motions do not stimulate me enough to bring me to orgasm.

I believe I have not been demanding or aggressive, being content with the pleasureable sensations of giving my man all he wishes or desires to reach his strongest ejaculation. We have used every possible position plus anal coitus, rear entry (dog fashion), and fellatio, sometimes to ejaculation and frequently in the act of foreplay.

Vic is and has always been a wonderful husband and I love him passionately after almost 28 years of marriage. He has never been a really good lover, but I can't blame him for his ignorance. He has always believed that a woman never takes the initiative or offers advice or suggestions in how to please her. This deflates his male ego, and a woman who does tell the man how to stimulate her is being whorish. This, of course, all stems from his early teachings and beliefs. Erroneous, yes. Double standard, certainly. But I can't blame him and still love him deeply despite all.

Since August 1968 Vic has become increasingly impotent, but this too is not his fault. On the above date I underwent a radical mastectomy of the right breast, this was followed in December of 1970 by a radical of the left breast. I feel like a female eunuch! Naturally, it has caused Vic to become impotent.

I tried to take it all in my stride, accepting it as my fate and living with it as best I could. I have done all in my power to help Vic understand that it is not his having reached 50 (which he did just before the first operation) but my disfigurement which causes his failure to get and maintain an erection. There's not a man alive that can get sexually stimulated by someone in my condition. He denies this saying it is his anxiety and failure to bring me to orgasm (which I have failed to accomplish since the first operation).

I have had almost two years of psychiatric treatment for depressive thoughts. I have no trouble reaching orgasm in masturbation alone, but while Vic has tried to bring me off both orally and digitally, it just doesn't work. This is not his fault either, but mine, because I know he does not like to perform cunnilingus. You see the female fluid (slime) has always been objectionable to him, to the point that he has always jumped up the moment he has ejaculated and rushed to the bath to wash himself thoroughly of the filth.

I would be lying if I said this had not hurt me at times, but I have tried to overlook this, though I confess I can't forget it as he still does it even though he has begun to read *Forum*, along with Masters and Johnson's *Human Sexual Inadequacy*, Reuben's *Everything You've Always Wanted to Know About Sex But Been Afraid To Ask* and a particularly good book for religious inhibited men and women by Ed Cray, *The Secret Libertines*.

My poor darling was totally unable to help me decide to have surgery either time and I don't blame him for that either. How could he possibly know what I would look like? I knew because my mother also lost her left breast but died two years later. I tried to get my doctor to just remove the growth and let me take the chance that it was early enough not to have spread beyond the one tiny growth, but he would not hear of it and I couldn't find one who would. Shortly after the first surgery, after I had fellated him to ejaculation, at his request, he told me that I was not to do so ever again because he felt it was immoral and vulgar. This I'm afraid I've been unable to forget though I have truly forgiven him and have done so many times since at his desire.

I hope I do not sound as though I am seeking pity or approval for I honestly am NOT! I understand his being torn between his early teachings and his normal sexual desires, also he has since retracted these beliefs. Still I must confess it hurt me deeply and added to my self-doubts and inferiority complex. I am not writing for myself as I know there is nothing to be done to alter my appearance as we are not wealthy enough for me to go to a plastic surgeon.

I have suggested Vic have an affair, but keep it secret from me unless he finds he wants to marry the woman, to separate on a trial period, or to divorce so he can be free to seek a new life with a whole woman. He swears he loves only me and will not consider anything with anyone but me. I love him too much to see him suffer through no fault of his own except his love for me and our long years of happiness.

Mrs V.C.,
Oklahoma

It is certainly not true that men inevitably go off women who have had a mastectomy. One such patient of mine has just married and is having a happy sex life with her husband who regards the disfigurement as being of little consequence to either of them.

The breasts are not an important component in the arousal of many men and women and in any case all men have to adjust themselves to the progressive deterioration of the breasts (and the rest of the body) of the women they marry. In general, women, being physical in attitude, place too much importance on physical factors, often failing to recognize that men are more romantic and place greater value on the relationship with the woman than on her body. (If this were not the case all women would be forsaken when they grew older.)

You illustrate the point very well by saying you are a female eunuch simply because you have had your breasts removed. Since many women all but lose their breasts as they get older the difference between them and you is not all that great.

Your attitude is a worry since a man seems to accept a woman basically at her own evaluation of herself. If she behaves as if she is worthless, it is hard for him not to slip into the same situation. I am not minimizing your misfortune but trying to put it into a reasonable perspective. There is no point in making bad things worse.

In the same way you seem to have it in for your clitoris but we know that the size and positioning of the clitoris is not related to a woman's sexual and orgasmic efficiency. Your notions about your clitoris presumably affect your response during intercourse. It seems as if you wish to blame everything on yourself and allocate some sort of near-sexless superiority to your husband. Whilst I agree that his upbringing will have affected his attitudes towards women and sex, it isn't necessary for you to make some sort of virtue of it.

An increasing proportion of men do become impotent after they pass the age of 40, and those who have been reared in an inhibited fashion and who are restricted in their sexual expression suffer first. It is not too much to say that some such men look for an excuse to exempt themselves from their sexual duties. This would sound to be the case here rather than your supposition that your husband has simply gone off you, otherwise he would have been likely to accept your offer of seeking extramarital satisfaction. However, when allowance is made for his inhibition it sounds as if he is really trying to help you and that his inhibitions are lessening.

If you want to help him I think the first step is to help yourself by changing the image you have of yourself. You could try to accept his statement that he loves you, and that you are lovable in spite of everything. I think if you generally tried be less sensitive things would improve. Your behaviour and attitudes are more likely to increase his difficulties rather than reduce them. Try to accept things as they are rather than resenting them.

If you were less neurotic about it all (and I don't blame you for being neurotic since you have had rotten bad luck) I think you would find that the things which seem so awful to you will

106

recede in your mind and you will be able to re-establish a happy and sexual relationship with Vic. Concentrate on intimacy and worry less about intercourse which will return with time.

If, as I suspect, you are always drawing attention to your thoracic region stop doing so; pay more attention to clothes, especially underclothes and perfumes. Try to enjoy being a woman again. Paradoxically, I think you will do best by talking less about sex to your husband.

Adversity can and does improve human beings if only they can overcome it. If you can you might even find that intercourse will be better than ever before. You might even get orgasms without your special technique. It is worth a try.

ORGASM, MY WIFE AND I

On the subject of clitoral/vaginal orgasm I think that Mrs A.G. contradicts herself. She refers to the 'intense almost electric shock of pure clitoral stimulation'. Then she goes on to say that her 'deeper (vaginal) orgasm came by a different route, a panicky situation involving a full bladder and crossed thighs'. She points out that this was not a sexual situation. There were no exploring fingers. However, she does say that she uses a full bladder and crossed thighs as a masturbation technique.

In view of her next statement: 'I can achieve something almost as good if on top, when I can control my movements at the crucial moment', I would suggest that it would be equally as good if her bladder was full when she had intercourse in the superior position.

As a mere male my opinion is that Mrs A.G., like other females, does not like her clitoris directly stimulated, hence her 'thigh pressure' method of masturbation and her satisfying orgasms when on top. I think that if her partner masturbated her manually on the 'outside', using heavy pressure on her labia, she would have what she calls a vaginal orgasm!

For years I have shared my life with a lady who rarely has an orgasm during intercourse. Most times she requires clitoral stimulation to arouse her. Once her clitoris is erect then she has to be stimulated via the labia majora, only then does she become 'wet' enough for me to enter her vagina. Although she enjoys the act of intercourse, as I have said, she rarely has an orgasm. However, heavy and rapid 'massage' will quickly bring her to orgasm after the act.

There have been times when she has achieved orgasm during

intercourse, but these have been after longish periods of absence from each other. She has been in a highly excited state. Normally she requires stimulation before she becomes wet, but on these occasions, when I put my hand up her skirt, I find her already moist.

There have been occasions when she has literally soaked her panties in anticipation. At such times she does climax during the act, but even so, still likes to be masturbated to further orgasms afterwards.

On odd occasions during love play my wife will take my hand and guide two of my fingers into her vagina. If I then suck her nipples and rotate my fingers in her vagina she will sometimes come. But no amount of 'finger-fucking' will have any such result. It must be rotation of the fingers.

On occasions we have fucked when her bladder has been full but at such a time she always prefers to be masturbated. In a 'panicky' situation, she will rub her vulva as though masturbating rather than cross her thighs!

Mrs A.G. makes no mention of oral sex in her letter. During cunnilingus my wife has multiple orgasms and all the time my tongue is in direct contact with her clitoris!

Mrs A.G. might like to learn of the time that I came in my underpants without manual contact. It was a sexual situation though! My wife is now 49 and I am 52. We met when she was 20 and a student nurse. She wanted to finish her training before marriage but when she did become State Registered she still wanted to carry on nursing. By this time we had become very attached to each other but had got no further than kissing and breast fondling.

However, one evening I met her as she came off duty and we went to the small flat she shared with another nurse who was at that time on night duty. After supper we began kissing and as usual I fondled her breasts, unbuttoning her nurse's dress to do so. Tentatively I pressed my fingers to her vulva through her slip and when she did not stop me I pulled her slip up until I discovered that she was wearing french knickers. I began first to stroke her labia and my penis was rock hard.

Our kisses became more passionate and suddenly her hand came down and she took hold of my fingers and guided them to the spot she wanted rubbed. In a minute or so she climaxed and as she did so I ejaculated also. That was the start of our 'trial marriage'.

I think it is only inhibited people who have to be 'told' how to 'handle' their partners. My wife needed no tuition into how to handle my penis, whether to excite it to erection or to masturbate it to ejaculation, which she has often done when menstruating. At such a time she is herself often on heat and will masturbate herself at the same time. As her excitement increases so her hand movements speed up, on both of us, and often we enjoy a mutual orgasm.

My wife and I have no 'signed and witnessed' contract to keep us together. Neither of us can seek divorce on the grounds of adultery of the other. During our 'marriage' we have both of us strayed from the straight and narrow. I was the first to fall when my wife's cousin stayed with us for several months. We became attracted to each other and so it seemed natural that we should sleep together when my wife went on night duty. We were caught out the first week. After one particularly sexy night my wife found us still in bed together when she arrived home. To my surprise there were no fireworks. Her only comment was: 'I wondered when I would catch the two of you in bed! It was obvious to me it just had to happen.' Later the three of us discussed the situation and the cousin and I agreed that it was just a passing fancy.

Several years later my wife fell for a male nurse. When I taxed her on the subject she admitted that she had had intercourse with him several times in his car. I felt very jealous and angry, but her attitude to me did not change, neither did her sexual desire.

After some months I met this man and found him a most charming person. He invited the two of us to his home and I met his wife. We made up a foursome and went to dances and other social activities. An attraction grew up between his wife and I and one evening he and I spent most of the time dancing with each other's 'wife'. Janet was a well-built young woman, with breasts much larger than my wife's. Janet took every opportunity to press them hard against me as we danced together and when I did my best to hide the fact of my erection she arched into me. Not only that but she would also make false steps which brought her crotch in hard contact with my upper thigh! Need I say more? That night we swapped. For five or six years we would change partners maybe three or four times a year.

Incidentally Janet liked direct stimulation of her clitoris both before, during and after orgasm. She would also have multiple orgasms, quivering and jerking under me as I thrust into her.

Unlike my wife she was very vocal, telling me not to stop, to keep on doing it, to make it last. When I did come she would have one final orgasm and then refuse to let me touch her vulva because she said it was 'too tender'.

These two ladies were as unlike as chalk from cheese when it came to intercourse, yet both experienced deeply satisfying orgasms, one by hand, the other with the penis.

C.N.,
London

MUCH MARRIED

I'm 52 and have been married, I am appalled to say, five times. I left my first wife of seven years in 1954 because of an unsatisfactory sex life with her, which was as much a result of my impatience as her apathy. I married the woman I'd left her for mainly because of sex, and when we parted four years later, it was for reasons other than sex. I went to live with a woman whom I eventually married and with whom I was extremely happy until she died seven years later. The next two marriages were short-lived because of general incompatibility and a lack of foresight on all our parts.

Counting a few adulteries and a great number of extramarital affairs, I have probably known 60 or 70 women, not including prostitutes. I've been single for three and a half years now, and although I'm pretty much a one-woman man, I've rarely had to go without sex for a long time.

My problem is what I would call semi-potency. My sex drive is about average in that there have been a few times in my life when I've managed to make it two or three times in a two-hour period, but now I find myself unable to go on for a second time. Even after an hour, no matter what I do I just can't make it again.

Something that has happened recently has most concerned me. When I had entered my partner, I found myself approaching climax after 20 or 30 thrusts, so I withdrew to slow down. I felt myself throbbing as though I was ejaculating, but there was no ejaculation. When I had regained control, I re-entered and as long as I stayed on top, everything was OK. However, this particular woman can only achieve orgasm when she is on top of me and stretched full length. When we switched positions I began to go soft. She stimulated me with her hand

110

until I was hard enough to re-enter and the same thing occurred again. I just could not make it.

What I would like to know is if heavy drinking (not necessarily before the sex act) could have an effect on my sex performance. I know, of course, that drinking to excess before the occasion does have a bad effect, but I am mainly concerned with general drinking, over a period of weeks. I would like to mention that one night, about six years ago, I was very drunk and despite this, I managed to take my wife twice within the same hour. Is it possible that I could have lost some of my sex drive to this extent in only five years?

I do have steady drinking evenings and I am a heavy smoker. As my performance has begun to deteriorate and I still have a lively interest in sex, what if anything, would you advise? Should I cut down on my drinking and smoking? Try Vitamin E? I'd appreciate anything you could suggest.

D.T.,
Address withheld by request

Would I be right in thinking that you have the traditional idea of the sex roles – that the man is the initiator of sexual activity, the active, dominant partner, while the woman is the 'victim', the passive and submissive partner?

Even if you say I'm wrong, I shall then suggest that though you may not consciously think like this, unconsciously you do. And why do I think I'm right?

Take this sentence of yours, 'I was very drunk and despite this I managed to take my wife twice within the same hour.' See anything wrong with it? What about the word take?

'I managed to take . . .' not 'I managed to make love with' or 'have it off with', or even 'I managed to fuck . . .' In the circumstances you describe, I imagine that you did 'take' your wife, made her submit, because unless she was very drunk herself, or really blindly in love, I can't imagine any woman finding it pleasant being sexually mauled about by a drunken partner.

I think you used 'take' unconsciously but readily in your letter because that is how you think of intercourse between a man and a woman. And unless I am wrong, it is because you think in these terms that when your recent partner got on top of you, thus symbolically reversing the sex roles, you lost your erection as a protest against her becoming the dominant partner and making you the submissive one. In other words, the cause of your loss of erection was entirely psychological.

Habitual heavy drinking and heavy smoking, especially at your age, will in time have an adverse effect on any man's sexual capacity and performance. It doesn't strike all of a sudden, it creeps up on one insidiously. It is bound to happen because habitual heavy drinking never allows the body to be free of alcohol, and over a period of time the alcohol attacks the general nervous system, of which the sexual nervous system is an inextricable part, and so deadens all our responses. As we rely for a good sexual response largely on our sexual nervous systems, our ability to respond sexually cannot avoid being damaged and eventually destroyed.

Isn't that depressing? But let me tell you a story.

I come of a line of highly-sexed men. My father died of pneumonia in October 1939. He gave my stepmother a guilt complex for the rest of her life, because, though desperately ill and aged 67, six hours before he died he insisted on making love and she had 'humoured him'.

His father, my grandfather Chartham, was three times widowered. He produced by his three wives 22 children and by his numerous concubines an innumerable brood of unofficial little Charthams. He died in 1925 aged 76, and we then discovered that he had 'drunk a coalmine', ie because of his drinking habits from the age of 60, when his third wife died, he had hit the bottle so hard that his coal mine had to be sold to pay his debts.

He lived with us for the last two years of his life, and one day in 1923, when I was 13, he came stumbling into my room as I was having a naked romp with my best (boy) friend and my stepmother's kitchen-maid, aged 15, who had already introduced me to the felicities of a fuck well fucked. 'Don't stop on my account, you lucky children!' the old man said, and withdrew.

Two or three hours later, I encountered him again. Without saying a word, he pressed a gold half-sovereign (50p) into my hand. After a long silence he said, 'I'm proud of you. You're a true chip off the old block. But let me give you a warning. Until five years ago I thought nothing of having sex three times a day. (Five years before he was 71.) But for the last five years I haven't been able to get the horn at all, and do you know why, my boy? Because when your last grandmother died, I took to drinking a bottle of whisky a day. Take my advice, if you like sex as much as I did, and if you still want to give it to a girl when you are my age, lay off the drink!'

112

My father and my (older) brother became confirmed teetotallers when grandfather died and they learned what had happened. I haven't been able to do that, but remembering always grandfather's example, I do not drink spirits before 6 pm, and I limit myself to three Scotches before dinner and a very occasional brandy. (Wine doesn't count.) And I can tell you, it is a policy that is paying dividends grandfather would have envied. (Robert Chartham)

ALWAYS TOO TIRED

The trouble is, I want sex and my wife doesn't. I do play around with her but it seems to make no difference. She just lies there like ice. She says I hurt her sometimes (I have a normal size penis), then she says I take too long. When I want sex, she is always too tired.

I have said I shall have to find another woman, but she doesn't seem to care as long as I don't bring trouble home or neglect the home. I think she knows I am too shy to find anybody else.

We have five children who are all at school, except for one who is at work. My wife works full time, I do shift work.

G.B.,
Kent

It is difficult to know how to respond in the most helpful way to your letter. I can see that you perhaps feel rejected and badly used so I won't wish to add to your distress.

However, your poor wife is having a very hard time. Rearing five schoolchildren and working full time must severely tax the capacity of any woman and unless you are using effective contraception this alone could account for her disinterest in sex. Her troubles are probably increased by your shift work and possibly you fail to give her as much help, support and comfort as you might.

She sounds as if she sets store by respectability and she might have been reared to believe that sex mainly exists for reproduction. Her disinclination and pain show that she actively dislikes intercourse and obtains no pleasure from it whatever. Tiredness and pre-occupation with the many anxieties that must result from her lot in life will also distract her.

If you really wish to alter matters I think it is likely that you will have to see life from her point of view and then act accord-

113

ingly. For example, if with more effort you could earn more money so she could work part-time or give it up altogether then this would help her enormously and would lessen any resentment. If you are self-indulgent over expenditure this should cease and if you are mean with her then this could alienate her affections. Similarly, if you do not show appreciation for her efforts through words, actions, small presents and 'treats' especially for her then you should start to pay very serious attention to this aspect of your life together. Any woman who does all she achieves must be praise-worthy so this should not present any problem. Perhaps self-pity or old-fashioned views of the respective roles of men and women make you seem unsympathetic or useless to her and if this is the case you will have to set about altering your image.

It may be, of course, that you see none of this applying to yourself but your view of yourself is of less importance in this context than hers of you. Alteration in this is likely to prepare the way for her to improve her sexual responsiveness towards you. After that it is a question again of trying to discover what she really likes as opposed to what you think she does. If she is inhibited this can be difficult but reading Forum *should help especially if you can interest her in it too.*

Your general shyness probably extends to your sexual behaviour and this could have had an inhibiting effect on your wife in itself. This, indeed, could have been the start of the 'misunderstanding' between you which has led to the present situation in which neither obtains or gives much pleasure.

KEEP AN INTIMATE DIARY

Lack of communication is one of the prime causes of difficulty and breakdown in marriage, as indeed it is in probably all forms of human relationships, and as the years go on the problem of communication can become more acute, or perhaps the results of its neglect become more serious.

Many of us find difficulty in expressing thoughts and feelings to our partners, or perhaps although we could later do so the opportunity is lost at the moment.

Whilst it is essential to a successful marriage to discuss everything together, often partners may have reached a point where they do not discuss some things. These are usually intimate sexual details, but the difficulty can extend to more general matters involving home management, work, money, children,

114

and so on. The problem then is to break through the barriers and actually begin the process of re-establishing proper communications.

All these problems can be helped, if not solved completely, by husband, wife or both keeping a diary.

The purpose and nature of the diary will vary considerably. Some may religiously make an entry every day, others may leave great gaps; some may confine it to more mundane domestic matters (at least to begin with) while others may deal exclusively with the sexual relationship, but at least a start will have been made.

For a time the diary should perhaps be kept secretly, but later it can either be shown to the partner, or 'accidentally' left around to be discovered.

After a while it may be unnecessary to keep it going, or one or both partners may decide it should be continued. In any event it can do nothing but good, for even if your diary were to be used as evidence in divorce proceedings it would have served a purpose in freeing two people whose marriage would not have succeeded since it could not stand up to full communication.

It will be obvious from this letter that I have tried this idea, and found that it is useful in helping my wife to understand a little more of me, and for me, through thinking about things as I write, to understand her a little better. We also discuss everything and read *Forum* together, but it sometimes helps to put down something in more detail, more fluently, or more exactly than we can express in spoken words. It is also enjoyable to re-read past intimate experiences, or plan future ones, and helps in that ever-deepening, varied, and enduring relationship which any marriage must be if it is to survive intact for a lifetime.

S.W.,
Kent

ORGASM

WHAT'S IN AN ORGASM?

My boyfriend recently brought me home a copy of *Forum* and I found it very helpful.

My problem is one that you must get fed-up with – yes, orgasm! I am 17 years of age and have been making love nearly every night for a year but I have never had an orgasm. Just lately my boyfriend and I have spoken frankly about it and he just can't understand why I can't come when he tries so hard to make me. He of course comes every time.

I do enjoy all the foreplay, but after reading about other women's experiences in orgasm and with my boyfriend wanting me to come so much, I really want this experience.

When we are making love, or just playing, my boyfriend can get me to a point where I sweat all over, my body stiffens, vaginal area and clitoris swell enormously and I really think that I will come any minute, as other women do, but then it just slows down, all the lovely feelings go and my body feels dead; my boyfriend hopefully carries on but I have to push him off as it's only aggravating, although I do let him go into me and work until he comes.

Please tell me am I normal inside and why doesn't the fluid 'come' from me (I do have regular periods)? What is it that stops me coming as we both try so eagerly until it hurts me, and when will I actually know that I will 'come'?

My boyfriend says he feels I'm not getting the full satisfaction that I should and I'm beginning to feel quite depressed about the whole thing. I feel jealous of women who boast about having eight orgasms in one session.

I wasn't really bothered about not having orgasms at first but now my boyfriend says I mustn't just want him to come, I should want his wonderful feeling also.

Please, please help me, I have confidence in you.

Miss L.E.,
Portsmouth

Without being able to do an internal examination on you, I still feel 99 per cent sure that you are a perfectly normal girl. What makes you so certain that you do not experience orgasm? What

*you describe, both in foreplay and in actual lovemaking sounds
remarkably orgasmic to me. Perhaps you have read about
'clanging bells and trumpet fanfares'? Orgasm is hard for me to
describe to you, because we all experience this pleasure in a
different way, but your description of the body stiffening, the
sweating, and the clitoral swelling fits very well what researchers
have found to be the bodily reactions.*

*One eminent sexologist writes: 'For my money the most sen-
sible and acceptable view of the female orgasm, since it covers
the wide individual variation which is inherent in human beings,
is elaborated by Josephine and Irving Singer. They recognize
three (and it may well turn out that there are more) types of
orgasm which are arbitrarily divided as follows:*

*(It is stressed that these are not mutually exclusive; all may
be experienced by any particular female, at different times according to circumstances.)*

*1 The "vulval orgasm" is characterized by involuntary rhyth-
mic contractions of the vulva as well as by the mainly
physiological changes which have been measured in the lab-
oratory by Masters and Johnson. This kind of orgasm is not
coïtus-dependent since it can be produced by a variety of other
procedures including masturbation.*

*2 The "uterine orgasm" does not involve any vulval con-
tractions but there are physical and emotional changes which
are certainly measurable. Characteristic of this type of climax is
a gasping cumulative type of breathing which culminates in an
involuntary breath-holding response. The orgasm occurs at the
moment when the breath is forcibly exhaled; it is immediately
succeeded by a feeling of relaxation and sexual satisfaction.
This kind of orgasm which depends largely upon the effects of
uterine displacement is a consequence of the penis impinging on
the cervix. Subjectively it is felt to be "deep within the pelvis".*

Doris Lessing in the Golden Notebook *describes the uterine
orgasm precisely.*

*"The stimulus is uterine jostling. That is what produces the
response. But the response is a kind of laryngeal spasm in the
throat, accompanied by tension of the diaphragm. The breath is
inhaled cumulatively, each gasp adding to the amount of breath
contained previously in the lungs. When the diaphragm is
sufficiently tense, the breath is involuntarily held in the lungs,
and the cricopharyngeus muscle tenses, drawing the larynx
down and back. The feeling is one of 'strangling in ecstasy'.
Finally the cricopharyngeus snaps back to a resting position,*

and the breath is exhaled simultaneously. The suddenness with which this occurs produces the explosiveness without which the term 'orgasm' would hardly apply. For a day or two following an orgasm, I sense a pronounced tonic state of the deep vaginal muscles. The satisfaction is so complete that subsequent climaxes are quite impossible for at least a day. For me, the relief from sexual tension which this cricopharyngeal orgasm brings is analogous to the relief from pent-up nervous tension which an acute sobbing spell may bring. Both involve cricopharyngeal action. Perhaps ethologists would care to know that my facial expressions are different in my two types of orgasm. In a clitoral orgasm, my teeth are bared and my brow is furrowed with 'anger' lines. In the other kind of orgasm my brow is smooth and the corners of my parted lips are drawn back, although my teeth are not bared; ie a typical 'fear' expression. The significance of this is not clear to me."

3 The "blended orgasm" which again is experienced as "deeper" than vulval experience, combines elements of the previous two kinds. One of the shortest and yet graphic descriptions came from one woman who said: "My vagina swallows once or twice and I have an orgasm".'

Your own mental sensation is less easy to clarify. I think you must realize that you do have the ability to enjoy an orgasm, so now you must learn to relax and to enjoy it. You do not have to come at the very same moment as your boyfriend. Be thankful that you experience your sensation before he finishes; many girls worry because they cannot come at all until their lover has finished, and it is less easy then to experience orgasm with a soft penis. If you can relax after you have experienced those feelings that you have described, and then enjoy having him inside your relaxed and comfortable vagina, then I think that one of these days you will find that you will come again, with no warning, and maybe yet again.

I am sure it is your anxiety, and the fact that you really are trying too hard at this, so making it heavy going work on you both, that is causing you to find it aggravating. The fluid will come from you with relaxation. Easy for her to say this, you will be saying, but how do I start to relax? Well first, don't feel you have to do it every night. Then, if you never feel enjoyably moist, I suggest you invest in a tube of my good old favourite for such occasions: KY jelly.

Apply it tenderly to each other, take your time and you're away.

CAN'T GET ENOUGH

I consider myself a normal 20-year-old male, except for one thing – I have never been satisfied! Of course, many of your readers would think I am bragging or trying to kid someone, including myself, but this is an authentic problem.

I first had sex with a woman when I was 16, and from then on it has been all go. I have had the good fortune of having women aged between 16 to 30, but still to this very day I have never been completely satisfied inasmuch as I have left their beds the way I got in – with an erection!

When I say that I have not been satisfied, it does not mean that I have not achieved orgasm – far from it. I usually manage three or four orgasms with a good woman on the right night, but still I want to fuck on. I have tried different methods of love-making and positions, but the more varied it gets the more I want, and in some instances, this has been the reason for the abrupt end to what could have been many really good relationships because they think I am an 'animal'.

At present I am living with a separated woman of 26. Some months ago, after making love a few times, I disclosed my 'secret'. Of course, she laughed it off saying that no man has ever left her unsatisfied and that night she set out to take me down a peg or two, but after two hours of solid fucking, followed by a cigarette and another two and a half sessions, she fell back crying that she had had enough and I was left with six and a half inches of solid flesh to play with!

I don't want this relationship to end the way so many of the others have ended, and it is for this reason that I have put pen to paper to seek any advice you or your readers may have to offer.

J.B.,
Germany

I don't think you are bragging, because when I was your age much the same sort of thing happened to me. But I am wondering whether you are using the right term when you say, 'I have never been satisfied'.

Like you I was multiorgasmic and could have several orgasms without losing my erection.

But though, as you put it, I 'left their beds the way I got in – with an erection', I was sexually satisfied; in other words, though I would gladly have fucked on, once I had given my erection time to subside (which would be in 15 to 20 minutes

119

after bodily contact had been broken off) there were no tensions left, and I felt completely at peace with myself and the world.

Fortunately, just before I was 20 I found a girl with the same capacity, and married her, and in the 32 years before she died, I think both of us must have crammed into our sexual life-time seven times as many climaxes as an average-sexed couple (4 orgasms a week) achieve in the same period.

If you think you and I are pace-setters, listen to this. Four to five years ago I was making some investigations into sexual capacity and performance. Among those who helped me were three young men aged 19 (A), 22 (B) and 23 (C). Under controlled conditions and with the help of two partners, in one session, A had seven orgasms in 55 minutes (with the same erection) and in a session some four hours later had 13 orgasms in roughly two and a half hours by masturbation (five orgasms in 45 minutes with the same erection, followed by a pause of six minutes when a second erection was induced within two minutes of looking at some blue pictures, with which he had four orgasms in 42 minutes, followed by a pause of seven minutes at the end of which a third erection was induced by about three minutes direct stimulation of the penis by hand and fellatio, which produced two orgasms by fellatio in 20 minutes, followed by two orgasms by self-stimulation in 25 minutes).

B, during intercouse had four orgasms in about 50 minutes with the same erection, paused for 15 minutes, restored his erection spontaneously during loveplay within three minutes and had two orgasms by intercourse in 35 minutes, paused for 20 minutes, restored erection by fellatio within five minutes, had one orgasm by self-stimulation and simultaneous loveplay by partner at the end of 15 minutes. Eight orgasms in two and a half hours.

C had seven orgasms by self-stimulation in 42 minutes with the same erection, paused for five minutes, restored erection with two minutes of hand stimulation, had two orgasms by fellatio in 15 minutes and one by hand stimulation in another 15 minutes. Ten orgasms in one hour 20 minutes.

It is, of course, well known that the average-sexed young man in his 20s can have one orgasm, if he has learned to hold back, at the end of say 35 minutes of lovemaking. This orgasm deflates his erection, and because of the post-orgasm tenderness of his penis-head, he is unlikely to obtain a second erection within less than 10 to 15 minutes. This second erection he can sustain for, say, another 30 minutes before he has a second orgasm, after which he is probably psychologically as well as physically sexually satisfied and is ready to call it a day.

Most average-sexed men of any age are satisfied by one orgasm and though most up to the age of about 40 could, if they wished, have at least a second erection and orgasm after an average pause of 15 minutes, after 40 it takes progressively longer to induce a second erection, and as release from tension has been provided by the first orgasm, there is little or no inducement to try for a second erection and a second orgasm.

When a man has an orgasm a number of nerves and muscles are brought into play.

The ability of these nerves and muscles to recuperate and regain their strength determines how soon after an orgasm a fresh erection can be induced and another orgasm can be obtained. The rate of recuperation, which depends basically on the original quality of the nerves and muscles, differs from individual to individual. We call the rate of recuperation 'sexual capacity', because it determines how many orgasms a man can have within a given period. The actual number of orgasms a man has on average we call his 'sexual performance'. Sexual performance very rarely matches a man's sexual capacity; performance is always less than capacity, because the man is usually so relieved of tensions by one (or two) orgasms that he is not encouraged to test his capacity.

Those men who can have multiple-orgasms (with the same erection), or a number of orgasms with different erections within a certain fairly short period of time, have been blessed with nerves, and especially muscles, of very high quality and out-of-the-ordinary powers of recuperation. When attempts are made to have multiple-orgasms or frequent orgasms with different erections over a given period, usually each successive orgasm takes a little longer than the last to obtain, and if different erections are being used, the pause between the subsidence of the last and the reconstitution of the next is also longer.

The fact that you 'get out of bed with an erection', even after having had a number of orgasms, results from the fact that you respond very rapidly to your sex-drive plus your high sexual capacity which allows you to produce seemingly endless erections.

As I said earlier, I always found that my orgasmic experience had satisfied me, and that if I turned my thoughts from sexual things, my penis would eventually subside and I would be per-

fectly happy. If this is also your experience, I can't see why you want to do anything about it, except to make the most of your luck in having such a high sexual capacity. (By the way, if you live up to your sexual capacity while you are young, it will stay high throughout your life. At 63 I can still achieve multiple orgasms, two or three, two or three times a month.)

If, however, you are not satisfied, and are worried by feelings of frustration, then go and see your physician, explain the circumstances to him, and he will prescribe medication which will depress your sexual desire, and thus your sexual response, so that the orgasms you do have satisfy you, and your penis won't always ask for more. (Robert Chartham)

MUSICAL CLIMAX

My boyfriend and I have developed a very firm and warm relationship but we have failed to achieve simultaneous orgasm. We have been going together for over a year and have intercourse a minimum of four times each weekend.

We both respond sexually to music so, recently, we spoke to a friend who works for a record firm, telling him of our sensitivity to music and our problem regarding simultaneous orgasm. This friend informed us that he himself, as well as numerous acquaintances, have been able to work their lovemaking into the love-death theme from 'Tristan and Isolde'.

He gave us a small 45-rpm record of this piece saying, 'If at first you don't succeed, try, try again.' For five weekends we tried. Both of us find that our orgasm rhythms do not in any way correspond to those of this music.

We were a little embarrassed at this and finally my boyfriend, with my permission, brought it up with the record company friend. This guy insisted that the rhythm of the orgasm, rooted in the anatomy, was as fixed in the time/release action as a falling body. This pattern, he claimed, had been captured by Wagner in this theme.

He even brought a tape of himself and his girlfriend having their orgasm in time to the love-death theme (both the orgasms and the theme clearly heard on the tape). We tried for the sixth time that weekend but again to no avail.

Do you think we should give up and try to find different

partners in order to achieve simultaneous orgasm? Or, are we simply freaks, out of step with natural orgasmic rhythms?

Name withheld by request,
New York

There is no such thing as a 'fixed' orgasmic rhythm as this friend suggests. You are certainly not freaks; many couples have difficulty coming to simultaneous orgasm.

If you really enjoy making love to music try using Bolero by Ravel, another piece said to have a particularly conducive theme. On the other hand, many people prefer enjoying each other's separate orgasms just as much, or more, than a simultaneous climax. So, enjoy your relationship and don't worry.

ORGASM DIFFERENCE

When I got married my wife told me about a difference between men and women which I have not yet seen mentioned in *Forum.*

Both sexes have muscular spasms at orgasm, but whereas the male can continue having these, and enjoying an orgasm, if stimulation stops after the first, the woman's pleasure is spoiled unless stimulation continues throughout. The peak of sensation, my wife says, recedes more quickly for women than for men and is harder to get back.

Is my wife unique, or have other readers also found this difference?

E.C.,
Yorkshire

There is a subtle difference in the sexual climax between male and female and also in its effect on each. It is quite true that once the male climax has been reached and the reflexes activated, ejaculation will proceed automatically whether stimulation continues or not. There are usually four or five involuntary contractions of the ejaculatory muscles, although a few further contractions may be made voluntarily in order to expel the last drops of semen from the urethra.

The situation in the female differs in two respects. First, the female has no ejaculatory apparatus and therefore no specialized muscles for this purpose. Instead, during orgasm and with continuing clitoral stimulation there occurs a rhythmic throbbing of the perineal muscles surrounding the vagina and urethra, and also a rhythmic contraction and relaxation of the muscles of the womb. These contractions are relatively weak compared with the powerful ejaculatory contractions of the male, and may continue for a somewhat longer period. So if clitoral stimulation ceases altogether immediately after climax is reached these rhythmic throbbings may cease or appear to cease, and orgasmic sensation, as in the male, will not reach the same peak of intensity as it would have if stimulation had continued. These perineal throbbings are not quite analogous to the male ejaculatory contractions and would not necessarily continue automatically, so your wife's observations are probably correct.

Secondly, although satisfying orgasm is sexually enervating for both sexes, it is much more so for the male. He loses his erection and, depending on his virility, will usually require 10 minutes or longer before regaining his potency. This is thought to be due in part to loss of seminal fluid during ejaculation causing a fall in pressure within the reservoirs, the seminal vesicles and ducts of the prostate gland. But the volume of fluid can at least be partially restored within a short period by further secretion from the cells of the glands. Women, on the other hand, are capable of continuing active copulation after achieving orgasm and of reaching a further climax after a shorter or longer period depending on their individual sexuality. On the whole, females are much less fragile than males, sexually speaking, and Nature can be congratulated on making this difference between the sexes. (Consultant)

ORGASM AFTER SYMPATHECTOMY

I am 34, married with two children. I married at 19 with no experience to speak of with other men, and I had no idea until about 12 months ago that I had never really had a climax, although I did enjoy sex very much.

Four years ago I had a sympathectomy to improve my circulation. For a time after, I was apathetic to the point of hating to be touched. My husband's attitude at the time was not very helpful. Gradually my sex life has improved and I now derive immense pleasure and fun with my husband, who in turn has improved his techniques and is more understanding, although I have to fake an orgasm to please him.

I cannot achieve that elusive climax without the aid of a mains operated vibrator going at full throttle. Once away I can have orgasms galore but if I turn the volume down, masturbate, or my husband takes over, the feeling quickly subsides.

From reading *Forum* I gather there could be some danger in using a powerful vibrator in that it could desensitize me still further. I do feel that my clitoris is not as sensitive as it should be – having used a battery vibrator without much success and also tried leaving all mechanical aids alone for a while and simply masturbating manually, again without success. I wonder if I am trying to achieve the impossible – a plain ordinary climax.

A doctor once told me that a sympathectomy affects the central nervous system and I am very lucky to have an orgasm at all. Do I content myself with that?

Mrs D.S.,
Cheshire

I have not myself treated any woman who has previously had a sympathectomy for a psychosexual disorder. In theory, the operation could interfere to some extent with the physiology of sexual response and I am sure that a number of women will have reported adverse effects after surgery – but whether these would be mainly of physical or psychological origin would be hard to determine with certainty.

However, as far as animal experiments are concerned, it is remarkable how many of the nerves supplying the genital region of the female can be destroyed and yet she will still undertake and apparently enjoy intercourse. Both men and male animals can be made impotent by quite small damage to the nerve supply.

In your case, I don't think the operation can have had much direct effect. I say this because most of your increased sexual pleasure has occurred since then. It seems that up to a year ago you were inhibiting (or denying yourself) your orgasmic responses.

Even now it seems as if you require a great deal of stimulation in order to 'batter down' your defences against orgasm but once they are breached you can enjoy multiple orgasms. The difficulty lies in getting going.

Some women do perhaps have fewer nerve endings in the clitoris than others and so may require heavier stimulation. In masturbation, some women only lightly touch the area but others press so hard that their knuckles go white. However, such stimulation could represent the need for massive physical sen-

125

sations to overcome psychic opposition. Women vary enormously in the ease or difficulty with which orgasm can be induced and the methods of inducing it. Nearly always, when a woman who previously had difficulty getting orgasms 'discovers' the knack of easy induction, it is because her inhibitions have been reduced. This applies to masturbation and to intercourse but especially to the former. The more a woman practises masturbation and the better she is at it the better her chances become of having orgasms in intercourse.

It perhaps seems to you a silly way of putting it – but the more willing you become to accept and enjoy orgasms the easier it will become to have them. It sounds to me as if you have settled down at a level where you can only accept orgasms after a herculean struggle. You even ask if you should be content at this level. If you practised arousing yourelf to higher levels initially by sexual fantasy or studying 'erotica', you should find your responsiveness steadily increases simply because you will be accepting your own sexuality to a greater extent in your own mind and altering your attitudes.

If you read your letter again you will perhaps see what I mean when I say that you almost speak of your orgasms as if they were not a part of you and your vibrator as a feared object. It is your mind and not your vibrator that will do you harm. A sign of progress will be that you will suddenly need more subtle and more specific stimulation than your vibrator can afford. You will then need to use your hand and one more barrier between you and sex will have been removed. You will then have to transfer from your hand to your husband's hand and thereafter orgasm with the penis in the vagina will be but a short step away.

CRY UNCLE

I am in my early 30s, married to a man in his middle 60s, with two small children. We have had a very satisfying marriage – including our sex life – up until a year ago. My husband's sexual appetite has diminished considerably, which I presume is due to his age. He wants sex about once a month whereas I feel I am at my sexual peak.

We discussed this fully, and my husband felt I should find more sex elsewhere. At first I hesitated, but after giving it much consideration, I decided to have some extramarital affairs. This was four months ago, and I have had relations with six different men during this time. Aside from a 'one-night stand', I have had sex with each man more than six times. Two of my lovers are in their 30s and the other four are in their middle 20s.

My problem is that I can experience an average of four orgasms during foreplay and intercouse, and I only feel satisfied if I have had these multiple orgasms. Even though my husband has infrequent sexual desires, he has always satisfied me by postponing ejaculation until I 'cry uncle'. These other lovers seem to have their orgasms so quickly (within 20 minutes, including foreplay). I have tried arousing them again after their first ejaculations, but they always say they've 'had it' and are surprised that I want more. They seem to feel that one orgasm is enough.

I would like to know if I am difficult to satisfy or if I just had bad luck in my choice of men.

Mrs J.C.,
Address withheld by request

It may be that your original choice of lovers was the best. Your husband's ability as a lover is probably the result of the extent of his sexual experience before marriage. Which is not to say that a younger man cannot be as good a lover, but your husband may possess the patience and experience that younger men lack. Also, because he loves you, he may have felt a greater desire to satisfy you as completely as he knows how. He may also simply be a superior lover to any of your other choices. He has had more opportunity than the others to discover how to please you most effectively.

I don't think that your demands are inordinate at all. You should expect your lovers to pay as much attention to your sexual needs as you pay to theirs. Your letter suggests your needs, but you don't mention your response to your lovers. Are you a passive sexual partner? You seem to be aggressively finding partners, but once in bed do you lie back and wait for them to make love to you? Sex is a reciprocal arrangement. Maybe the lack of excitement in your sex life is as much due to your lack of effort as that of your lovers. It is certainly something to consider.

Your husband has graciously given you a free rein, but maybe you still have some degree of guilt about your extra-marital affairs. In which case, it's time to reopen the matter with your husband. Perhaps both of you can work this out of your system.

Furthermore, and perhaps most importantly, you sound as though you've given up on your husband altogether. Mid-60s is not too old to be a good lover. Many older men see this age as the prime of their sexual drives. It may be that your husband is simply going through a difficult stage. Perhaps he feels he's too old for you and doesn't want to impose on or repress your youth, so he has decided to play second fiddle to younger lovers.

Since he is the best lover you have had, I think you should start actively to reassure him and excite his sexual drive again. If he was active sexually in the earlier stage of your marriage, there is every reason to believe that he still can be. Turn him on as best you know how. His lack of interest in sex may be due to things other than a diminished drive. Maybe he just has to know you still want him.

MASTURBATION

NURSING CARE

In a recent *Forum*, a South Carolina woman told of being brought to orgasm by a nurse on several occasions during a stay in hospital. I had a similar experience in a hospital.

Several years ago I had a minor operation in Florida. The day before my operation a nurse shaved me from the waist down. The exposure was embarrassing, but the nurse turned out to be a talkative girl. Our conversation put me at ease, for a while at least. While she worked I learned she was married, had two children, and had just turned 30. She was also rather nice-looking and had a good figure.

I was gradually becoming sexually aroused despite my effort to distract myself, and I found it increasingly difficult to keep up my end of the conversation. Inevitably, I developed an erection.

Shortly after this happened, without a pause in her conversation, the nurse put aside the razor and began to manipulate me. I was surprised, to say the least, but I followed her lead in seeming to ignore what she was doing to me. She was in the midst of telling me about a boat she hoped to buy when I reached orgasm. When it was over, she finished shaving me, continued our chat, and never in any way acknowledged what had just taken place. I made no comment either, for what could I have said?

She made the act appear routine and almost non-sexual, yet I've never heard of anyone else having this experience until I read the letter in *Forum*. I should add that for me it was definitely not non-sexual! I still find excitement in just recalling the incident.

D.G.,
New Jersey

CAN'T COME INSIDE

My husband of a few months is having a major problem. He is 50, I am 49.

We are both very passionate and indulge in sex nightly. He has masturbated excessively in the past, having previously been married to a woman who did not want much of a sexual relationship. Most of the time he cannot climax inside of me and has to masturbate, which now upsets him, as he wants to complete the love act naturally. He is used to hard, fast, and vigorous masturbation.

Can you suggest a way of undoing the damage?

Mrs C.D.,
Pennsylvania

Both you and your husband seem to think that his earlier masturbation has done him harm and accounts for his inability to have an orgasm whilst inside you. You even use the word 'excessive', which implies that you believe there is some norm which he has exceeded with the consequence that a penalty must be paid.

This attitude (but not his earlier masturbation) alone could be sufficient to give rise to difficulties, since our sexuality is as much in the mind as in the genitals. For example, a man who thinks – no matter how unconsciously – that frequent ejaculation is a punishable waste of precious resources may well have difficulty in undertaking satisfactory intercourse regularly.

In your husband's case however there is no apparent impediment to ejaculation as such – only to ejaculation in your vagina.

Most women regard this as a fault in themselves and believe that if they were only more attractive or more exciting the man would make it. In fact, the trouble nearly always lies with the man and relates to the circumstances or his past experiences or his attitudes. If your husband was a sexual failure with his former wife – and this could have been the cause of her disinterest – then it will take time for him to recover his confidence and it is very important that you remain uncritical, warm and appreciative.

It will take him time to learn and you have only been married a few months.

If this is so it would probably help if you could learn to masturbate him in ways which excite him more than when he does it for himself. In any case don't feel excluded, and do take an interest in his masturbation, watch him, try to feel excited by it and partake in some way such as playing with his anus or scrotum. Perhaps too, you could tell him a fantasy whilst he masturbates or you masturbate him. The idea of all this is to involve yourself in his eroticism so that he feels increasingly excited by you.

All this would help with one common cause of the problem: that unconsciously a woman that such a man loves is perceived as his mother who must not be despoiled by ejaculation within her vagina. The more the woman can show that she is not 'pure' but is psychically sexual the better; but if it is done too crudely the man may reject her. The essential point is to give him the impression that both he and his sexuality are not only acceptable to you but are actively desired.

Another possibility is that he prefers masturbation because he is better able to concentrate on some fantasy theme which he feels unable to reveal because he thinks it is perverted. Only reassurance and communication would reveal this and when revealed the solution is usually obvious.

Finally, turning to your own theory, namely, that his penis has become adjusted through masturbation to a form of stimulation which cannot be reproduced by the vagina, I must admit that this does seem to be a possibility in some cases. Presumably all men try to provide themselves with the type of stimulation they have learned to like best, through masturbation, when they place the penis in the vagina. Some, for example, like to make quick, hard, short movements and it seems that your husband falls into this category.

Apart from enhancing your psychic sexual value to him as suggested above you can increase physical stimulation in various ways. Try adopting a position where the penis enters the vagina at an angle so that its top surface rubs against the lower edge of the pubic bone. Another possibility is for you to lie under him but to close your legs when he has penetrated. A further technique is for you to use your hands to compress and stimulate the shaft of the penis as it moves in and out of the vagina. This last manoeuvre, if done correctly, can be a big help. Training your perineal muscles to contract hard as the penis moves inwards is also useful and if done well can bring a man to orgasm without the penis actually moving within the vagina at all.

FEMALE MASTURBATION

I only recently discovered *Forum*, and I can't sing your praises enough! I have worked hard and conscientiously over the last few years to accept my feelings about sex and rid myself of the inhibitions and guilt instilled in me by my parents. I love sex, I love bodies, I love sharing with other people.

I felt very guilty when I began masturbating at the age of 20 (I'm 26 now, by the way), but I thoroughly enjoy it now. I love masturbating in many different positions and places. I enjoy using my fingers, a dildo, a massager, carrots, candles, cucumbers, pillows, the bed sheets, and any other item that strikes my fancy at the time. It excites me to sit on the floor in front of a full length mirror and watch while I insert different items into myself. I have very sensitive nipples, and I enjoy rubbing them against the wall mirror while in a standing position. I especially enjoy manipulating my nipples and clitoris after I have applied a small amount of body lotion or baby oil to each area.

Masturbating while in water (in a full tub, under a shower, in a swimming pool or pond) can be delicious. I have two different types of bead curtains hanging in my flat and they feel so beautiful when I hold them still and rub my nipples and pussy against them. I enjoy masturbating manually when driving on motorways in light traffic. I like to play when talking on the telephone to people I like, both male and female. They don't usually have any idea what I'm doing unless I tell them. Once a man was so excited by the knowledge that *he* began masturbating and we both had very exciting orgasms!

I enjoy pornographic films and either masturbating myself while watching them or masturbating a willing partner who's gone along with me while he or she reciprocates. Porno photographs and books also get me started!

I enjoy pressing my pelvic area against the front of public juke boxes playing records while I am supposedly seeing what records are listed. I have never achieved an orgasm like this, but the vibration is wonderful. I imagine a woman could get the same effect from a washing machine or dish-washer.

I have found it very helpful, when with a new partner, to masturbate in front of each other in order to understand better how each likes to be stimulated and manipulated.

I certainly enjoy all forms of sexual activity, including one or more partners of either sex. I'm not stuck into only masturbating, but I felt sparked at this moment to share my masturbatory practices with you and your readers. Hope it gives some women some new ideas about taking advantage of the sensual possibilities surrounding them of which they may not be aware!

Ms J.A.,
Address withheld by request

132

PLEASE YOURSELF

I was extremely interested in the article in a recent issue on our reticence towards masturbation. Several of my women friends have freely confessed to adultery when we have talked about sex and two of them have given the most lurid details of these extramarital affairs. Yet on a couple of occasions when I asked whether they masturbated they appeared to be shocked. Yet I am quite sure they do.

I am a confirmed masturbator, yet I am married and enjoy sexual intercourse with my husband and never have the slightest trouble achieving first class orgasm with him. I began when I was 11 years of age when a schoolfriend came to stay with us during the holiday. We shared a big double bed and at night we used to show each other our private parts and then stand in front of the mirror on the wardrobe and rub ourselves off.

I am now 20 years older and I still delight in standing in front of a mirror and tossing myself off. My husband knows this; in fact he loves to lie on the bed doing the same thing for himself while watching me perform.

On average I masturbate three times a week. I have no special day or time for doing it. I just do it when I feel like it. Sometimes I get in the mood when I have had a bath, other times when I have just completed my housework and the place is quiet. Nor do I choose any particular room in the house. I notice a neighbour of mine often has her bedroom window curtains drawn in the afternoon and I suspect she is masturbating because usually the curtains are pulled back after about half an hour. If I happen to get the urge while I am in the sitting room I just pull my pants down and lie on the couch and if I am in the loo I proceed to do it there. I never feel any sense of guilt or shame. In fact I usually feel absolutely marvellous especially when I succeed in getting an extra large orgasm.

As for being ashamed of anybody knowing, far from it, though I don't go about boasting about it. Recently a friend came round to my house unexpectedly. I was feeling frightfully randy at the time and had taken my knickers off and was about to indulge when the door bell rang. Of course I had to invite her in. I offered her a cup of tea, wondering why she had come.

Apparently she had had a bust-up with her husband who she discovered was having an affair with a secretary at his office. She was full of self-pity and kept saying that she blamed herself for not giving him satisfaction in bed. I told her not to be so

133

bloody silly and to think of herself. I asked her whether she ever got any satisfaction and she said sometimes.

I asked her straight out whether she ever gave herself any pleasure. She pretended not to understand me and I repeated the question in more explicit terms. She hesitated for several seconds and then said no. I knew of course that she was lying and asked her why on earth was she so ashamed of admitting she did masturbate. I told her that I frequently do so and thoroughly enjoy it. I lifted up a cushion and showed her my pants which I had stuffed there when the door bell rang. I explained that I had been about to have it when she came.

She wanted to leave immediately saying she was sorry. I invited her to stay and watch me if she felt like it. She seemed undecided so I took off my dress and lay down on the couch with my legs wide open. I began to play with myself and she then said she would stay if I didn't mind. I applied some face cream to my fanny and began to work myself very slowly, chatting to her all the time. Gradually I could see her becoming agitated. Finally, she took her knickers off and began to masturbate. We both finished at the same time. I had an absolutely huge come-off, presumably because of the circumstances, and I think my friend didn't do too badly either. I asked her how she felt and she said marvellous.

She came round to my house once a week for about two months after that just so that, as she said, she could relax. She had tried to do it in her own home but felt tense and nervous in case anybody came. On a couple of occasions I had to assist her to get really going, usually by allowing her to fondle my breasts and once by applying cream to her cunt.

She suddenly stopped coming to the house for her weekly sex lessons (as she called them). I asked her why and she said that she had finally overcome her fears about doing it in her own home. Apparently one evening she was feeling very badly in need of masturbation but her husband was due home in a few minutes. She decided that he could like it or lump it so she stripped and lay on the couch. When her husband came in she was about to reach a climax. To her astonishment he seemed delighted, took his penis out and while fully dressed and standing in the middle of the sitting room tossed himself off. She told him firmly that although he could have intercourse with her anytime he felt like it she was definitely going to continue with masturbation; that it gave her enormous pleasure and had made her feel a new woman.

I have read several surveys which suggest that fewer women masturbate than men. I am not at all certain of this. I believe just as many women do it and do it regularly but because it has been dinned into their heads that it is 'filthy' they refuse to admit to performing a perfectly natural function. For instance, a close friend came to see me recently in apparently great distress. She had walked into her 14-year-old daughter's bedroom and found her masturbating. You would think she had found her daughter murdering somebody! I got very angry with her and asked her if her son, who is 12, masturbates. She said she didn't know but thought he probably did. That didn't worry her at all. It was quite all right for the boy to indulge but a dreadful thing for the girl!

Such a cockeyed attitude made me even more furious and I was determined to have it out with my friend, not for her sake but for her daughter's because I suspected that she was going to be watched and chastised and made to feel like an outcast. I first told her about my own masturbatory habits, their frequency and their variations. I explained that this did not interfere with my relations with my husband.

When she quietened down a bit I asked her had she never masturbated. She said she had when she was young. The family lived on a farm in Sussex and she used to go to the hayloft and play with herself. One day an old maiden aunt had discovered her secret and kicked up the most dreadful scene. Why then, I asked, did she make such a fuss herself when she found her own daughter doing just the same thing. Couldn't she understand the girl's urge? I told her I believed she was making such a song and dance simply because she had been stopped, that it was just frustration. She agreed that I was probably right. Would she like to do it now, I asked her. She didn't reply so I suggested that if it helped her I was willing to indulge myself at the same time. I was astounded at her reaction. She practically ripped her clothes off and before I had time to get myself ready she was frigging away at herself. A week later I had a visit from the daughter. She said her mother had told her she had come to see me and that I had explained things properly to her.

Why must women adopt this attitude? So far as I know men don't make such a fuss about their sons masturbating. Are women genuine in their attitude or are they just carrying on in the tradition of their grandparents that women are not supposed to enjoy sex in any form, and that their cunts are just a receptacle for their husbands' sperm?

As I have said, I have been masturbating for the past 20 years and hope to go on just as actively for the next 20.

Women would be a lot happier if they accepted the fact that their bodies are to be enjoyed by themselves as well as their husbands.

Mrs P.L.,
London

TECHNIQUE

HOW TO DO FELLATIO

Could you please brief me on how to do fellatio really well? I don't want my man to be disappointed with my efforts!

Miss M.T.,
London

Fellatio is not just a matter of putting the penis-head in the mouth and sucking it. Naturally, this simple activity would give the man a good deal of pleasure, but to provide him with the maximum enjoyment, you must know the sensitive areas of the penis.

These are – in descending order of sensitivity – the frenum, penis-tip, rim (both round the edge and in the groove under it), the base of the penis all round about an inch and half above the root, the whole length of the underside of the shaft; and finally, the rest of the skin of the penis.

Since the frenum (the little band of ordinary skin which joins the skin of the shaft to the membrane covering the penis-head), and the penis-head and rim, lead in the sensitivity stakes it is essential to draw back an uncircumcised man's foreskin as far as it will go before beginning fellatio. Otherwise some of the effect will be lost, because the mouth and tongue cannot be in direct contact with the extensive masses of nerves in these three closely located areas. Also the warmth of the mouth and the saliva it contains are extremely stimulating in their special way.

One thing about fellatio a woman must never forget. The head of the erect penis is extremely sensitive and she must take particular care all the time not to bite or scratch it with her teeth. Should she do so she can be absolutely certain of disaster. Nothing makes the penis deflate more rapidly than pain. A sharp nip, and within two seconds it will be completely limp, and will take a great deal of the friendliest persuasion to get it back up again.

So the first thing the woman must learn is to draw her lips down and under (or over) the edges of her teeth to shield her delicate target from their sharpness. She should not draw them in so much that they are completely rigid, but just enough to cover them.

In my opinion, the position in which fellatio is performed is important. Many men find being fellated standing up very exciting, and to do so the woman nearly always kneels on the floor, on a cushion. This is a good position because the frenum is directly available to her tongue and so is the underside of the penis. Besides, unless the man is very tall, she will not have to depress the penis very much when she takes it into her mouth.

Some men find this standing position too exciting, especially if they are fellated until they come. The rising excitement can make the knees quiver uncontrollably, and the shaking can be so violent as to cause difficulty in keeping balance.

If fellatio is used only as a foreplay technique and the session is going to end with the penis in the vagina, then I suggest the couple should lie on the bed. The woman should have her face towards the man's face, and her bottom towards his feet, rather than the other way round, because, once again, the frenum is directly presented to her tongue. This does not happen in the '69' position.

Before taking the penis into her mouth, the woman gives the frenum, penis-head and rim a warming up by licking them, or teasing them with rapidly moving tongue-tip. This can be followed by a number of varieties of caresses, like running the tongue round the edge of the rim, working the tip of the tongue under the edge of the rim, licking the frenum and penis-tip with the tongue, and very, very lightly nipping or rolling the frenum between the lip-protected teeth. Blowing on the penis-head and under the rim is also extremely stimulating.

When the woman eventually takes the penis into her mouth, she should take as much in as she can without gagging. Simultaneously with her sucking of the penis, she must move her mouth up and down the shaft and head. Most men like to control these movements, so if her partner puts his hands on her head to do this, she should follow the rhythm of his hands.

Since the penis must be held away from the man's belly in order that this manoeuvre can be carried out, the woman should move the hand holding it up and down that part of the penis which will not go into her mouth. With the other hand she should fondle his balls – again very lightly.

As the man's arousal sensations begin to build up, the woman will notice that his balls now and again move up towards the root of his penis, pause there for a second or two, and then move down again. When he is approaching the point-of-no-

138

return he will begin to breathe heavily, and will automatically make rhythmic movements of his pelvis.

At the same time his balls will rise and lower more frequently, and they will not now descend so low as they did previously. When this begins to happen the woman will know that he is going to come within 30 to 60 seconds.

The really sensuous woman will have no compunction about letting a man ejaculate in her mouth. I am quite convinced that if it were not for the pulsating of the penis, women would be unaware that their partners were ejaculating. However, I must concede that some men's semen has a distinctly acid taste which very slightly stings the back of the throat when swallowed.

If the woman is not keen, for this or any other reason, to accept the semen in her mouth, as soon as the man's balls begin to get agitated she can withdraw her mouth and continue with her fingers, or take his penis into her.

If the semen tastes at all, it is not a strong taste, except in a few fairly rare cases, and a drink of water will immediately dispel any slight stinging sensations there may be. Certainly, swallowing semen never did any woman any harm. It cannot, because for the most part it is made up of salts and vitamins.

There is also a 'deep throat' technique for advanced lovers which consists of taking the penis head down past the epiglottis, but this should only be done with great care.

FELLATIO TECHNIQUE

There is one method of fellatio that hasn't been mentioned in Forum, as far as I know, and which I have used for over 10 years of marriage very successfully. I recommend it to those couples where the woman dislikes the taste of semen.

Simply roll on an unlubricated type of french letter, either the plain or teat end variety, before starting. It is still very exciting for the man, and there is no risk of the woman receiving semen in her mouth.

With the teat end type an added thrill is obtained after ejaculation by the woman rolling the filled teat between her lips, feeling the semen trapped without having to taste it. Even with playful bites on the french letter I have never split one when doing this.

Mrs L.H.,
Essex

139

COOL LIPS

We have been married only three months and my wife and I really enjoy our sex life. Before I married I was well informed about sex and found that I enjoyed everything I tried. At first I was hesitant to mention oral sex to my wife but with a little love, anything can be accomplished.

Recently we found a new technique which gets me very excited. My wife performs fellatio on me after she has eaten a bowl of ice-cold jelly. Her cold mouth on my hot penis feels incredible. I am not saying that my wife should eat cold jelly everytime she wants to eat me, but if she has trouble getting me excited, the cold sensation of her mouth really gets me excited quickly. Ladies, cold lips and a cool tongue are a real turn-on, so give it a try.

D.K.,
Address withheld by request

MOTHER NATURE'S INSTANT FOAM

My husband and I have just returned from a camping trip in Canada. On the first morning after our arrival, my husband awoke early to wash and shave. He called to me in the tent and said he couldn't find the shaving cream. I realized that I had forgotten to pack it and since there was no shaving cream within miles of our campside, I jokingly suggested that he masturbate and use mother nature's shaving cream. My husband took me up on the suggestion and after a few strokes he collected a good handful of semen. He spread it on his face and began to shave. Which watching the proceedings I got so excited that I reached into my panties and started masturbating. By the time he had finished I had experienced several fantastic orgasms. We repeated this several times during the week with the same lovely results.

The next time you go camping with your favourite man, leave the shaving cream behind. Take it off with Mother Nature's instant foam.

N.C.,
Address withheld by request

For safety's sake the Forum *editorial staff has consulted a number of dermatologists about the effect of semen on the skin. They all agree that there is nothing in 'Mother Nature's instant foam' that is harmful to the face. In fact, it probably causes fewer allergic reactions and irritations than shaving cream, although it might not give as clean a shave as the products on the market sold specifically for shaving.*

ADAPTABLE TOOTHBRUSH

This letter is for those who may find it difficult, for one reason or another, to purchase a vibrator of the phallic variety. If one has easily purchased without embarrassment either a plug-in or cordless-electric toothbrush, the problem is solved.

A few years ago I sawed off the brush end of one of the many extra brushes accompanying our electrical unit. I then filed and sanded the end of the plastic remainder to a smooth, round contour. Inserted into the electrical unit, it serves as a clitoral stimulator. This small cylindrical vibrating head – about the size of a little finger – may appear as an unlikely candidate, but I dare say that there is none other as vigorous. The intense orgasms of my wife are testimony to its effectiveness.

C.S.,
Minnesota

LOVE AQUA-STYLE

My new husband of a few months, aged 50, took me to a beautiful Mediterranean island for our second honeymoon recently. Here we were at last on our own and able to discover each other afresh. Neither of us had, in spite of previous marriages, realized before what wonderful pleasure you can give to each other just in fucking. We were both very inhibited when we first met and had never even thought of anything but the 'missionary position'.

In the Mediterranean we discovered what we think is the ultimate in sex between two people! About 100 yards out at sea – in broad daylight – my husband produced the most wonderful erection which I was able to sit on with my legs wrapped around his waist – a position we couldn't even consider on dry land. The buoyancy of the sea and the gentle waves did nearly all the work for me, making me rise and fall on his penis, and before we knew what was happening we were beyond the point of no return and having it off good and proper. It was fantastic. The sea kept me wet, which I didn't need for long, and there was no question of any foreplay – I saw it, I wanted it and I took it.

141

Has anybody else tried this 'aqua-fucking', or are we old-fashioned after all and just very much in love with each other?

Mrs M.N.,
Kent

HOW TO MASTURBATE A MAN

I'm 21 and single. Along with my friends, I have what I consider liberal sexual views; I'm just not the type of girl who can successfully pull off a naïve act, and as a result have a sort of sophisticated aura which I prefer to keep. This is the reason I am writing to you.

It has been several years since I was a virgin. I consider myself good in bed and have never had any complaints in the fellatio department. The one thing I have never done, though, is to masturbate a guy. At this point in my life I'd feel kind of silly asking a guy how the heck you do it. I really started to think about it after a guy told me that he would actually prefer a good hand job to fellatio. There are times when intercourse is out of the question, and I don't feel like fellatio, but when I don't want to leave my date with no relief at all.

Now I certainly have some idea of what to do, but I'm asking about how to give a really good one. Is a light touch preferable, or is medium to heavy pressure better? How would you do a guy who has been circumcised, and whose skin is stretched tightly during erection; is it necessary to carry a lubricant around? Should the strokes be fast or slow, long or short?

I hope you won't consider this a silly question, but fellatio is so much in vogue, I really don't think that many of your female readers would be particularly adept in this particular thing.

Ms M. R.,
Rhode Island

No one is too old or too 'sophisticated' to learn. I suggest you consider dropping your 'aura' and find out precisely what turns your man on. There is no better teacher than the man you are trying to please. There are, however, certain basic techniques which may be useful to know about if you want to master a good hand job.

Masturbating a man is an experience filled with fantasy and tactile sensuality. A careless tug or a raspy whisper could put a damper on the act as well as the erection. You should be aware of how you look to him and, if you talk to him, the tone of your voice and the words you speak.

Now for the essentials. Circumcised or not, you proceed the same way. Equip yourself properly before you begin by removing any jewellery that might interfere with those pleasurable sensations. Moisten both your hands liberally, not pouring anything directly on him because the abrupt sensation may turn him off or make him shutter. Your mouth can replace any additional lubricant if you are so inclined. However, if you choose to use something other than nature's own, be certain that it has an oil base and smells pleasant. Place your palm around the penis and slowly coat your partner with the lubricant. (Don't worry about the mess; he won't mind!) Close your fingers tightly enough to have a firm grip, but not a stranglehold.

As his penis begins to grow to erection, place your other hand around it as well, the fingers of both hands intertwined. You are stroking him in a way that simulates the feeling of having a penis in a vagina. Your hands should be kept moist enough so that, in this position, you can both hear the sound of this moistness. (Most men find this extremely exciting.) You can alternate between the one and two handed approaches and light and heavy touches, including in your repertoire corkscrew motions and the fondling of his testicles (not so lightly that it tickles).

Watch his facial reactions to your ministrations. This is how you will learn what he finds the most stimulating. Increase your speed as he's nearing orgasm, but don't emulate a piston engine. You can change tempo by using long, gentle strokes, extending from the base up to, and including, the tip, or by employing shorter, firmer strokes. Don't hesitate to relubricate your hands if they begin to feel dry; this pause will also give your partner a chance to calm down so that you can build him up again to an explosive climax. Do not stop stroking when you either feel or see the first spasms. Continue to fondle him (a little more gently) until he has finished ejaculating.

Once you have perfected your technique, there is no end to the variations you can use to make your man come. However, don't hesitate to ask him how he'd like you to handle him.

THE SCROTUM

I have heard that touching a man on and around his scrotum arouses him very much.

Perhaps you could help me by explaining in ordinary terms

where it is as I'm sure there are many women who would like to know.

Miss J.E.,
Cornwall

The scrotum is the bag of skin hanging behind the limp penis and below the erect one (when the man is standing). It contains the two testicles. In very hairy men, the skin of the scrotum may be thickly covered with hair, and even less hirsute men usually have a few hairs growing on the scrotum.

When the man is sexually aroused, the skin of the scrotum becomes very sensitive.

Often this happens even before he has an erection. Like most highly sensitive areas, the skin of the scrotum responds best to very light caresses, usually by the partner. (There are not many men who can arouse themselves sexually by caressing their own scrotum.) In any case, the testicles are always very tender and must never be gripped hard, or hit, or punched, or bitten; so it is just as well that the skin of the scrotum responds best to light touch. In fact, if the caresses are not gentle, the skin loses all its sensitivity.

Most men find that they respond very quickly and very intensely if the fingertips are lightly moved backwards and forwards over the surface of the scrotal skin. They have the same intense response if the scrotal skin is licked. Many are also turned on if the palm of the hand is lightly passed backwards and forwards over the tips of the hairs growing from the scrotum, without touching the skin at all.

There are few men, too, who do not find it very arousing if the whole scrotum, including the balls – if they are not too big – is gently drawn into the mouth and gently sucked, or gently moved round the mouth with the tongue. If the balls are too large for both to be taken into the mouth at the same time, sucking on one and then on the other is just as effective.

There are very few things that give a man more feelings of comfort than to have his balls lightly held in the palm of his partner's hand.

While we are in this area, there is another very sensitive spot which is too often overlooked. This is the ridge between the back of the scrotum and the anus. (It is called the perineum.) Light caresses with the finger-tips or tongue from the anus, up and over the scrotum, up the shaft of the penis to the penis-tip, and back again to the anus can send most men wild.

Because the nerves in the perineum are part of the sexual nervous system, pressure with the finger-tips at the mid-point of the ridge, can often induce an erection, or restore a flagging erection to stiffness.

Women also possess a perineum, between the rear of the vagina-entrance and the anus. It is just as sensitive as the man's.

HOME HELP

I recently discovered that two common household items, the shower hose and the hand hairdryer, make great sex aids.

We bought a shower hose a few weeks ago. One morning my husband came out of the bathroom grinning and said to me, 'You know I bet you could bring yourself off with that hose.' I love masturbating, so I immediately rushed into the bathroom to try it. It was marvellous.

Initially, I use lukewarm water and just move the stream around the outside of my labia and the very top of my pubic area. Once I get excited, I can comfortably rotate the water in a circle around my clitoris, sometimes making the temperature warmer or colder. I get a lot of unique sensations this way, and a slow, very nice orgasm. My husband likes to do it to me, and also to go down on me afterwards. He says the combination of my juices and the warm water is delicious.

We have also found that my hand hairdryer is a nice sex toy. During foreplay, one of us moves the stream of hot air over the other's body. My husband gets especially excited when I spread his legs and direct the air back and forth between his anus and his testicles. He also likes it in the armpits. I enjoy the air along my back. On hot days, we sometimes turn it to cool and use it to evaporate the sweat. After I've had an orgasm, I like my husband to run the cool air up and down between my legs.

I hope some other *Forum* readers will try using these devices.

Mrs G.,
Address withheld by request

ORAL SEX

ORAL SEX TRAINING

At last, after five years of trying, I have succeeded in fulfilling my greatest desire to have my husband perform cunnilingus on me.

Like a lot of men, he encouraged me to fellate him, but he refused to reciprocate and give me the same thrill. But recently, I had my way, and how I achieved this may be of some interest to your women readers who have had problems in getting their desires fulfilled.

Realizing my husband's fondness for kissing and sucking my breasts, I tried wetting them with my own vaginal juices. To my surprise, he sucked at each nipple more eagerly, and as I continually carried on wetting them, so he transferred his attention to each one in turn. It was obvious to me that the wetness or taste on my breasts excited my husband – not the nipples. I then began rubbing my vaginal juices on other parts of my body and I noticed that he transferred his attentions to these new spots. I even invited him to suck my wet fingers, which he did.

Gradually, I succeeded in getting him to go lower and lower down my body, licking wherever I wet it, until eventually his face was against my thighs. I just had to part my legs and he soon buried his face between them and began sucking me off within seconds. I had the most explosive orgasm I have ever had.

I then changed my position so that I could fellate my husband at the same time. We stayed like this until he had filled my mouth twice and I lost count of my own orgasms.

My husband has confessed to me that he now enjoys oral sex more than anything else.

Mrs W.M.,
Hampshire

You seem by some happy chance – or intelligent thought – to have reproduced fairly precisely the sort of gradual approach a therapist would have recommended in this situation. Getting people used to things a bit at a time is an excellent method where any kind of fear or distaste is involved. The essentials are not to put any pressure on the 'patient', not to let him – and especially not to force him – to do anything that makes him anxious, to adopt a fairly light-hearted attitude to the 'treatment', and to reward every sign of progress verbally or, better still, sexually, so that the thing which was previously disliked becomes associated with pleasure.

Other readers must at some time have used similar ways of getting their partners to like things which initially turned them off. We'd be interested to hear how they went about it.

AGE-OLD APHRODISIAC

Mrs W.M. writing from Hampshire recently described how she diverted her husband's attentions from her nipples to her vulva using, apparently unwittingly, the ages old and only authentic aphrodisiac of her own juices.

I was first made aware of this use of juices more than 40 years ago in Africa. Once weekly I used to hold what present day politicians call a surgery for the tribes people; at one of these, surrounded by foremen and women who acted as my advisers, I found myself faced by a furious woman whose complaint was that her daughter alongside her had been beaten by her husband. No ordinary beating, against which she would not complain, but vicious and cruel – 'Look!' As she said the word she hoisted up the girl's skirt, and I was shown the girl naked from the navel down; she was light skinned and the weals on her thighs stood out clearly as did the bruises on the customary smooth plucked vulva.

The demonstration over, I asked what the girl had done to deserve all that. Nothing! She was a hard working and respectful wife unfortunately married to a good-for-nothing rascal who neglected her for other women. I stalled by telling them to go away for the present while I sent for and questioned the husband, and made my own inquiries.

I found out that the husband had a reputation as a good getter of offspring on wives with impotent husbands, or those who just wanted a child by a man of their own choice rather than the man they married with no choice, or perhaps who just wanted a change. He was kept so busy with others that he neglected his own wife. Consequently her mother's incessant inquiries as to whether she was pregnant yet had to be answered with a No. This went on till the mother got suspicious, stepped up her pestering and eventually got from the weeping girl the information that it was months since her husband had had intercourse with her.

Mother went into instant action, and hauled the girl to the local wise-woman who inspected her inside and out and pronounced her quite fit for breeding from. Mother mentioned the essential omission, and the two older women went into conclave.

The neglected wife was given her instructions and she was told to put them into effect at the first opportunity, which she did thus.

When her Lothario husband, because some wife had failed to keep her appointment, came home and told his own wife that he was going to fuck her she did not, as she would normally have done, hoist her skirt and bend over but instead stripped naked and put her rolled up clothes under her rump as she lay on the floor. Lothario took this to mean that she was randy from neglect – a good sign – and with this in mind omitted to say his customary prayer or carry out the traditional inspection of her vulva. Immediately he mounted her, her vagina clasped his penis, sucking and squeezing it alternately at every thrust. But eventually she mis-timed and inadvertently squeezed him out of her altogether. Automatically, because he was about the point of no return, he jabbed at her to get into her again; but instead of the squelchy comfort of a hot vagina his penis hit something that made him yell with pain.

It did not take him long to discover that what he had hit was a flat round one-ounce tobacco tin. This his wife had placed under her bottom to collect the secretions from her vagina as they flowed out. Not wanting them to be mixed with any of his ejaculate had made her concentrate on that and mis-time the actions of her muscles – hence the disaster. Disaster indeed – because Lothario knew full well that her intention was to put the contents of that tin into his food and thus make him her slave!

What frightened her was that he did not immediately beat her but told her to put a halter into a bucket of water; that told her that she would be beaten in the morning with the hard wet rope, something to think about all night. But it was worse than that. He made her carry the wet halter while he took the long cow-rope (lassoo) and she walked behind him to their cassave patch in the bush. There he slipped the noose round an ankle, threw the end over the branch of a tree and hoisted her so she hung head down naked from foot to waist, her skirt falling over her

148

head so she could not see when and whence the blows would fall. Being suspended by one leg only, most fell on her vulva; only when she passed out did he lower her down.

Many years later, I learnt that women in another part of Africa put dates into their vaginas and keep them there until they are well steeped in the secretions thereof, when they offer them to the men of their choice in order to ensure that the men will be attracted to them.

I firmly believe there are lessons to be learned from the tales travellers tell and which stay-at-homes dismiss as fanciful nonsense. In those same tropic climes about which my story is told, they had and still have an oral contraceptive that grows on a bush that is found both wild and cultivated. Unexploited, because there is no profit to be had from what grows in nearly everybody's back yard! I also learned out there that, illiterate though they might be, those people were aware of the effects of hormones if not of hormones themselves. But that is another story...

J.J.,
Wales

INTO ORAL

My initiation into sex at the age of 14, 30 years ago, was not like that of most of the lads of my age, with young teenage girls but by a middle-aged woman, the same age as my mother. The experience that I was subjected to by this lady (who incidentally I had always called Auntie) when she succeeded in seducing me in her bedroom, became the future pattern for my sex style. She succeeded in enticing me to perform oral sex on her. This first time sexual thrill was so exciting to me, I climaxed twice, and when I had finished begged her to let me visit her again. She agreed and soon I found myself calling three times a week and this I kept up for four years.

The smell, taste, and feel of a woman reaching her orgasm during oral sex, to me is the greatest thrill I have ever had. My auntie was also a very rare type of woman I've since discovered, inasmuch that she was capable of ejaculating just like a man when she reached her orgasm, and often filled my mouth with her vaginal juices which I enjoyed swallowing. Since my introduction to oral sex I've practised it with hundreds of women, but I've only come across a few capable of 'ejaculating' like her.

When I was 18, I succeeded in introducing a young girl with whom I worked to oral sex. She was known as the office lay but she had never experienced oral sex before. She went mad with excitement and had numerous orgasms. After this she went completely off normal intercourse and preferred oral. She obviously mentioned her new-found thrill to some of the other girls, and who had been responsible. I soon became the main attraction in the office and very much in demand by the rest of the girls who wanted the sexual thrills without the fear of pregnancy. I have never yet found any woman who has not enjoyed being sucked off and quite a number I have succeeded with have since told me that straight intercourse no longer excites them. One married woman with three children whom I introduced to oral sex, was beaten up by her husband when she tried to get him to do the same, and she left him for a time because of his refusal.

I've performed oral sex with many different women from 16–50, fat, thin, short and tall, they have all enjoyed it. I do, however, show a preference for the well-built ones who seem to get much wetter with natural juices than slim ones. Also I prefer those who do not use deodorants.

I happened to mention recently to a woman doctor I had started having an affair with that I had come across a couple of women among the hundreds I have had oral sex with, who were capable of ejaculating like a man. She said that this was physically impossible and that it was more than likely that they had succeeded in simulating ejaculation by controlled urination. Could this be so? But she assured me that, providing the woman was healthy, it was unlikely to harm me, she had known of cases of couples who regularly imbibe each other's urine.

T.M.,
Kent

Women can't 'ejaculate' – their vaginal secretions are a continuous moistness, not a separate burst of fluid. Drinking urine (urolagnia) is harmless. (Consultant)

ORAL MARRIAGE
In the 35 years of our marriage, we had coital intercourse more times in the first week than in all the years since. Since our honeymoon 35 years ago, we have only had coitus on six occasions, and this was only because we wanted a child.

150

Nevertheless we have still made love to each other three and four times a week bringing each other to a climax every time and still do. The relationship between us now is a completely oral one.

It was a recent letter on learning oral sex that encouraged me to write to you, and while I agree with the advice given, I must warn the reader that if he is successful in getting his wife to succumb to his wishes and her desire for oral sex becomes as strong as his, they may become completely addicted to it as we did at the expense of any other practice. We have no regrets, but he may.

The relationship between my husband and I began four days after being wed, after a very active three days and nights. I was awakened one morning by my husband kissing me all over and finally burying his head between my legs; he kissed my vagina. This excited me so much that I had a number of quick orgasms. He had never done this before, his tongue darted in and out and explored every part of my sex. I just lay petrified while he continued sucking me.

Eventually I was exhausted by continuous orgasm and my husband returned to his pillow. I noticed that he had climaxed at the bottom of the bed. I 'put my foot in it'. This experience excited and thrilled me so much I begged my husband to repeat it that same afternoon. Once again I found that this oral, onslaught on my sex was intensely satisfying and thrilling and once begun, I was powerless to stop it until completely exhausted.

That same evening when we went to bed I soon began pushing my husband down beneath the sheets again to suck me, but this time he reversed himself and offered his penis to my face. I soon began kissing and sucking him, retaliating as he was sucking me. Within minutes he came off in my mouth, I swallowed his semen and still carried on until he lost his erection.

Instead of returning to his pillow my husband just lay there, his head between my thighs. After about an hour he had another erection and like two leeches we greedily began feeding off each other sucking and swallowing each other's love juices until we were both dry and exhausted.

Since that time we both agreed that this form of lovemaking is the ultimate thrill for us and we regularly engaged in oral sex three to five times a week, and we still do although we are 57.

As for the effects after all these years of indulging in oral intercourse, unlike the claims made by some of your readers, my bust size has not altered 1 cm, but my skin and figure are just as they were when I was in my 30s. I still menstruate regularly, in spite of my age, and there appear to be no signs of it stopping. I still run, swim, and am considered very active for my age. I've never required any vitamin pills or medical treatment in spite of my continued sexual activity.

Mrs P.F.,
Surrey

ORAL LOVEMAKING

I am hooked on oral love; but – being a man – on cunnilingus. I have been doing this for over 25 years, and enjoy it just as much today as when I first started.

The desire first came to me years ago, when my then girlfriend and I were indulging in horseplay and wrestling. I allowed her to pin me down by her knees on my arms, and she squatted on top of me. My face thus came into close contact with the crotch of her knickers and the delicate smell excited me to an erection. I willingly surrendered to her, and allowed her to sit on my face for some minutes. She must have been aware that I was excited as my breathing became heavier, for she released one of my arms and I was able, with her help, to pull open the crotch of her knickers and press my mouth to her now very excited vagina. Within seconds I ejaculated, without her even touching me.

Although we had often had intercourse before, it always took several minutes before I could reach a climax.

I have, since my initiation into cunnilingus, pleased many women in this way.

Most love it, and I certainly do. Whether they touch me or not, I always reach a climax when they co-operate by pressing my head towards them.

Women vary considerably in size, taste and smell, but I have never yet been with one who is offensive to me. Some prefer lying on their back while I lie with my head between their legs, others like to sit on my face and work themselves up and down; some masturbate me while I am doing it.

I don't expect my partner to reciprocate, as I have never failed to reach a climax.

I am married and have been so for 10 years. My wife soon became aware of my delights and adjusted herself to them.

Our lovemaking begins with fingering each other followed by ordinary intercourse. When she becomes very wet, we separate and I drain every drop of her juice from her orally. She usually has three orgasms before I climax.

I get greater satisfaction and feel much more relieved when I climax in this manner and my wife likes it too.

Anyone who hasn't tried oral love is really missing out.

R.M.,
Devon

EAT YOUR WAY TO BED AND BACK

My husband and I very much enjoyed reading Annie Howard's erotic menus in *Forum* recently.

But what about the many people who would find her dishes far too expensive? We can't afford asparagus spears in melted butter, Chartreuse or secreted liqueur chocolate, to name but a few items. Fortunately, economy and eroticism can go hand in hand – as we have found out.

My husband, who has a wonderfully inventive attitude to sex, has often given me the marvellous pleasure of eating from my vagina. The sensation as he draws a ripe, large banana through my labia, passing his tongue over my clitoris, is often sufficient to give me several orgasms of ever-increasing intensity. Then I, too, can give him enormous pleasure when I kiss and lick his penis, having prepared it with a deliciously cold yoghurt of the fruit variety, eating the dessert, sucking and swallowing, while caressing his testicles and thighs.

I have always loved having my breasts stimulated, and often my husband will anoint them with his share of creamy yoghurt, and thrill me by pulling and sucking at my nipples. He tells me he gets great pleasure from imagining that he is drawing a fla-voured milk from my breast, produced especially for him. This in turn leaves my nipples swollen and erect, indeed begging for more!

We can together experience what we call 'an oral orgasm', which we achieve by passing chocolate bars and delicious sweets from one mouth to the other. This is a delightful and erotic part of our foreplay and one which we tend to prolong because it is so enjoyable.

One can visualize endless variations on this theme: cream, thick and yellow; ice-cream; cider to tickle his erect penis; even champagne if 'in the money'; honey dripping golden and slow

... everyone can find hours of sensual pleasure in the imaginative game of marrying all the senses and literally 'making a meal of it'!

*Mrs V.H.,
Hampshire*

*Annie Howard did say in her article that: 'Some of the loveliest, sexiest food and drink is, alas, also the most expensive. So I suggest you save these suppers to serve on special occasions'.
(Editor)*

CINNAMON TEST

In my opinion, my wife has come up with a very unusual discovery. It is so nice and satisfying that I felt it should be passed on to other lovers so they can enjoy it too. There is not that much to it, but it has never failed to work.

My wife has always practised and loved fellatio. She does it beautifully, but she always used to hold my emission in her mouth. When I returned to earth, she would get up and spit it out. One day she got the urge to suck me off and she aroused me slowly. After many minutes, she brought me to a climax. As I poured forth my essence into her mouth, she kept moaning delightfully. She seemed to enjoy swallowing my semen more than I had ever remembered. She looked up at me with a sparkle in her eye and told me that I tasted like cinnamon. She insisted that I had never tasted like that before and said that she had loved it.

We talked about this unusual occurrence and I recalled that I had eaten three cinnamon rolls for breakfast that morning. Every time I eat cinnamon she can taste it in my semen. We have experimented and now we're absolutely sure that this works and it never fails to turn us both on. I've told friends of mine about our discovery and they all agree that for some reason this adds spice to a man's system. Their wives also swallow semen, which is the way we like it.

When my wife wants to suck me off, she will feed me cinnamon. This has got to be the most secret erotic signal I've ever heard of.

Another little delicate touch she has added is claiming that all my semen with the cinnamon comes from my right ball (which seems to be larger than my left one). She gives this side her

154

special tongue and sucking caresses. The sensation is overwhelming.

We love our little discovery and hope that others benefit from it.

W.K.,
Address withheld by request

FANTASY

SHOULD I TELL?

I am 24 years old and have been married for two years. My husband and I have had a very happy sex life and, just when it was beginning to need variety, we started reading *Forum*, which has taught us many new ways of making love.

Now *Forum* has done it again. I read Nancy Friday's recent article about women's sexual fantasies with great interest. About half the time when my husband and I are making it, just before I come, I have the same fantasy over and over. I have never told my husband about this.

I think about a gang of motorcycle hoods. They have me strapped down across two bikes, with my legs dangling over the wheels. Then, one by one, they rape me, taking turns in a 'round robin' kind of thing.

This dream or fantasy has always made me enormously excited. I close my eyes and each time my husband thrusts I picture a different pair of sinister eyes and another huge erect penis thrusting up inside me. It always gives me a wild orgasm.

I have never told anyone about this fantasy and I'm ashamed to tell my husband. Nancy Friday said that when she first started asking women about their fantasies, with their husbands there, all the men became very uncomfortable and mad at their wives. I love my husband and I want to know if you think I should tell him. I'm also worried that there's something wrong about my becoming so excited by the thought of brutal rape. My husband has always been a very gentle and considerate lover and I really don't want him to be any other way.

Name withheld by request,
New York

Most women do have sexual fantasies and a rape fantasy is fairly common. It doesn't mean that you really want to be raped but, for some women, it is simply a way of letting the mind loosen the controls all of us have been taught to impose as children which, of course, is fresh and exciting. If you think of yourself as tied down, then you can be abandoned and give yourself up to pleasure.

There's absolutely nothing for you to be worried about

because of this fantasy. From what you say, your husband sounds like a sensitive lover, and you also say you're happy with his lovemaking. I would only suggest that you try to broaden the kinds of fantasies you have – the one you describe has a lot of details in it that particularly appeal to you. Your legs must be a certain way and you picture the eyes as well as the penises of the gang members. Though there's nothing to be concerned about in this, you might try to think of other fantasies that also excite you so you don't become fixated on just the one.

Frankly you will have to decide about telling your husband. I don't think it's necessary, but if the guilt you feel about this fantasy starts to interfere with your lovemaking, then it could help to talk about it with him. Maybe you both can get into it by using scarves gently to tie you down while he makes love to you. If the fantasy excites you and doesn't get in the way of lovemaking, I see no reason why he has to know about it. As Nancy Friday pointed out, a husband (or wife) can also be very hurt to discover that their partner's thoughts are 'elsewhere' during lovemaking.

FRIGIDITY

We've been married four years, and I adore my wife. But she's never been terribly sexy. I don't mean that we haven't enjoyed sex together, but there's an air of aloofness about her. Even in bed I never feel as though, as the poets say, I am one with her.

She's never made the first advances, but until a few months ago she responded to mine and we made love regularly. For the last six months, however, we've had sex perhaps only three or four times. I've talked to her about it and she says that most of her creative energies go into her work. She's an artist – quite a good one – and her work sells well. She's accused me of being too physical and says that I should seek spiritual satisfaction in marriage.

Because of my frustration I've had an affair with another girl for whom I feel no love at all.

A couple of weeks ago, while my wife was away for the weekend with her family, I decided quietly to study her canvases and drawings to understand better what she is trying to express. Most of her paintings are abstract into which, I'm afraid, I can't read a meaning. But she had a private drawer full of drawings which made my hair stand on end.

The faces are hers and mine. She depicts me tied in chains, in elaborate harness to a cart in which she's standing whilst whipping me, trotting around a room that looks like a dungeon.

In another drawing I'm trussed up like a chicken while she towers over me, carving a beautiful pattern on my back with a dagger. In yet another I'm hung from the ceiling – she has cut my throat and is catching the blood in a goblet.

In all the drawings I'm shown with a large erection and she is in black costume with the breasts and buttocks exposed, wearing a small black mask. There are many designs of costumes for her and boots, some waist high with the genital area exposed and finely drawn in.

For hours I sat fascinated, then horrified. I see she wishes to torture me and perhaps despises me because I haven't shown any inclination for these practices.

I think she's torturing me by being frigid and I don't know what to do. If I tell her I know what her real desires are I may lose her altogether. On the other hand, I don't really want to experience these things she dreams about. I'm not a masochist. What should I do?

Name withheld by request,
Devon

Your wife is expressing her sexual fantasies and sadistic incli-nations through her work. She might know of your extramarital affair and this may have brought these urges to the surface in her artistic creations. But this doesn't necessarily mean that she wishes to put her fantasies into action.

You have two courses open to you. Either say nothing but try a new approach, a bolder technique of lovemaking. Her fri-gidity may well be due to your inadequacy or hesitancy. Or she might like you to encourage her to take the dominant role.

Alternatively, you might like to bring it into the open and discuss the matter with her frankly and tolerantly. Perhaps she deliberately left the drawings for you to find in order to bring about such a showdown. If so, feel free to let her know that you don't relish the idea of playing a masochist role but that you're willing to get a clearer idea of what her desires in lovemaking might be so that some compromise in doing what turns you both on can be reached.

In any case, unless your marriage is on much shakier ground than you describe, it's very unlikely that you'll lose her by raising the matter. In fact it would probably give both of you much more insight into each other's needs.

PET PROBLEM

I haven't told anyone about this worry I have. And you're the only place I can be honest.

I recently bought a German Shepherd because I live in a big city by myself and I felt better about my safety with a watch-dog. My dog is very affectionate and on nights when I'm feeling blue, he snuggles into my bed and licks my face and tries his best to cheer me up.

Well, you can see where I'm leading. I haven't done anything yet that I need to feel ashamed about. But I catch myself fantasizing and once I had a dream about my dog. I'm much too ashamed to tell you the details of the dream but you can imagine how I feel. Should I see some psychiatrist or someone who can help me? Am I perverted? Should I get rid of my dog? I'd hate to do that because I really love him and I'm sure he would be heartbroken too.

Please help me with this problem.

> (*Miss*) *Name and address withheld*
> *by request*

Your feelings aren't really so uncommon, you know. Many – perhaps most – people have sexual fantasies or dreams involving acts they'd be ashamed of in real life. The important thing is not to lose sight of the vital difference between reality and fantasy. Because something turns you on in imagination, it doesn't follow that you'll be inexorably swept along into trying the same thing in real life. You're still in control. It doesn't even follow that you'd enjoy the activity if you did try it. And don't worry about being a 'latent' zoophiliac; it's your behaviour, not your thoughts, that indicates what you are.

I get the impression your emotional life is pretty empty. We all need to love and be loved, unless our development goes badly wrong; and we are capable of displacing this need from its 'natural' targets, if none are available, on to anything that offers. Hence the relationships that can build up between otherwise heterosexual men in prison. What is confusing you is not so much the love you feel for your dog (in our culture, it can be more acceptable to feel love for a dog than a member of one's own sex!) as the sexual impulses that go along with it. You can't

159

disentangle sex and love – there are sexual components even in the normal parent–child relationship. What you can do is see these erotic impulses for what they are – the unwanted, but quite normal, by-products of your inevitably over-intense feeling for the only creature who is currently offering you affection, understanding, comfort, and loving body contact.

The way through your present difficulty lies in that last sentence. Keep your relationship with your dog in perspective (and don't, of course, actually involve it in erotic activity – you would clearly be overwhelmed with guilt and remorse). And, somehow, find human companions who can give you what your dog does now. Encounter groups or something of the sort might be a good starting point; I suspect that you find it hard to form relationships with people at the moment.

STREAK OF FANTASY

The recent fad of streaking now seems to be fading, but during a warm spell in May I did my best to keep it going. I had gone to a party which was an utter flop but became friendly with a redhead, so I invited her to come for a drive to a small country pub in Epping Forest.

I waited in my car but she appeared with two other girls. My spirits sank. One is great, but three get in each other's way. I will call them Jane, Jean and Joan.

It was about a seven mile drive, a very pleasant night and, over a few gins, the girls relaxed. Jean and Joan were pretty gigglers, but it was Jane who attracted me. Somewhat older, perhaps 25, she had that cold sardonic look that I find most sexually attractive. Returning to the car park, I asked them if they would like to do a little streaking. 'What, strip here and run up the road?' 'No, much longer than that. You take off all your clothes, get in the car and I drive you home.' 'It is really streaking in a way, isn't it?' There was some hesitation, then Jane undressed.

Jean and Joan argued a bit but, seeing Jane naked and willing to go along with the gag, did likewise. I put all their clothes in the boot, took my trouser belt, a belt from Joan's jacket and my tie and tied their hands behind them. Just what are you up to, asked Jane, seated beside me. I kissed her breast and thigh for a minute and said, you'll see.

I drove off, feeling more excited as the minutes passed. The success of this streak depended on surprise and the more daring

160

and dangerous the surprise, the greater the intensity of the sexual excitement.

I drove reasonably and to cries of 'Oh no, Christ, what are you thinking of?' pulled in at a filling station. The attendant's mouth fell open and I delayed events as much as I could by asking for the oil and tyres to be checked. He called his mate and the chit-chat followed.

'Are we allowed to touch?' 'Help yourself,' I replied. Jane, being at the front, had four hands wander all over her, but she made no attempt to object. We left, Jean and Joan calling me every name available, but Jane saying nothing.

A mile further on I pulled in to a quiet secluded road and began caressing Jane all over. I knew she did not mind as she edged forward to the edge of the seat. Only a fool would have missed the message. I put one finger in her anus and my tongue in her vagina and brought her off. I moved to the back and performed likewise on her friends who, to my surprise, co-oper-ated as best they could. All three girls tasted beautiful.

As we continued our journey, I realized that it was not the sexual excitement that appealed to all three girls but the know-ledge that they were being completely dominated. Sexual thrills plus the real fear of being arrested was a combination of emotions not one could resist.

I decided to go the limit. In another 10 minutes we passed a police station. I stopped and called out to two police officers standing by a panda car. Jean and Joan nearly collapsed with fright. 'Please don't!' 'Don't call them over!' 'We'll do anything if you drive on!' 'Please go on!' I must hand it to Jane. She said nothing, except to open her legs even wider.

The policemen ambled over and I asked them the way to a certain block of high rise flats. They answered, I thanked them and as they left us, one said, 'Don't catch cold girls!' I swear that all this time Jean and Joan literally stopped breathing. Now, in what other country would police act as kindly as this?

As we went on I asked all three how they felt. The two at the back called me every form of bastard known to man. But Jane said nothing. 'Save it, girls,' I said, 'the best is yet to come. I have one trick left that will turn your legs to jelly.' I stopped at the end of Joan's road, opened the car door and told her to come out. 'What, without my clothes?' 'That's it. You're going home naked.' I untied her hands, smacked her behind, jumped back in and drove off. I saw her in the rear mirror running across the road and wondered if I was overdoing things. When

Jean's turn came she sobbed 'Please don't make me!' 'What will you give me?' I murmured. 'Anything!' 'I want that for starters! Out you get. Come on.' I took back my belt and left her to it.

Jane now saw I was in deadly earnest, especially as she lived on the 14th floor of her block of flats. It was a neighbourhood full of yobs and hooligans who might give her a rough time if they caught her in a lift. But if I was to master her completely, to break her in utterly, I had to go ahead with my plan to make her mine. I knew she had always got her own way with men, but it was about time her bluff was called.

She was no longer cool and supercilious but begged me to give her clothes back. I told her that whatever she said would have no effect on me. The streak must finish properly with her naked at her own front door.

I opened the car door, she stepped out and indicated I untie her. 'No, you go home as you are.' She trembled and said could she come home with me instead? 'No, the streak must finish as it started. You, bound and naked. Now get going.' I drove off but there she stood, frightened but defiant. I found out afterwards that she met a couple she knew at the ground floor entrance. The husband offered her his coat but she refused, saying that she had to arrive at her own door tied and naked. There, he untied her, found the key on a string and in she went, as silent as a shadow.

Since then we have met many times and as we lie naked on my bed she will murmur, would I like to tie her up? I do and then feel her beautiful wet lips gliding over my prick. She does not want any other man now as I aroused in her the perfect combination of sex and fear. That night her excitement almost reached suffocation point but I have a little time to invent an encore. We get married in September.

D.H.,
London

Congratulations, D.H., on the neatest piece of fiction! A fetishist's dream. Not one but three submissive females! And not a male orgasm in sight ...

Male readers, roused to bloodlust by D.H.'s Walterscapade, who may feel tempted to carry around to parties a ball of twine and a few neckties and belts, please take heed of the following gaol warnings.

I think of our police just as kindly as D.H. But I doubt if a promotion-conscious constable would react as complacently as

D.H. would have us believe. (Even on the road from Epping to London!) The sight of three full frontals might initially send a pleasurable twinge to the average PC's groin. But it would also send urgent thoughts of arrest for indecent exposure racing to his brain.

Anyone who exposes himself in a place where others can see commits a public nuisance. And 11 years ago a case ruled that even if only a police officer witnesses the flash, the offence is proved.

The police can also arrest, under the Town Police Clauses Act of 1847, without warrant, anyone who 'wilfully and indecently exposes himself in any street in any urban district to the annoyance of the residents.'

A while back a court decreed that a person in a car was in the street! Indeed all 'open lewdness' and whatever openly outrages public decency amounts to a crime which attracts a fine or imprisonment or both without limit! And the prosecution don't even have to prove that the accused's behaviour actually disgusted or annoyed anyone.

Certainly the three girls seen close up by the police as D.H. described it (one of them opening 'her legs even wider' and all three presumably displaying some visible marks of their recent sexual arousal and climaxes) all but invite prosecution for these highly embarrassing offences.

Suppose, also, for example, that the strain proves too much for one of the victims and she screams for help. Or imagine what could happen if she went running to the police afterwards complaining that the man had terrorized her, that she had submitted in silence to his evil ministrations once she saw that the other girls did nothing to defend themselves. The sexual superhero of D.H.'s fantasy would look pretty rueful in the Crown Court dock charged with indecent assault. And pitiful if he gets the maximum sentence of two years inside!

True, by undressing themselves the girls can't afterwards pretend they were totally innocent bystanders (and consent of course constitutes the defence to indecent assault).

But a court will take a dim view of a man who ties up a naked girl and humiliates her publicly against her will. Especially if he invites complete strangers (the garage attendants) for a gratis grope. Even D.H.'s inventive picture of the reactions of the two girls in the back concedes that they were at times speechless with fear and embarrassment.

Nowhere in his fairy tale does D.H. suggest that he had it off with one of the girls. Is this the traditional impotence of the domination fantasy? Or the knowledge that the moment he admits to entering a girl in this situation he admits to committing rape? I have little doubt that any man who treats a woman in the circumstances D.H. sketches for us would also lay himself wide open to a rape charge. For the law defines rape as unlawful sexual intercourse with a female without her consent by force or by 'putting in fear'.

In fact a jury listening to the story of one of D.H.'s victims could very well reach a verdict of attempted rape. The mere fact that a tied up woman 'co-operates' means little when judge and jury hear that she afterwards calls her attacker 'every form of bastard known to man'.

D.H.'s final flourish – chucking the three naked girls out of the car, one of them still bound – would put the mockers on any mercy a judge might feel inclined to show when passing sentence. Lawyers have an unwritten rule: judges don't like men who strike women. I hesitate to think what they'd do with someone who tried to translate D.H.'s vicious dream sequence into reality.

SCHOOLGIRL FANTASIES

At the risk of boring you – my particular kink and the subject of my fantasies is schoolgirls. Nothing peculiar in that you may say. But I really do believe that my case is different, and I think that I know the reason for my 'perversion' and I have a theory about how I may cure it if I could legally put it into practice.

To begin with, my fantasies do not include spanking, sixth formers or dirty old men, which appear to be the standard fare for books on this subject. In my fantasies I do not appear as myself (middle-aged bachelor), but I see myself as a boy of the same age as the girls involved. This usually ranges from 11 to 15, mostly at the lower end of the range. In fact the only adult to enter my fantasy world is the occasional schoolmistress, who is invariably attractive, 25-ish but virginal.

The girls are also virgins in the beginning and in most cases remain so throughout. In most cases they are unwilling to give me any sexual gratification, but I achieve my ends by trickery rather than by force. A typical example of my fantasies is the one in which, as a 12 year old, I go swimming with a girl of similar age. I have just become aware of her newly developing breasts and this arouses me. After the swim in a deserted open air pool we both go to our respective changing rooms to change. I burst in on her as she is clad only in her knickers, and she covers her breasts with her hands and shouts for me to go away. I take her clothes and place them in a heap near a busy highway.

I then say that I will only bring her clothes back if she takes off her knickers. She refuses, but I insist. She then offers small sexual privileges, such as a closer look at her breasts but is adamant that she will not remove her knickers. We continue to bargain until she finally offers to let me feel her breasts for half an hour and feel outside her knickers for 10 minutes. I eventually agree to this.

After this I return the clothes to her and watch her dress. We then walk back to the school. On the way back I disclose that I know of something she wanted to keep secret and use this threat to make her strip off completely. I grope around her genitals for a while and she begins to cry and say that it is unfair for boys to treat girls so, and how would I feel if the position were reversed. Feeling sorry for her, I bring out my penis for her to play with. Our session of mutual fingering is then interrupted by the appearance of the schoolmistress. She takes us to her room. I then blackmail the teacher into letting me just feel her breasts initially, but she gets a liking for it and eventually seduces me, when I have my first ejaculation. (This is one of the few fantasies which actually ends in copulation.)

Another fantasy is that a group of girls offer me sex in return for doing their homework, the rewards depending on the results obtained; a third is that through a two-way mirror I photograph a girl in the bath and threaten to show the pictures around the school unless she lets me have a feel.

I believe these fantasies arise from being deprived of sex at the onset of puberty. Up to the age of 10 often I would ask a girl to remove her knickers, and in a few cases they obliged and permitted a little gentle exploration. When these same girls began to develop breasts, though, they would not let me see or touch them, and also refused to remove their knickers or let me touch them in any way. From then on I had no sexual encounters until a little light petting when I was 18. At the age of 19 I patronized prostitutes. My sex life has been practically nil since then. I am ill at ease with mature women and feel that they don't fancy me.

I sincerely believe that I shall have to get through this sexual 'block' before I can move on to a full 'normal' sex life. There is a whole age group of females missing from my background and somehow I shall have to explore this experience, then perhaps I can leave these stupid fantasies behind me. The question is how to do this legally. Obviously I cannot have intercourse with a girl under 16 but what degree of intimacy is permitted?

I should like to start with a girl of 11 and go through all the ages, living through my fantasies, culminating in copulation with a 16-year-old.

Then I feel that my problems would be solved.

I should hate to hurt or embarrass any of these delightful creatures, and if there is no other way of relieving these feelings, I hope that there is literature available which will keep them in the world of fantasy. It may be argued that literature about young girls may actually have the opposite effect, but I feel that it will help to control my obsession. I welcome your views on this matter.

I must be the only person who believes himself to be a young boy in search of sexual experience. What do you suggest?

A.G.,
Hull

What interests me particularly about your fantasies is how basically inhibited and self-protective they are. For instance, although middle-aged, in your daydreams you always appear as a boy of the same age as your 'victims'. This apparently squares things with your conscience, which even in fantasy apparently finds the idea of a middle-aged man interfering with young girls too hot to handle. Similarly, you never go the whole way with the young girl but only with a grown woman. Even then you seem to require the reassurance that it is 'not your fault', since you are invariably seduced.

The most likely cause for your regressive fantasies is that you are basically afraid of mature female sexuality and are loath to attempt a relationship in case you can't make it sexually and are rebuffed. The feeling that women 'don't fancy you' is a clear projection of this insecurity.

Up to this point I think your understanding of your problem is admirable but I'm afraid I cannot go along with the ideas you suggest for treatment.

As far as the law is concerned, the petting you envisage would lay you open to a charge of indecent assault, even if the child were willing. So I would strongly discourage you from approaching anybody under 16.

But even if they were permissible, I cannot agree that the methods you propose would allow you to 'work through your problems' and make you capable of a sexually mature relationship.

I personally think that the more immersed you become in your fantasy world the less likelihood there is of you ever making it with a female adult. Although you may shrink from it, I think your best bet is to try to start a relationship with a sympathetic mature woman. When you feel you know her sufficiently to confess your difficulties, she may just feel that she is able to offer you the understanding and help that you need.

If on the other hand you feel unable to take the risk then by all means continue to indulge your fantasies, just so long as you don't act them out. I am bound to repeat however that the more your daydreams come to dominate your life the less likely it is that you will ever be able to cope with a sexually mature relationship.

'Social retraining' therapy could help you feel more at ease in adult relationships.

SEX THERAPY

THE 'HONEY' APPROACH

When I got married four years ago I had difficulties with my sex life at first as my wife has a large vaginal passage and my penis is only four inches long. There was no feeling at all when we had sex, and she had difficulty in getting an orgasm, till one day I told her of a method I learned whilst doing service in the Pacific. It has worked for us, and perhaps it would for other *Forum* readers with this problem.

I was stationed on an island in the Philippines for five years and a very attractive native girl taught me their method of sexual approach.

First, we washed each other's genitals thoroughly – they are very keen on hygiene. Then we lay on a mat or bed. I would rub her all over with delicate coconut oil, which was perfumed, then we would play with each other. When my penis was hard she then rubbed it with clear honey.

For intercourse, she would lie on her back with raised legs and her knees drawn up to her chest. With my legs apart and my back to her, I would guide my penis slowly down into her vaginal opening, and she would lower her legs on to my back at the same time crossing her legs and contracting her thigh muscles

As I moved slowly up and down she would contract her vaginal muscles which, together with the honey, increased the vaginal friction.

At each thrust the honey gave a wonderful, stimulating sound which added to the excitement.

Since my wife and I have been using this technique, she can now achieve five orgasms at a time and will not have sex any other way now, she enjoys it so much!

My daughter was having trouble with sex in her married life until she tried this way at our suggestion. Now, she and her husband use it almost exclusively.

The native girls who taught me this technique believe that it makes the man's sex organ stronger and that the honey will give him strength. They swear it strengthens the woman's vaginal muscles and also develops the bust. This certainly seems to have happened in my wife's case.

G.B.,
Cheshire

SEX TALK

I have been divorced for the past two years and have done my share of 'bouncing' around. A year ago I met and fell in love with a man. His divorce will be final next month and we anticipate marrying within a few months.

We consider ourselves to be sexually liberated and have a fantastic time in and out of bed. We both agree that in almost all respects we are perfectly suited to one another, and we cherish our wonderful relationship.

There is, however, one problem. It's my 'hang-up' – I just can't verbalize in bed. I can write pornographic stories to excite him, I can and do think about what I'd like to say to him but I just can't get the words past my lips when I'm in bed with him. It turns him on to hear me say things to him while we're making love and he's asked me to try but outside of asking him to fuck me and saying things like, 'It feels so good', I can't say anything.

I'm 33 and I enjoy my sex life. I really like it when my man talks to me in bed but I can't respond. I have various erotic items at my disposal, films, books, dildos, vibrators, French ticklers – nothing turns me off sexually.

Please help, I'd like to be able to surprise him. Everything else is so perfect. I might add that I've spoken to a few girlfriends and we agree that rather than heightening the excitement of lovemaking, talk brings us back to reality and detracts from our enjoyment. The only other item I've heard about talk being distracting was while I was in labour. The nurses told me that talking made it easier for women to get their minds off the contractions and as a result, the contractions slowed down a bit. Could this be the same process?

Can you suggest how I can get over my hang-up about telling my lover sexy things when we are making love? Any suggestions would at least get me moving in the right direction.

Mrs M.S.R.,
Address withheld by request

Sex at its best is play, and the nature of play is that it is spontaneous. That means doing or saying whatever feels good at the moment. Each of us has our own way of being spontaneous, of being playful, of being sexy. The degree of our playfulness increases the more we feel at home with our partner and feel safe letting ourselves go. For now it is sufficient for you to be aware that you want to be more verbal with your sexual partner without putting pressure on yourself to perform verbally. This relationship is relatively new. Give it time and allow yourself to go along with what comes naturally to you, and do not get into a bind over whether or not you can say sexy things while making love.

You mention that you can already say that you want your partner to make love to you, and that 'it feels good'. Perhaps you can build on what already comes easily by adding qualifying adjectives or phrases when you say you want your boyfriend to make love to you. How do you want to be loved? Specifically what do you want your partner to do to you? Tell him. Spell out the 'it' when you say what feels good: his chest, his eyes, his penis, his buttocks, etc. Just begin by adding a simple phrase or adjective to what you already can say; then go from there. A lot of words are not necessary; what is exciting is to say what you feel as you feel it. This is not conversation, but exclamation often. Yells, moans, sighs, screams, tears, laughter – whatever comes to you, let it all happen and don't hide your feelings.

Be patient with yourself; it takes time to change. Perhaps in your first marriage you were the silent partner and now you want to be the opposite. No one becomes comfortable making sounds and saying words, if it is a totally new experience. Trust the process, and know that you will let go as you are able.

ORGASM DIFFICULTY

My wife cannot achieve orgasm through intercourse or oral sex, although she can with a vibrator or one of those hair rinse hoses.

Except for this our sex life is great; we have oral sex, try different positions, different places, make up fantasies for acting out, and we also communicate beautifully.

The first two years of our marriage she said she didn't care one bit about having an orgasm, but now she does. I have tried to get her to stimulate herself while we are having intercourse but she says she does not like to touch herself. She doesn't masturbate now and says she has never done so.

H.M.,
Address withheld by request

Difficulties in obtaining orgasm quite often occur to women who have not masturbated during adolescence, and I think this

170

*may be the main cause – though possibly not the only one – of
your wife's experience. It seems that in a fairly large number of
women, the clitoral mechanism has to be provoked into action;
or, to put it another way, to be shown what is expected of it,
before it will respond of its own accord. The earlier this is done
the better; and the way it is done is by self-stimulation or stimulation by a partner. The longer this teaching is delayed, the
longer it takes to get the clitoris readily to respond.*

*The fact that your wife responds to the more aggressive
forms of vibrator-and-hose stimulation, but not to the much
more gentle forms of oral stimulation, seems to suggest that her
clitoris has not reached the stage where it will respond easily.
This I think can be overcome by patient, gentle but persistent
and frequent stimulation by you. As she has now begun to
stimulate herself, get her to teach you exactly how she does so,
and follow her instructions faithfully.*

*Don't, however, fall into the trap of relying on this one
method of stimulating her alone. The constant use of one
method may get a woman fixated on it, so that eventually she
becomes unable to respond to another method.*

*I suggest you bring her off by her own method, then, after a
pause, apply oral stimulation, or some other way of stimulating
her. If at first these other ways do not produce orgasm, never
mind; keep on with them, because the more readily she
responds to her main method of stimulation – (the more the
clitoris learns its job) – the better she will come to respond to
other types of stimulation.*

*In various cases of this kind which I have treated, I have
found that it is essential on occasions when you are stimulating
her by her method (which will almost certainly be a manual one,
or a vibrator) you should have your penis inside her vagina. (By
the way, lots of women don't like stimulating their own cli-
torises during penis-vagina contact, though I would like to encourage them to do so.) Quite probably, you will only be able to
reach her clitoris when you are inside her by using one of the
rear-entry positions, so that you can reach a hand round to the
clitoris. If it takes a long time to bring her off, one of the most
comfortable rear-entry positions is for you to sit on an armless
chair with her sitting astride you with her back to you. Don't
worry about deep penetration at this stage; I advocate this
method because I believe it is very important for her to experience orgasm while the penis is inside the vagina, and so long as
the penis makes contact with her orgasmic platform (the first*

*third of the vagina, nearest the entrance) this is all that is neces-
sary.*

*There is another position which also gives you full and easy
access to the clitoris. Find a table about the height of your
genital area. Put some cushions on it, and lay your wife on her
back on them, with her buttocks on the edge of the table. She
spreads her legs and draws her knees up towards her breasts.
You stand between her legs and put your penis into her vagina.
She can then either put her ankles on your shoulders, or cross her
feet in the small of your back. (The raised legs give you deeper
penetration.) You can then stimulate her clitoris with one hand
and play with one of her nipples with the other. Don't move
your penis very much until she has come off. When she has
climaxed, then bring yourself off. She will find the sensations
caused by your movements inside her very pleasant, even stimulating, at this time.*

IT ISN'T MY FAULT IF HE CAN'T EJACULATE

I am 31 and engaged to a 45-year-old executive. Our relationship is very satisfactory apart from two problems.

The first is what I have seen described in *Forum* as
retarded ejaculation. The second is my over-lubrication, which
I think is largely to blame as I cannot provide the vaginal tension and friction which my fiancé says he needs to achieve
orgasm.

I have never experienced this situation before in any other
relationship and it is making me feel very inadequate. I cannot
discuss it with my fiancé because he is incredibly, almost patho-
logically sensitive about his age, and would be very hurt and
angry if I told him he had a sexual problem. It would be tan-
tamount to accusing him of impotence – so I tell him it is my
fault he cannot ejaculate.

Miss C.A.,
Yorkshire

*While you do have two problems, they are not quite what you
think. For your 'over-lubrication' is simply a sign that you are a
healthy, sexually responsive woman. As you say, you have had
no difficulties in earlier relationships; don't blame yourself for
your fiancé's troubles. Do you want to go through married life
taking the blame for his faults, to spare him pain? I am not
proposing an attitude of hard-hearted callousness – which, I feel*

172

sure, from your letter, you would not be capable of anyway. But he is an adult in years and if he is not yet mature enough to accept the responsibility for his own behaviour it would be doing him no favour, in the long run, to play along with his immaturity.

Retarded ejaculation, in itself, is generally curable. But curing it without the sufferer's knowledge and active co-operation is another matter. The therapy, which is fully described in Masters and Johnson's 'Human Sexual Inadequacy', basically consists of accustoming the man to ejaculate with you masturbating him and then getting him used to ejaculating inside your vagina. You kneel astride him while masturbating him and as he reaches the point of orgasm lower yourself so that the tip of the penis enters the vagina. Once the barrier has been overcome, you can begin substituting vaginal for manual stimulation earlier and earlier in the arousal process until 'special measures' are no longer necessary.

I suggest you start by putting your hand over his as he masturbates after intercourse (you do not say that he does so, but this is the usual pattern; if he goes and does it secretly in the bathroom, you will have to begin by encouraging him to do it in bed with you). If he objects even to this, it is your turn to get hurt – tell him you just want to feel closer to him by sharing his pleasure. Without a few home-truths, your campaign has no hope of success!

Once he is used to this, and you have learnt the rhythm and pressure that please him best, ask if you can bring him off entirely by yourself. It's natural enough for you to want to do this for him, so no suspicions should be aroused.

When this, again, has become a frequent part of your love-making, and he has ejaculated several times (the first time will be the hardest to achieve, but don't give up), begin occasionally kneeling astride him while you do it. His penis will be right in front of your pubic bone; easy enough to vary the stimulation while stroking it with your vulva from time to time.

By now you should have learnt the subtle physical signs that mean his ejaculation is irrevocably at hand. Your next step is to position yourself over him so that you have merely to move down a little for penetration to take place; this you do as his orgasm commences. Whether or not you warn him of your intentions in advance, I leave to your judgment; doing this without warning might upset him, but his reactions might also help

173

clarify for you the motivations underlying his inability to ejaculate in the vagina. This knowledge, however, will not be of much use if he is so disconcerted by the experience that he refuses ever again to put himself in a position where it could be repeated! So you must be tactful.

If all goes off successfully, you need only take him inside you earlier and earlier in the arousal process for normal intercourse to be the eventual result.

A possible shortcut, if you really cannot succeed in giving him an orgasm by masturbation – take up the kneeling astride position while he masturbates himself, and have him tell you when he is going to come so that you can insert his penis at that moment. Perhaps, if you said that it was emotionally important for you to make love in this way (occasionally) he would co-operate to this extent.

Throughout the whole process it is important that you demonstrate not the least anxiety about whether or where he comes. Tell him you've got used to the way he makes love and are quite happy if he never changes. The point of this is, of course, to remove any worry he feels about coming; as a woman, you must know from your own experience how destructive such worry can be. Most of your fiancé's tension, however, may be unconscious; he may not even admit to himself that there is anything wrong. You can best get at this by measures designed to relax him generally; I suggest massage and lots of relaxed, sensuous caressing as part of your loveplay. Alcohol or tranquillizers might also help. (Robert Chartham)

SLOWING HIM DOWN

Forum, I'm going crazy! For years now my husband has had a problem of coming too quickly. At first, it seemed like an occasional mishap. We had just been married and were making it pretty often, at least once a day. Sometimes, he came immediately, too fast for anybody's comfort. I had to go to the lavatory a few times to relieve myself but nobody's perfect. Every time we now try to make love, his ejaculation is premature!

This is making both of us nervous wrecks. Not only is his ego in a shambles, but I'm getting crazy for a good lay. The problem is that I love my husband. I love to fondle and caress his penis, the inside of his legs, and all that, but I hesitate even to touch him these days. I am constantly afraid that he will come before he even enters me. (That hasn't happened yet, thank

God!) Furthermore, I think he is getting a little nervous about working me up to orgasm because he's afraid my excitement will make him come too fast. In other words, we both feel as frigid as mummies whenever we try to have sex.

I hope your advisers can come to the rescue. I'd hate to leave him, but this tension is going to drive me out of the house. I'd feel more comfortable at my mother's house, and that's getting pretty serious.

Mrs R.D.,
Address withheld by request

An excellent and very effective way of curing premature ejaculation is outlined by Masters and Johnson in their 'Human Sexual Inadequacy', which I suggest you both read. First, you tell your husband that intercourse is out for a while. Then, after sessions of pleasant mutual massage and foreplay, with no sexual demand, you masturbate him until he tells you that he's reached the point of no return. With a thumb on his frenum (the little strip of skin joining the head and shaft of the penis in the midline on its underside) and the first and second fingers of your hand on the top side of his penis, your first finger just above the rim and your second just below it, you squeeze hard. His ejaculation will be stopped and his erection subside a little. Then repeat.

Do this several times a session. Eventually, your husband will learn to tolerate high levels of sexual arousal and will regain confidence in his ability to control himself. There will be the occasional failure, of course, but neither of you should worry about that. Your own sexual needs he (or you) can take care of by methods other than intercourse, since it's important that he should not feel any pressure on him to perform.

When you both feel fairly confident with the squeeze technique, begin having intercourse in the woman-above position. Once he's penetrated, stay quite still for a while, so he can get used to the feeling; if he becomes too aroused, lift yourself off him and apply the squeeze technique again.

The position, and the staying still, will be exciting for you as well and help restore your own relaxed pleasure in sex. (Women married to premature ejaculators tend to get a bit frantic, working away like mad to come before their husbands do and worrying all the time about whether they'll make it.) Just squatting astride your husband, savouring the feeling of him inside you and knowing that there's no need to hurry or try to come, since

175

you're in control, will help rid sex for you of the anxiety that has become associated with it.

It should not be too long before things are back to normal between you and your husband, though Masters and Johnson recommend that the squeeze technique should still be used once or twice a month to prevent slipping back. In general, the woman-above position is best for premature ejaculators and it may be best to stick to this whenever he's anxious or tense.

Throughout the 'treatment', it is vitally important that you don't pressure him, or denigrate him, or criticize him. Accept it as a shared problem, think of the 'treatment' as being as much to reduce your own anxiety as his. Ask for his help as well as offering him yours. Don't, in other words, put him in the situation of being inferior to you in that he's 'sick' and you're 'well'. Any element of this between you is going to cause more resentment and estrangement, not less. Remember Masters and Johnson's primary doctrine, 'it takes two to make a sex problem', and investigate the probability that you share the blame for your mutual difficulties.

WATER THERAPY

I am in my middle 50s and over the last few years have had a considerable falling off in sexual ability until I eventually found it impossible to get an erection at all.

In desperation I tried everything I could think of: tonics, tablets, massage, raw eggs in quantity – even aphrodisiac creams – without success.

A few months ago because of an article I read, I decided to try douching my loins with alternate hot and cold sprays. This I did daily, hot spray first until maximum bearable temperature was reached and my balls hung low, then I changed the spray to cold, until my shaft was numb and my balls pulled right up in the scrotum. After about a week of this treatment to my delight, my penis reached involuntarily with powerful jerks to a good size.

After that, every day produced improvement until now, after several months of the treatment, it attains seven and a half inches hard and straight and now, during the spraying, will ejaculate without any further stimulation other than the water, with powerful spurt and copious gushes of sperm equal to 30 years ago.

I am completely revitalized by this new ability and experience

176

the greatest thrill and satisfaction merely by watching myself standing stiff and throbbing, eager to perform.

You will no doubt know why this treatment should have this effect. I would be interested to know the medical reason. I can thoroughly endorse the efficiency of it.

R.C.,
Worcester

Hydrotherapy – the use of water in the treatment of illness – has been valuable since time immemorial. It was used by the Assyrians 5000 BC and by every major civilization since. It acts by stimulating the blood vessels of the part so treated to contract or dilate, according to the temperature of the water used. This has a reflex action on the part supplied by those blood vessels. The stimulation also acts through the segment of the spinal cord which supplies the nerves to that area of skin, and so there are effects on remote and deep organs also supplied by that same segment of cord.

In general, benefit is chiefly felt from the toning-up qualities when cold sprays are used, and the soothing and relaxing qualities when warm douches are applied. A great number of different modes of application have been invented, fine sprays under pressures from mild to very strong douches of great torrents of water, baths, all temperatures from cold to very hot, sometimes alternating to increase the stimulation of the skin and so relax the deep structures. Exercises can be performed with the water being used to support a weak limb, and various medicaments added to the water to make artificial 'waters', where 'natural waters' containing mineral salts of various types and dissolved gases are not easily available.

The cost and time consuming processes needed for adequate treatment make this service increasingly hard to get, and many natural Spas have closed down. Although modern drug therapy has replaced much of the benefit obtained from hydrotherapy, there is without doubt a place for almost every type of treatment, and many people would benefit emotionally and physically from a course.

STIMULATION NEEDED

I have a problem which is slowly but surely getting me down. I am a single man of 39 years of age. I am courting a girl of 31, and we are both very much in love. Just recently I failed for the fourth time to achieve intercourse with her. As you can imagine, we are both very unhappy about this situation. For me it is shattering.

After the usual loveplay, I go almost fully erect, but my penis is simply not hard enough to penetrate easily and when I have entered, it is not solid enough to complete the act. In fact, by this time, I am not even fully erect. My girl, who has been married before, has taken me by hand and mouth in an effort to reach a full erection but the stiffness required is simply not there. She has masturbated me by hand and I have ejaculated. This is the maddening part of it.

I went to my doctor about a week ago and explained my problem to him. He gave me a prescription for some small white tablets which I take four times a day. I have taken them for a week now and there is no improvement.

I have been thinking about going to an adult aid centre. You know the places I mean. Usually a book shop with different devices to help your sexual problems. Would 'erection creams' help?

I would really appreciate your comments as I could not bear to lose a girl I think so much of.

Name and address withheld
by request

Your problem may be less serious than you think, since you can at least obtain an almost full erection.

If it is possible to get professional treatment based on deep relaxation and desensitization (known as 'behaviour therapy'), I am sure this would help. If not, try a 'do it yourself' treatment based on Masters and Johnson's techniques.

To begin with, abstain from any sex play and concentrate on mutual massage using body lotion, each of you taking turns to massage and caress the other and of applying creams to your body avoiding genital areas. After a few sessions you can touch the genital areas. The next stage involves your partner kneeling astride you (with you lying on your back). It is up to her to judge whether your penis is erect enough for penetration and she will then insert it into her vagina. Later more conventional positions can be attempted but this initial position is very important.

For a full account of the procedure I would advise you to read 'Understanding Human Sexual Inadequacy' by F. Belliveau & L. Richter. It would help to find a psychiatrist or

178

psychologist who uses these techniques as it is preferable to have some supervision if possible.

This programme works best with a 'stimulation course'. I suggest that if possible you should see some sexy films. Also, buy some pictures of whatever type of fantasy turns you on and look at them before intercourse. It would also help to try mutual oral sex, in the '69' position.

Finally, try never to lose your sense of humour during fore-play or intercourse. Don't make sex into an anxiety-provoking experience but turn it into a light-hearted pastime enjoyable whether you have full intercourse or not.

There is no scientific evidence in favour of the efficacy of 'erection creams' – so don't waste your money.

IMPOTENCE SOLUTION

You recently published a letter from a woman faced with the problem of her 60-year-old husband's impotency. He agreed to her having affairs with other men in order to satisfy herself. I too was faced with this problem, but fortunately due to a very considerate husband, he made it unnecessary for me to want a substitute.

When he realized that his potency had decreased and that no longer was he able to perform as frequently as I wished, he quickly tried to find an alternative method to satisfy me. I always used to find oral sex distasteful but faced with the fact of not being able to have a normal coital relationship, I allowed him to perform cunnilingus.

My reactions to this were amazing. I had orgasms the like of which I'd never before experienced. My husband sucked me until I couldn't stand it any more, bringing me off six or seven times in half an hour until I had to push him away. The experience thrilled me so much, that I soon begged my husband to suck me off nightly. He willingly obliged.

Even if he was still able to have intercourse, I would now prefer to be sucked off and, as for wanting a substitute, no thanks! My husband gets no erection nor reaches a climax while he is down on me, but admits that he loves it. It's not just to satisfy me, he enjoys it too.

In 25 years of marriage, until four years ago, we never in-dulged in this practice, but since then I have found complete satisfaction and contentment. I'd always recommend your women readers faced with the same problem to try the same solution.

Mrs J.M.,
London

TOO BIG

My husband and I get along great and we have a fantastic relationship in bed except for one terrible problem. His penis is so large that I can't really get it in my mouth in order to perform fellatio. I like sucking his penis and he certainly enjoys having me go down on him but I have such trouble getting his penis in my mouth. Can you give me some suggestions about how to go about performing fellatio on him without choking to death?

*Name and address withheld
by request*

It is difficult for a woman to perform fellatio for lengthy periods of time on men with very large penises. Your mouth gets tired, and there is a tendency, provided your mouth is big enough to engulf the penis, as yours appears to be, to choke.

The best thing to do in your situation is to find a replacement technique which most easily simulates fellatio. Take a dry washcloth, soak it in hot water and wring it out so that it resembles the hot wet towels used in Japanese restaurants. Using the washcloth like a glove, caress your husband's penis much as you would caress him with your mouth. I think your husband will find the results most satisfactory.

You may find the next technique difficult to believe, if you've never tried it before. Treat your husband's big toe as if it were his penis and suck it. I have no idea why this should feel so much like oral sex, but take my word for it, it makes a fine replacement.

ANAL SEX

ANAL INTERCOURSE

I am sort of unofficial leader of a group of young people of various ages who with the help of *Forum* are becoming very enlightened sexually, especially over the last two years. We think your mag is fantastic and sometimes hold various discussions about different aspects of sex. We were having one of our usual discussions when the subject of buggery cropped up. We know what it is and legally what it means, but we would be grateful if your experts could answer the following questions for us:

One of our group was recently put through various tests by a police doctor to see if he had had anal intercourse with an older man. He states that a glass instrument like a thermometer was inserted up his back passage and certain measurements taken, but no explanation was given for this action. Could you please tell us why this was done? How, medically, can it be established that two men have had intercourse with each other?

Could you explain what actual damage is normally done by this sort of sexual act to the back passage or is it reasonably safe with the use of a lubricant?

Apparently the reason why some males become bisexual is that their anal area is very sensitive sexually. Is this common?

Could you tell us if any advance has been made recently to lower the age of consent so that younger men can legally have homosexual relationships together? We think that if women want equal rights, certain members of the male sex should be equal as well. Why should female homosexuality be allowed and male homosexuality under 21 be illegal?

J.M.,
London

The best way to answer your letter is under its own four sections.

The device the police used could have been a thermometer but it is much more likely that it was a disposable plastic proctoscope. This enables the user to look inside the lower end of the rectum and anal canal. The information sought would be such things as how far and how easily the proctoscope goes in,

181

was it painful, was there any damage or inflammation of inside tissues? Habitual anal intercourse may result in thickening of the orifice walls and development of a characteristic funnel shape in the region around the orifice. A swab could also be taken of the contents of the canal to allow a microscopic search for sperms.

Providing gentleness and adequate lubrication is used, and the penetrating organ is not vastly too big for the canal, no physical harm is likely to result. The process may be painful to start but will become less so with repeated use.

The muscles around most body orifices are called sphincters. Many people feel pleasure when they are stretched, eg mouth, vagina, anus. Additionally, when an object is introduced into the male rectum it may rub the neighbouring prostate gland and the sperm storage vessels. To many this is intensely pleasurable and can lead to swift orgasm.

There has been no significant movement to lower the age of consent in this respect. However, now that at the age of 18 you can fight and die for your country and vote in parliamentary elections, it is difficult to see how the minimum age of 21 for male homosexuals can be arbitrarily continued for much longer.

DOES ANAL SEX CAUSE PILES?

I'd like to try anal sex but I'm worried about getting piles. Does anal penetration cause these? I've been told that heredity has something to do with developing haemorrhoids and since a few people in my family suffer from them, I wouldn't want to chance anal intercourse if I might get them as a result.

P.H.,
Address withheld by request

We have to point out that anal intercourse is illegal between consenting heterosexuals. But there is no medical foundation for the ban. You need have no fear of getting piles. So long as you go about it gently, use plenty of lubrication, and never allow a penis or finger that has been in the anus to touch the vulva (bacteria that are naturally present, and quite harmless, in the bowel can cause cystitis if they reach the urethra) you should have no problems.

There is a tendency for varicose veins, whether in the legs,

rectum (piles) or scrotum (variocoele) to run in families. It's
by no means a certainty; just an increased risk.

AN UNENLIGHTENED LAW

I think it's absurd for it to be an offence for a husband and
wife to perform anal intercourse when it's not illegal for
homosexuals.

My husband and I are both 54 and have been married for 30
years. During the early years of our marriage we had intercourse every day or more often and we both loved it. Unfortunately I had two miscarriages and was advised to avoid a
third pregnancy. We tried every form of birth control available
at that time, but none seemed to suit us or allow us to be
completely spontaneous.

We tried withdrawal, but had a failure and I became pregnant yet again, causing another miscarriage.

This time I was in hospital for three months. I asked for
sterilization but was refused.

When I returned home, penile–vaginal intercourse seemed
out of the question, so we tried oral sex. We both found this
completely satisfactory, and soon began regularly having sex in
this way. We were able to control our orgasms so that they were
simultaneous.

But eventually I began to want my husband to come off in
me. I wanted to feel his penis jerking inside me. True intercourse
was out of the question after my experiences, so I suggested
anal intercourse.

We tried a number of times but failed, because it was too
painful. So, unknown to my husband, I started to exercise my
anus, beginning with small objects, and gradually increasing the
sizes until I was able to accommodate my husband's penis easily
and without pain.

Our marriage took on a new lease of life when we started
anal intercourse. If we had not begun it, we might have split up.
I can see no difference in our relationship than that between two
males, yet we are committing an offence. Is it not time this
particular law was quietly dropped?

That first time was 20 years ago, and led to multiple orgasms
for me. Anal intercouse has been a regular part of our sex lives
ever since.

Mrs M.M.,
Wales

I tend to agree with you, Mrs M.M. Unhappily, many lawyers don't.

I think I should clear up a few misunderstandings first, though. The law certainly hasn't given a good housekeeping seal of approval to buggery – the legal term – between homosexuals. At best the official attitude amounts to no more than reluctant tolerance (the leading textbook refers to anal intercourse as 'this horrible offence'). You will find that the Sexual Offences Act 1967 merely exempts homosexual acts in private when the parties have reached 21 and both consent. The law has so strictly interpreted these conditions that if a third person takes part or if one of the couple is only 20 (an adult for all other legal purposes) they risk penalties of 5 to 10 years' imprisonment.

You say you can't see any difference between your relationship with your husband and that between two men. Quite frankly, neither can I. Except that you have formalized yours with a marriage certificate. But I'm afraid that three years ago an Appeal Court judge adopted the opposite viewpoint. 'We see strong reasons,' he declared, 'for making a distinction between acts of buggery committed upon a man and upon a woman.'

Unfortunately, he does not appear to have stated those reasons. In the case in question a 19-year-old 'model' had posed for the accused on a deserted moor. What began as a photo-session quickly degenerated into an erotic jamboree which included straight intercourse, fellatio and buggery. Throughout the festivities the defendant seems to have clung to his camera and recorded a most enlightening pictorial essay of his activities. Conveniently for the prosecution, who produced it as evidence at the trial.

The girl complained to the police, ironically not about the sexual gymnastics but because she thought the defendant had stolen her watch. From there the whole story emerged. Convicted of buggery, the defendant received an 18-month sentence. He appealed.

The appeal judge accepted that 'the act of buggery was with the lady's consent' and even referred to the expression on her face in the snapshots 'displaying with apparent pleasure her vagina and other parts of her body'. Nevertheless he approved the 18-month sentence as 'fully justified'. He commented: 'Whatever Parliament may have provided as regards consenting male adults . . . nothing of this kind has been done in the case of

184

*buggery of a woman where the maximum sentence prescribed
by law is still life.'*

The only consolation I can offer, Mrs M.M., is that the police
and the courts appear to go easier on married couples. The
above appeal judge even referred to the various cases 'when in
the matrimonial bed a husband has done something of this sort
to his wife and such offences have been treated with great leniency'. Prosecutions of spouses rarely occur even though a consenting wife is an accomplice to the offence. And a few years
back a court described a £20 fine as 'a very proper sentence'.

Nevertheless I still cannot see as a matter of common sense
why it should be perfectly lawful for a man to come off in his
lover's mouth and yet risk a savage legal revenge if he as much
dares to penetrate her rectum.

And a conviction for buggery doesn't even require proof of
ejaculation!

POWER TO THE PROSTATE!

My wife and I are regular subscribers to *Forum* and always
find something of interest in it. Your recent articles and letters
concerning the prostate gland have been most appreciated since
information of this type is seldom found in conventional sex
manuals. We have noticed, however, that your discussions of
the prostate almost always emphasize the various maladies it is
subject to, and we believe that too little attention has been paid
to its erotic aspects.

The prostate is an erogenous zone, a source of unparalleled
sexual stimulation and gratification. Of course, homosexuals
have long been aware of this, but for this very reason a social
stigma has been attached to the idea of male-passive anal sex
that prevents heterosexual couples (who may otherwise be uninhibited) from experiencing the joys of this very exciting form
of intercourse. It is in the spirit of power to the prostrate, therefore, that we would like to share our experiences with your
readers!

I am 32, my wife is 28. We enjoy a very uninhibited sex life
which has led us most recently to experiment with male-passive
anal intercourse. We have come to the conclusion that a man's
capacity for sexual response is far greater than most people
realize.

Naturally, like most men I always have enjoyed anal stimulation during sex play. Usually this consisted of little more than

my partner lightly running her tongue around the outer rim of my anus, or perhaps inserting a finger a half-inch or so during intercourse. This always excited me tremendously as my anus is very sensitive, and any such stimulation causes my cock to throb wildly. I always secretly desired full penetration of my rectum even though I never had experienced prostate massage and didn't really know what to expect. I was afraid to ask for it, however, for fear that my partner would find the idea repulsive or think me a latent homosexual. I can see in retrospect that it was my own fear of homosexuality that prevented me from expressing my desires. I felt somehow that to admit a desire for deep rectal stimulation was to confess some kind of deviation.

These needless inhibitions were swept away when I met my wife, a vital and very erotic lady who didn't hesitate to stimulate my anus manually and orally. One day I gave myself an enema before my evening shower and later in bed asked my wife if she would insert her finger all the way. Without hesitation she fetched the vaseline, began massaging my anus slowly in a circular motion, and then slid her finger deep into my rectum, wiggling it rapidly. The sensation was shocking and incredible. I had never felt such deep and exciting pleasure. She probed for my prostate, the location of which neither of us was certain about. 'Is it here?' she asked, hooking her finger back and forth inside me, 'or here? or here?' I was absolutely wild with excitement and when at last she found the target a warm electric vibration surged through my balls, lubricating fluid began pouring copiously from my cock, and I wanted to immediately fuck her. She withdrew her finger and, in a state of wild abandon, I made love to her for more than an hour, bringing her to orgasm several times before I finally came. It was the best sex we'd ever had.

Since my initial 'deflowering' several years ago, male-passive anal intercourse has become an important part of our sex life. We don't do it every time we make love, but we do find it mutually desirable about once a week on the average. Some weeks we do it two or three times. We use two basic positions: lying face down with my legs spread and my hips arched upward, or lying on my back with my knees drawn back to my chest and my feet above my head. In either position my wife enjoys stimulating me orally before inserting her finger. Either I spread my cheeks with my own hands or she does, and then she slowly licks and tickles my anus with the tip of her tongue,

186

working gradually deeper until her tongue is in as far as it can go. She keeps this up for several minutes and needless to say it makes me crazy. Then she lubricates her finger, sometimes two fingers, and penetrates me very slowly so that I can relish the sensation. Once in she wiggles her finger-tip rapidly against my prostate and alternately pumps in and out of my rectum in a rapid motion. I am driven instantly into a state of blind ecstasy and fluid begins flowing abundantly. This sensation is almost exactly like ejaculating since prolonged manipulation of my prostate produces a feeling almost as intense as an orgasm. The important difference is that we can sustain this level of excitement indefinitely, the juices pouring out of me all the while. More than once she has fucked me this way for half an hour, after which I am quite out of my head with lust.

That my wife can enter my body and bring me to orgasm as I do to her is a most gratifying erotic resource. We both have come to think of my rectum and prostate as masculine counterparts of the female vagina and clitoris. I must emphasize 'masculine' here, for we definitely do not feel that there's anything 'feminine' about my enjoyment of anal sex. The prostate and the profound pleasures to be derived from it are uniquely masculine characteristics. My enthusiastic response to rectal stimulation has only increased my confidence in my own masculinity and is a source of great erotic excitement for my wife. My desire for her has increased since she began fucking me, and I believe the feeling is mutual. Even when we make love without anal sex – which is more than half the time – the level of excitement is much greater than before since we are now aware of the greater sexual potential that is available to us when we feel like it. I do not need anal penetration to enjoy fabulous and completely satisfying sex with my wife, but it does greatly enhance these pleasures just as manual manipulation of a woman's clitoris during intercourse is better for her than intercourse without such stimulation.

Indeed, so completely have we accepted passive anal intercourse as an integral component of male sexuality that we have had to revise our attitudes about homosexuality – or more accurately in our case, bisexuality. So voluptuous are the pleasures of anal sex for me that I couldn't help wondering how it would feel to have a live naked penis throbbing, pumping and ejaculating inside me. My wife says it would excite her to watch a man fucking me and that she would like to suck me or to have me inside her while I was being fucked by a man. Although we have not yet tried this I think it definitely is in the future for us, at least as an experiment.

I would appreciate some feedback from other readers regarding their experiences with heterosexual male-passive anal intercourse. I suspect that many couples enjoy this form of sex but are reluctant to discuss it, and that many men secretly desire stimulation of their prostate but are hesitant to ask their women to do it. Likewise, I suspect that many women would find pleasure in satisfying their men this way once they understand that it's not a threat to anyone's masculinity and once they appreciate the incomparable pleasures to be derived from it.

G.Y.,
Address withheld by request

ANAL RISKS

One of my chief sources of sexual stimulation has always been connected with the rectum and anal areas. Enemas and vibrators give me erections without any contact with my penis.

I wonder whether you or any of your readers can tell me of any safe stimulants for the rectum. I have read of champagne and spirits being injected but wonder whether these might cause damage to the rectal lining.

Also, would the introduction of suitable-sized fruit (of reasonable size) lead to any ill-effects, so long as such introduction causes no pain? I have in mind such things as bananas (peeled) and plums.

J.B.,
Worcestershire

The mucosal lining of the rectum is not very sensitive to pain, but the skin lining and anal canal are. Hence injections into the rectal mucosa (used in the treatment of internal piles) are relatively painless, whereas injections into the anal skin are actually painful.

Thus care must be used when dealing with the rectum as splits and tears of the mucosa can occur without any preliminary protecting pain. Such injuries can lead to serious infections.

Soft fruits are unlikely to do much harm unless they are large enough to cause splitting of the anal canal – these can develop into very painful fissures.

Alcohol of any sort in the rectum will act as a strong

irritant and constant repetition will produce an inflammation of the bowel which can become chronic and lead to internal haemorrhoids. Even repeated enemas using strong soap solutions can do this.

On the whole then, the rectum and anus are worth treating with care as inflammations and infections of this area are always painful and disabling, and dangerous complications can arise.

Whereas in youth one's body is marvellously adaptable, as one gets older practices which used to cause no harm can produce unpleasant effects. The usual protestation, 'but I have been doing this for years with no problems' will not help much after 45!

INCEST

FATHER AND DAUGHTER INCEST

A couple of days ago a friend of mine brought over a copy of *Forum*. It was the first time I had ever seen it so I glanced through it. I came to a consultant's comment about how parents can be too over-affectionate towards their children. This could have been written especially for my family; I could not agree more with your consultant's warnings.

My daughter Cheryl is 12 years old and she started acting peculiar towards her father about three months ago. All of a sudden she began getting up half an hour early for school so she could have breakfast with her daddy. When Danny left for work she would always give him a big hug and a kiss. When he arrived home she would give him another hug and kiss as soon as he walked in the door.

Before bed she would change into her pyjamas and come and sit on his lap for 10 or 15 minutes every night. When Danny and I retired to bed he would be very sexually aroused and on more than one occasion we would have sex two or more times that evening.

I never thought much of any of this until one Saturday morning. I always get up early on Saturday to start house cleaning, and when I get out of bed, usually around nine, Cheryl began coming downstairs and getting into bed with Danny.

After about a month of this I became somewhat curious. Why was the bedroom door always shut when Cheryl was in our bedroom? (She said there was too much noise with it open.) So one Saturday I opened the bedroom door to find out – and was really shocked. There was my daughter with her panties down to her ankles masturbating my husband who pretended to be asleep!

Can you imagine my husband pretending to be asleep when he was sexually aroused? I questioned my husband about this and he just told me it was nothing to worry about.

Well, I had to get a social worker for Cheryl and my husband has been ordered to see a doctor.

Reading about this sort of thing in *Forum* was like reliving the whole incident over again. I only wish I'd seen your comments earlier – if I'd been a little more suspicious, my husband and daughter might never have passed the danger point.

Mrs D.K.,
Indiana

The doctor and social worker you are in touch with are in a better position to offer you specific advice than I am, because they know all the circumstances.

But I should like to offer two comments, in the hope that they will help you in this very distressing situation.

First, incest is not as rare as most people think, and what your husband has done is something many men would like to do. Similarly, young girls of around Cheryl's age often develop very strong attachments to their fathers and fantasize sexual relations with them. This is, of course, only a phase on the way to becoming interested in men outside the family – the danger of acting it out is that the girl may get stuck, so to speak, at this stage of her development. I don't wish to condone what your husband did; he should have had the self-control to hold out against the provocation which I feel sure your daughter offered him. But I do feel that your best policy is to try to understand, not condemn, if your family relationships are to get back on an even keel.

And secondly, in many cases of father–daughter incest it is found that the mother is not receptive to her husband's sexual needs. After all, a sexually happy and satisfied man is far more likely to withstand a feeling of desire for another woman than a frustrated one! You give no information on your own sex life, so I can only offer this as a point it might be worth your thinking about and perhaps discussing with your husband. (Consultant)

BROTHER BOTHER

I am a 14-year-old girl and am not sure how to write this letter. I see *Forum* around the house a lot because my parents have a subscription. I think they want me to read it, or they probably wouldn't keep leaving it about.

My problem is this: my brother and I have shared the same room ever since I can remember, and since we were kids we've played with each other's bodies. Living in the same room, that always seemed natural to both of us. He could get a hard penis even when he was a kid. He plays with me, and we both get so excited, we want to make love. When he was smaller (I'm two years older), it was easy to tell him to get away from me, but now he is taller than I am and is getting really pushy. It worries me because I began to have my periods about a year ago, and I don't want to get pregnant by him.

I know I should start using a contraceptive now anyway, and Mom is pretty open about those kinds of things, but I still don't want to hurt her by telling her about my brother and me. Anyway, I don't want my kid brother to be my first real lover. What do you think I should do? I am getting really scared about the whole thing because he won't get off me.

Name and address withheld
by request

Since your parents seem fairly open-minded, I suggest you speak to them about your problem. If they read Forum *regularly, the chances are they have seen letters about such situations and understand more about such things than you dare hope.*

The extent of sexual contact you have had with your brother has not reached serious or reproachable proportions, but I suggest you bring things to your parents' attention before your brother's impatience gets the better of both of you.

You have a right to a certain amount of privacy. I think you should explain to your mother that you are becoming sensitive about your womanhood and would prefer having your own room. If this is absolutely impossible for financial or other reasons, it is up to you to make major changes in your living habits with respect to your brother. You should try not to lead him on and you shouldn't make it difficult for him to comply with your request to be left alone — get undressed in the bathroom, don't allow him to approach you sexually any more!

It is perfectly natural to have a potent sex drive at your age, and there is certainly nothing wrong with this. If you feel you are emotionally prepared to make love, I suggest you discuss this with your mother.

If you do not act embarrassed and broach this subject quite openly with her, perhaps you will put her at her ease too. These are difficult moments for mothers because they must face the fact that their daughters are women. Sometimes, it is difficult to speak frankly to another woman about sexual matters anyway, so you should try to be patient with her. I suggest, however, that you do have a full and open talk with her as soon as possible, before matters get too far out of hand.

INCEST

I am just 16, and I recently left England to join my parents who live in Nairobi. It is a completely different climate here and at first I had difficulties getting to sleep. I told my mother this, and she gave me some sleeping pills, but with not much effect.

After a couple of weeks my father was called for a month to Zanzibar on business. That evening when I was in bed my mother came to my room, sat on the bed and asked me if I was sleeping any better. I said no. She then slipped her hand under the blanket and got hold of my penis, which almost immediately got hard. Then she pulled off the bedclothes. (I was naked, I never wear pyjamas.) She admired the size of my penis, moving her hand up and down. A few minutes later, I ejaculated. She dried me up with her hankie. 'Perhaps now you will sleep better,' she said, and kissing me goodnight, she left the room. I did indeed go to sleep almost immediately.

The next night she came again, this time in her dressing-gown. She sat beside me and after asking me if I would like the same 'sleeping pill' again, began to masturbate me, leaning over me with her dressing-gown falling open.

This became a normal routine for about 10 days; then one evening she said she was going to bed and asked me to come and see her before I went to sleep. When I went into her room she told me to get into bed and take my pyjamas off; then she cuddled me. Mutual caressing soon led to oral lovemaking.

When my father returned we could only enjoy our lovemaking in the morning, when he was at work. At other times my relations with my mother are quite normal.

I do not think that this has done me any harm, rather it binds my mother and I together and I can add that thanks to my mother I have learned all about oral love. I've tried it on several girls and on two married women, friends of my mother, and they all wondered how, being so young, I had got so good at it.

We have never had actual intercourse as this, I am sure, would spoil our beautiful intimate relationship. So what we do is not incest, is it?

J.B.,
Nairobi

Exactly what constitutes incest legally varies from country to country; it is quite possible you are breaking Kenyan law. Morally, however, most people would certainly describe your relationship as incestuous.

The real risk is that of becoming 'fixated' on your mother and ceasing to be interested sexually or emotionally in other women. My advice to you would be to cool off your relationship with your mother, if not immediately, then as quickly as possible, while taking every opportunity to make friendly as well as sexual contacts with girls your own age. After all, it is such a girl you will eventually marry, and it could harm your marriage prospects if you get hung up on older women, whether your mother or her friends. A period of interest in older women is very common at your age, but you must give yourself every opportunity to grow out of it.

Don't feel too guilty about what has happened; see it as something that was appropriate at one stage of your youth, and taught you a lot about sex, but which must be put aside, like many other things, so that you can go on to become a mature man. Grown-up men don't rely on their mothers for sex – that is the mark of childhood.

ALL IN THE FAMILY

In our modern culture, the male reaches his age of greatest sexual need and potency years before he is able to support a wife and start his own family. This urgent sexual drive may then be distorted into homosexuality, 'Jesus freakism', drug usage, or in some other way incline him to failure to realize his fullest potential. Our social custom of husbands who are several years older than their wives is also stupid and impractical. This results in having the husband declining in sexual needs and ability during the very years when his wife reaches her fullest sexual maturity. In countless families this coincides with the time of puberty of their sons. Among my friends are several whose husbands advised and consented to initiation of home sex for their sons' benefit, so you see it is not confined to widows and divorcees.

My gynaecologist tells me that in her 32 years of practice she has always had a few home sex participants, but the percentage began to increase astronomically with the advent of the Pill. Before then many pre-menopause mothers frankly feared the high sperm count and potency of their sons. However, when the news media began publicizing the high venereal rate among the school age group, and then the medical profession became worried about the mutated form of gonorrhoea brought back

194

from Vietnam that has resisted the entire spectrum of anti-biotics, home sex really accelerated.

One of my dearest friends is the wife of a military officer who really laid down the law to his wife, before he left for two years' overseas duty. He instructed her to give their 15-year-old son at least two nights in bed with her every week during his absence. He knew she was a normal woman with strong sexual needs, so he wanted her to stay free from emotional entanglements that often come with sexual intimacy with older men, and, at the same time, to keep their son safe from disease and the drug and vandalism crowd. She still sleeps with her son two full nights each week and gives him a roll in the hay at other times when they both want it.

Another fine woman is now 60 and has two sons married and well established in their professions. Both usually drop in at her ever-open flat once or twice a week and enjoy a nice bed session with her. Both tell her that she is a very enjoyable and satisfying sex partner. She mentioned that each son really gave her a sex workout in the last month of their wives' pregnancies and for about six weeks afterwards.

Intra-family home sex – call it 'incest' if you have to – is a very real fact of life in our modern culture, and increasing every day. Just as laws against homosexuality are being wiped off the law books, you may see laws against 'incest' being repealed in the foreseeable future.

Name withheld by request
Hawaii

Your letter is extremely interesting. It may well be that the incidence of incest is underestimated, although from my own observations as a consultant psychiatrist I should be extremely surprised if incest is as common as you report it to be. Statistics on the subject are far from satisfactory. In the Forum *readers' survey, the proportions reporting that they had ever in their lives had sexual activity with a close relative was 0·5% with father, 0·9% with mother, 4·9% with brother, 4·7% with sister, 0·2% with son and 0·5% with daughter. These figures may or may not be representative, but in any case they must include many instances of transient, experimental, guilt-ridden sexual contact in no way comparable with the full scale adventures in intra-family sex in which you and your friends are engaged.*

In our own culture, sexual freedom among adolescents does not, in my experience, appear to be inhibited by fears of anti-

biotic-resistant VD. I can see the charm of the incestuous matings that you describe, but I wonder just how many of these mothers will suffer rejection and depression when their sons cease to find them sexually desirable.

PARENT VOYEURISM

In reply to a letter about child sexuality a point to which your consultant seems to take exception is not so much that an adolescent might, or should, be initiated into the pleasures of masturbation by someone, but that the initiator shouldn't be one of the parents. I accept that the existence of a parent–child relationship might complicate the situation and that some undesirable results could follow. But what is the alternative?

It is most likely that a youngster will be introduced to sex either by an adult or by another young person who happens to have had some experience and who is probably very much the same in age. Therefore do you think that any effort ought to be made by the parents to ensure that a youngster gets good and satisfactory initiation, or should matters look after themselves?

If we accept that it shouldn't be the parent who gives practical instruction and guides the development, then it would seem that he (or she) ought at least to make suitable arrangements, with either a responsible and friendly adult or a suitably instructed and acceptable young friend of the boy (or girl) to carry out the initiation and practice.

In short, are we doing our duty properly if we leave everything to chance?

J.D.,
Middlesex

There are still parents, although their number is happily diminishing, who feel that it is perfectly within their rights to control every step of their children's social relations. They are the ones who judge who the 'right' people are to be their children's companions, who the suitable escorts would be in a dating situation, and where the 'proper' places are to go. They expect their children to go along with these choices because they, the parents, know what's 'best'. Rarely do such parents regard their children as having rights of their own or valid individual opinions.

In advocating parental control over every detail of a child's sexuality, you are being just as patronizing about children's sex

196

feelings as these other parents are about their more general social lives.

What makes you think that what you regard as 'good and satisfactory initiation' would be seen in the same way by a child? When you give 'matters looking after themselves' as an alternative what you're really implying is that youngsters who decide on their own what kind of sexuality they want, with whom and when, are really getting a second-best deal because their choice is not likely to be as good as yours. You, the all-seeing parent, can give them what is best and you know what they want better than they do. (If it's a question of contraception then that's a different matter. You are likely to be more in the know about such purely technical matters and your advice on this can be most helpful.)

But there's another element in your approach – voyeurism. People who want to interfere in their children's sexuality give me the impression that they want to be in on the action, even if it's second-hand. The constant use of the word 'initiation' suggests a kind of sex ceremony at which the parent imagines himself to be an eager spectator.

Such feelings, in fact, may reflect an unconscious fantasy, like masturbating a child, perhaps, or being a child masturbated by an adult.

YOUTH

Young people are subject to violent emotions at key times in their maturation. Starting with loving relationships within the family, sex, on an unconscious level, is always present in a child's life. Teenage is the recognized time of sexual questioning and exploration, and a little later, there is that period of liberation, so eagerly anticipated, that comes between leaving the family and eventually starting a family of one's own.

CHILDREN AND SENSUALITY

INFANT MASTURBATION

After six years of marriage my husband and I still adore each other and we don't hide our feelings. We hug and kiss each other in front of our little girl without embarrassment, although we rarely go further than that when she is around. We both believe that masturbation is good for everyone and have no guilty feelings about it. But there are a few things I would like to know.

My daughter, who is three and a half, uses the thigh-squeezing masturbation technique while lying on her tummy, although she has started putting her hands on her genitals lately. She masturbates quite often, when she's overtired, scolded or excited, sometimes three times a day, other days, not at all. Although I know that masturbation relieves tension and helps one's later sex life, I wonder whether she is doing it too often.

She is not shy or embarrassed when she masturbates in front of us. How does she know how to manipulate her genitals in this manner, as no one has shown her and she has never seen us making love? How can I explain to her that masturbation is fine, but one doesn't do this in front of parents or friends?

Will she cool down as she gets older? I have talked to her only once about this, asking her what she was doing (very gently) to which she answered 'My exercises'.

I would very much appreciate knowing whether this kind of masturbation is normal in a child of her age. She is quite bright, with the mentality of a five-year-old in some areas.

Mrs J.S.,
Quebec, Canada

You obviously have a well-adjusted, precocious child. In her early formative years, you can expect her to explore and experiment with her body and external resources with perhaps more than the usual interest and curiosity. Rest assured that her masturbatory exercises are certainly not abnormal. From three to five are the hot years for most children; it is simply that most children are not as overt about their habits, satisfying their physical impulses during their private hours or in their sleep. Their secrecy is often due to the unfortunate fact that parents taught them from infancy that touching their genitals was wrong.

It is to your credit that you have been so open and understanding of her natural inclinations. For her, rubbing her genitals in public is as natural as scratching your head or any other part of your body. An infant discerns pleasurable physical sensation just as readily as he will react to pain or discomfort. Your little girl has discovered various mechanisms for relieving her excitement or disappointment through a healthy physical response. Happily, she has not yet been introduced to society's misguided censure.

I think you can encourage her lack of inhibition about her body while gently teaching her at the same time that some activities are best performed in private – a question of manners. Just as you have toilet-trained her through tolerant discipline, you can gently and gradually indicate to her that she should not probe her genitals in public.

First of all, you can assume that she won't always be as active in this manner. Chances are that in the next two or three years her masturbatory impulses will tone down considerably. In the meantime, gently persuade her not to do her exercises in public view. Don't take her hands away from her body, but speak to her reasonably and forcefully (she should be old enough to understand) about masturbating in privacy. At the same time, reassure her that in private such practices are perfectly fine.

FATHER AND SON

Eight years ago I had born to me a son from a girl I used to sleep with.

She left me two years ago and I have continued bringing up my boy.

I will get straight to the point. At night he does not want to sleep in his own bed and refuses defiantly.

I am not worried about this and have not been before, but he is indirectly seeking sexual stimulation by cuddling his tender body close to mine.

I am a warm-hearted, open-minded person and know there is nothing wrong about it at this tender age but what happens as he grows older?

Either he will grow closer to me or I will have to be overpowering and force him into his own bed.

201

You will also appreciate the fact that I don't want to lose his love for me even though it is more than I expected it to be.

A.F.,
London

Your son was six years old when his mother left you and him. Assuming that the relationship between him and his mother had been reasonable up to that point, her departure would have been a severe loss to him. Worse than this, however, he may have felt that she abandoned him because of his 'naughtiness'. A component of this naughtiness is the sexual interest that a little boy has in his mother.

This, obviously, could be harmful to his sexual development, unless he manages to come to terms with the blow. For example he may conclude, deep in his mind, that sexual interest in a woman leads to the loss of her love. He would not be capable of expressing his feelings in this way. But the behaviour of some men who experienced the loss of a mother at about this age is only to be explained in this way. And they are influenced by it for ever.

However, the fact that he is turning towards you, his father, emotionally and sexually, is not necessarily due to this distrust of women. A boy of eight is usually more interested in the father and his pursuits than he is in his mother. In addition, you are the one who loved him and stayed with him. Further still, you are probably the only person available for him to love. All love carries with it some sense of libido, and although children at his age are said to be in the stage of latent sexuality, they are still sexual.

Turning to yourself, it is not impossible that you are not too keen on women. Perhaps this is why the girl left you. It is not obvious from your letter why you didn't marry her. Possibly you already are married, and that relationship failed too?

You seem to find your son's love very acceptable and to an extent you depend on it for your own emotional satisfaction. This is usually a sign that the adult feels unsure and unconfident in a mature heterosexual relationship. Maybe you take your son into your bed to express, in part, your own sexual and emotional feelings through touch, closeness and cuddling? In short, although you do not realize it, your son's behaviour arises in relationship to your own. I feel it would be wrong not to say that this situation could have an adverse effect on his

202

*subsequent capacities to form a loving and sexual relationship
with a woman.*

*It is best for all of us that we grow up with parents, or parent
substitutes, of both sexes. Where a natural relationship exists
between the parents, the child finds it difficult to obtain excessive or sexual love from either parent and so develops normally.
In this case, your son would clearly be very jealous if you introduced a woman into the household, and yet this would be the
best solution to the problem.*

*If you could find a sensible, sympathetic woman who could
form a good relationship with the boy, and then gradually introduce her into the environment, this would be excellent.
Otherwise you should try to limit physical contact between you
and your son while, through your behaviour, reassuring him
that you are still devoted to him.*

*As far as possible, he should be encouraged to play with other
boys, to go to their homes, and bring them to yours. He should
have the choice of following 'boyish' pursuits.*

*Finally, you should try to speak in a kindly way about
women in general and his mother in particular. Even if it
involves a slight distortion of the facts you should try to supply
adequate reasons why she left. Getting him a female dog may
help in his development and take the pressure of his emotional
expression off you.*

*You, of course, would have to guard against being jealous of
the dog.*

*Beyond this, the only other measure I can suggest is that if his
behaviour or interests seem strange in any way you should consult a Child Guidance Clinic.*

NINE-YEAR-OLD SEX PROBLEM

This is, by proxy, a request for advice from Dr Chartham
from what may well be one of his youngest fans. Sebastian is
nearly 10, and has got sex problems (!!), and thinks it a good
idea that his parents should write to you. Before setting out the
problem, perhaps I could assist you by giving the briefest run-
down of the background.

Father is in his early 60s, and highly-sexed. Mother is 20
years younger, a trained nurse working with a local Group
Practice. Her sexual appetite is very healthy too; you name it,
they do it, or have tried it . . . A happy set up.

Sebastian has two older sisters, 11 and 12. The flat is large,

Victorian, full of music, musicians, and books. At the place of honour, next to father's chair, are back numbers of *Forum*, Dr Chartham's works, books on J. S. Bach and novels of merit with a strongly sexual content. The children have unrestricted access to all books, just as they have unrestricted access to all subjects of conversation. There has, however, been no thrusting of sex under their noses: as the questions come up, usually prompted by reading, they are truthfully answered, matter of factly, and in detail.

Sebastian's problem is that he gets erections and is unable to obtain relief by orgasm or masturbation. The problem is probably exacerbated by a tight foreskin, upon which local medical advice is to be sought shortly. About five years ago he was in hospital for the repair of a congenital hernia, when it was noticed that one testicle had not descended. Attempts to 'get it down' failed, and will be renewed, we understand, when he is 12. I feel it is possible that this, coupled with the failure to obtain relief by masturbation, is worrying him.

He is, at the moment, frustrated and miserable, and unable to get to sleep in the warm weather. He has discussed the problem with both of us together.

Your advice would be much appreciated.

Mrs H.M.,
Berkshire

Poor Sebastian! This is no time of life for him to get a sexual hang-up and I hope it hasn't amounted to that. But in any case, he has very wise parents, and I am sure you will be able to help.

Will you therefore tell him that Robert Chartham would be very surprised indeed if the undescended testicle had anything to do with Sebastian's failure to reach orgasm?

In fact, I'm pretty certain that it's the tight foreskin which is responsible. If the foreskin is so tight that it cannot be pulled back at all, lesions under it could be inhibiting the orgasm-producing nerves in the penis-head, under the rim and in the frenum.

(Whatever you do, if his foreskin won't come back at all, don't try to pull it back or let Sebastian try. Not only will it be very painful, but if you do get it back, there is a risk that you won't be able to get it forward again without medical help!)

I think it would be worthwhile checking if Sebastian knows how to masturbate. The mechanics of the business don't come naturally to quite a lot of small boys. The majority of boys are shown how to do it by older boys who themselves have been taught.

I had three or four friends with unretractable foreskins when I was Sebastian's age and older, and none of them found that the whole-hand technique worked. They used to be quite successful with two fingers underneath, directly on the frenum, and the thumb on the rim on the top-side, making very small massaging movements without removing the fingers from the frenum and oscillating the thumb backwards and forwards over the rim. Some of them found vaseline helped, others had to be quite vigorous, and others only responded to very light, very rapid movements.

You appear to be such understanding parents and to have such good rapport with Sebastian that I am going to suggest that one of you, probably dad, asks him to tell you how he masturbates, and if he is using the whole-hand method, or some other method, explain the method I have described above and see what happens.

He may have to experiment. (Chartham)

ONE INCH PENIS

Our son, aged 11, is becoming very distressed about the size of his penis. He is refusing to go swimming at school and is now getting into a state about taking showers at his new school, where he starts next week. All this is because he gets his leg pulled.

He is circumcised and his penis (flaccid) is about one inch in length. He is 5ft 2in tall and weighs four and a half stone.

We have read that a child with a small penis can be treated to improve growth, but that nothing can be done once puberty has been reached.

Has our son a problem, and if so what sort of treatment should we get for him?

Name and address withheld
by request

Firstly, your son is somewhat above average in height and somewhat below average in weight for his age. Since an average is a myth and it takes all types to make a world there is no need for concern here. His height shows that his pituitary gland is functioning normally.

As to the penis I can see no need for concern here either. Its

205

current size shows that it has kept pace with his general development. In due course, under the influence of his sex hormones when these are produced, it will begin to grow fairly rapidly. The sign that the penis is due to develop in the near future is an enlargement of the scrotum and testes. This occurs as a result of activity in the pituitary gland.

The flaccid penis is no guide to its erect size – both before and after puberty. Neither is the pre-pubertal size of the penis any indication of its final size. Some small boys seem to have a quite large (for a small boy) erect penis and yet after pubertal development its size is average. The final size of the penis is determined by genetic inheritance. In other words a boy's final penis size will be governed by the penis size of not only his father and relations on the father's side but also by genes from the mother and her side of the family. The actual increase in size is brought about by hormones. If your son knows this, it will perhaps stop him worrying.

The age at which the sex hormones are produced is much more variable in boys than girls. In some boys they arrive at about 11 years and in others not until 14 or 15. Genital development may be complete by 13 years or as late as 17 or 18 years. Since boys bother so much about their 'manliness', both penis size and pubic hair development have an effect in our culture. Early developers feel superior and because their muscles develop at the same time they can dominate the later developers in every way. Late developers have to learn how to cope with the adversity involved and if they can do so successfully it accentuates certain aspects of their personality which can later stand them in good stead. Mary Jones, who did years of research on the subject, found that as men, the late-developing boys are adventurous, flexible and assertive.

Although you don't mention it, your son may have been teased. Many, if not most, children who are teased become unreasonably sensitive about the topic involved. It is the child's response to teasing rather than the characteristic selected for comment which matters most to the other children. Whether he is being teased or not your son is reacting by withdrawal rather than facing up to the problem. He is developing a poor image of himself based on his penis or, alternatively, if he feels inferior to most of the other boys he is focusing his discontent on his penis.

Rather than bothering about his penis, which I am sure is and will be normal when it develops, you would be better advised to try to encourage him to face up to the issue of relationships

206

with others. For example, apparent unconcern or even amusement about his penis, if he is being teased, will deprive the teasing of any effect. If he is not being teased you will have to try to get him to see that the question of his penis is probably not the real issue involved. If he is feeling isolated you should take steps to prevent it, and so on. Boys at his age often play genital games and if he could become happily involved in these his problem should be over.

In short I think you will help him best by not concentrating on his penis but on his interpersonal relationships. It is much more likely that these are the real problem.

SHOULD I SHOW HIM?

I was raised in a sexually repressed environment and was taught that masturbation was both sinful and harmful to my health. This did not prevent me from masturbating frequently as an adolescent, but I did have serious guilt feelings. As a result, I believe I am more interested in my son's feelings about masturbation than the average father. At the proper time, I will tell my son in explicit terms that masturbation is a normal, healthy sexual outlet which should be enjoyed and positively encouraged.

It has occurred to me that one way to get this across is to declare frankly and unashamedly to him that I masturbated as an adolescent and continue to do so as a happily married man. But would it be inappropriate for me to casually masturbate in my son's presence on some occasion when he sleeps with me (when my wife is out of town, or another child is ill or we are on a camping trip together)? I would not allow myself to become sexually involved with my son by masturbating him or asking him to masturbate me. I only want to demonstrate in a concrete, but undemanding way that masturbation is normal and healthy. What would be an appropriate age for my son to watch me masturbate? What do you think the effects of such an experience would be on him?

D.W.,
Address withheld by request

I think you are over-reacting to your own guilt feelings about masturbation. I don't believe that it is necessary that you demonstrate so graphically to your son the value and acceptability of masturbation.

First, he will learn, as you learned, to masturbate when he is ready. Second, you must realize that a child has more to contend with in terms of sexual attitudes and feelings than merely the attitude of one or both of his parents. If you were to masturbate in front of him, he would be forced to deal with his sense of confusion over your reasons for doing something so unusual and the difference between your actions and the actions of the rest of society.

I believe you can accomplish the same end by merely presenting to your son an accepting attitude about sex in general and answering specifically and directly any questions he might put to you as he reaches puberty.

SUMMER OF 74

I am a 28-year-old housewife, married to a prominent attorney, and the mother of a son and daughter. My husband and I have a normal sex life and are financially secure.

Two summers ago at our summer cottage in North Carolina, I met a 13-year-old boy while my husband and children were away on a fishing trip. The boy was alone, having wandered down the beach by himself when we met. After hunting sea shells and enjoying the sun, we went back to my cottage. It was there that I got the strange idea to seduce him. After having a snack, I convinced him to take a shower to wash the salt off his skin. He was a little reluctant to get out of the shower knowing that I was in the same room, but he finally came out with a towel around him. We joked and kidded around until I pulled the towel from him. I eventually fondled him on the bed, and, after hearing him say it felt kind of funny, I decided to bring him to a climax. I found this terribly fascinating, especially when I felt his first spasms and saw his body become stiff. This was his first orgasm and he obviously enjoyed it. He had a dry climax which was probably due to his age. We met several more times that summer, doing the same thing, except that I allowed him to see me naked on the bed. He had never seen a woman before, and I explained to him the basic physiology of the female organs.

Last summer, we met twice and on the second meeting, I explained intercourse to him. With some difficulty we had relations that one time. The problem was that he had started to ejaculate a small amount, and I certainly had no intention of getting pregnant by him.

Fortunately, and with much relief, I found out that he was

moving with his family to the mid-west. I was starting to have guilt feelings about the whole affair. I just hope that no irreparable harm has come to this youth. I did it out of curiosity, in fun with no seriousness attached. I can't seem to rationalize it or decide whether this was probably just an enjoyable experience for a young boy or whether he will grow up thinking he was raped.

If a man did this type of thing, he would be prosecuted to the full extent of the law, and yet as a woman I too feel like a rapist. If someone does the same thing to my son when he is older, fine, as long as that someone is gentle and I don't hear about it. Obviously, I can't discuss this with my husband or clergyman or even with my close friends. If I were in the same situation today, I would never attempt or even think about doing what I did.

Name withheld by request
Kentucky

The manner in which you describe the seduction of a 13-year-old boy is distinctly different from the way you describe your marriage. The latter you seem to treat with detachment: your husband is a prominent attorney. But is he a prominent lover? Was the seduction a result of sexual frustrations with your current sex life with your husband? Or, was it just a pleasant fulfilment of a common fantasy. Most women find the idea of seducing a young boy erotically stimulating. You are not the first one to conceive of the notion, nor the first to satisfy her curiosity. (Don't be so afraid to admit that the experience was more than simply 'interesting' and not sexually stimulating as well.) However, perhaps you should consider injecting some life, some mutual excitement, into your marriage. Your attitude towards it sounds pretty deflated.

Under the circumstances there is nothing you can do to change what has happened. You cannot seek out this young man and tell him to forget everything. In this respect, guilt is a waste of time and the energy you could be devoting to your immediate concerns. The actual experience seems to have been pleasurable for both of you. Seduction is not necessarily rape, and it is not as if you brutally attacked the boy. I gather from your description that you were quite gentle and loving in your caresses and that you gradually introduced him to the pleasures of sexual excitation. There appears to be nothing sordid about the relationship in that respect. He actually had almost a year to

assimilate the reality of his relations with you before inter-
course.

*Many experts feel that learning sex from an older woman is
more healthy than awkward fumbling in the back of a car. If
one is unstable or particularly immature, sex at any age can be
damaging to some extent. This boy seems to have adjusted to
the idea quite well, returning on many occasions. Obviously he
also had the peace of mind to keep the relationship discreetly
between only the two of you.*

*I don't think that there is any sense in cultivating a guilt
complex over your experience. Nor do I encourage your seeking out another such situation. Why not accept that it has happened, and that you were largely responsible but not necessarily
culpable for the occurrence. Be at ease and attend to the present. I hope your son is lucky enough to have such a gentle
initiation into the world of sexuality.*

CHILDHOOD HANGOVER

Since I reached puberty, I've always had a problem with my
parents touching my breasts and grabbing my bottom. I used to
try to push them away because it never seemed normal to me,
but my mother always acted offended and said I didn't love her.
I never felt that feeling my breasts or my private parts was the
right way to show me love. My mother did this in public too
and harassed my sisters and my friends also, which embarrassed
the hell out of me. But my parents always ignored my complaints.

There were many times that I'd be awakened by my father in
the middle of the night. He'd tell me that I was masturbating in
my sleep and that I should stop. He kept telling me that if I
didn't start behaving, I'd get myself pregnant by the time I was
15. I would tell him he didn't know what he was talking about
and that he should leave me alone so I could sleep. Because of
my parents' constant prodding, I started sleeping around a lot
just to get back at them. My only regret is that, in the process, I
hurt my boyfriend (now my husband) by my looseness.

I feel extremely frustrated now, even though I love my husband very much. I am plagued by dreams in which my father is
chasing after me, trying to take my clothes off and feel me. I
scream and struggle in my dream, until my husband rescues me.
My father walks away laughing as he used to in real life when
he touched me all the time.

After one of those dreams, I can't stand to have my husband touch me for days. Feeling his penis reminds me of my father and sickens me. (I can't understand why I never dream about my father's penis). I can't help feeling that my father screwed me on one of those nights when he woke me. I was always groggy and never stayed awake for too long. Although my husband was the first one to penetrate me, he doesn't believe that I had never had sex before because, he says, my hymen was already broken.

Although I can satisfy myself by masturbating, I'd much prefer having sex with my husband because it is more meaningful. But when we do make love, my orgasms are few and far between. I understand that this is probably due to these past experiences, but I'm not sure how to work them out of my system. Any suggestions you may have would be appreciated.

Mrs R.M.,
New York

All parents have sexual feelings for their offspring, as do all children for their parents. Most parents and children in our society are quite uncomfortable about this. They have been taught by their culture through thousands of years of tradition to push such feelings down, which they do so well that usually they are expressed only in very limited and indirect ways. The feelings are especially apt to be a problem when children reach puberty.

Families find different ways to manage the pressure created. Eric Berne, in his study of Games People Play, found, for example, that many fathers and teenage daughters play a game of door slamming which at once expresses their sexual attraction for each other but also keeps the doors safely closed. In a very few families, people are comfortable enough about their own sexuality so that parents and children can talk easily of their sexual feelings for each other and even to express them. Things seem to work out, on the average, about as often for children in either of these kinds of families.

Your family appears to have been caught somewhere in the middle – not comfortable with sexual feelings or their expression, but not keeping them really in check. And now what you experienced as a problem then is showing up in your marriage.

In one sense your situation is common. The story of Oedipus, the Greek ruler who unknowingly married his mother, is not

211

such a timeless and moving tragedy because Oedipus was so unique, but because he was Everyman. Unwittingly, almost everyone marries his or her mother (or father or brother or sister), then blinds himself to the fact. We repeat in our new families many of the same patterns of behaviour with the same kinds of co-operation we grew up with. After all, these are the ones we know best, even if we don't always like them.

Dreams, like the ones you write of, are the ways we try to reprogramme or reorganize ourselves to solve such dilemmas in our lives. We dream about things we want and don't want all at once (like making love with your father).

The question of whether or not you actually had intercourse with him seems important to you now. It would have been difficult, if not impossible, for him to have had intercourse with you without you being awake. There are other questions, however, concerning the sexual and relationship problems with your husband, which are probably more important for you to solve. Putting the blame on yourself and past experiences with your father, hoping to 'work them out of your system', bypasses the very real problems you acknowledge in your marriage today.

The problem is to begin to separate your reactions to your father when you were young from your reactions to your husband now. Your sexual experiences with your parents, even to intercourse with your father if it did happen, need not become a block to happiness in your marriage and won't unless you let it. Work on this relationship here and now, perhaps with professional help for you and your husband as a couple. Not an easy assignment, but you have a head start in recognizing some of the problems involved.

OVERSEXED

I wonder if many people have any idea of the miseries of being born what used to be called 'oversexed' in a puritan section of society.

It started when I was very young. I used to like to comfort myself with a hand at my vagina and my mother would smack me if she caught me. Later when she found how much I preferred to have a bath with my year-older brother she suddenly stopped that too.

I loved playing with boys even at eight or nine, especially forbidden games like 'Doctors and Nurses' or 'dares' which usually ended with my hated navy blue knickers off. By this time my brother and I were in separate beds. When my mother saw me naked at the mirror examining the first swellings of my breasts, I was hastily given a separate bedroom.

I think she was also oversexed and worried about it and saw reflected in me her own failings. When I was 11 years old, I was dragged to a shop for a bra which I kept finding excuses not to wear all my school life – even being brought home by a puritanical mistress from school for 'not having it mended'. The other girls derisively called me 'sexpot' because I would always join in a group of boys going down to the river.

I was about 10 or 11 when with the help of my brother I first discovered my cervix and how in the dark the tip of his prick seemed to feel the same. Perhaps as a result of this experimental fumbling I was nicely opened up and had no problems or pains the first time he put his prick right inside me. But somehow it was more interesting when his pals did this, and less alarming when I could get another girl to come along on these early experiments – which was unfortunately rarely for they didn't really enjoy them. I did, and never had any trouble reaching climax.

I was very chuffed, when at last I got some decent pubic fuzzy and thought it would never start to grow under my arms like on our sexy French 'Assistant' whom I idolized. My clit also at last grew and got very sensitive and sometimes I got very moist (and I think smelly) between my legs.

My parents were always asking who I went to play with, what time I would be home, why I had so few girlfriends. So I took to cultivating girlfriends as a cover, and wearing my bra and knickers to school but removing them in the loo at four o'clock before taking the 'long way' home. Luckily my parents did not get home till 6.30. But a couple of teachers got suspicious one day we had slipped away from class. Some of the others had time to get their slacks up and their skirts down somewhat but I was climaxing and squealing a bit and a boy and I were caught right in the act!

After that I had to report to my parents' shop at 4.30 daily, and work till six! I joined everything from Guides to dancing classes to get away from home and see my boyfriends. But then I thought I was pregnant. The magazines said 'first, tell your mum', and like an ass I did, and was dragged off to the doctor. I wasn't preggers – just late, but I was dragged to a psychiatrist who said I was a fine healthy girl who should go on the Pill.

Mum put a stop to consulting him and took to locking me in my room at times. I wore myself out with masturbation.

By 15 I had had a couple of serious love affairs. One was with a boy who satisfied me but was a gangleader and I was really quite relieved when jail stopped this. The other had a great big prick which I was very proud of being able to take when older girls were terrified of it. But he could seldom 'bring' me and I was back to masturbation till I met a smaller boy who liked me to come at the same time and joked and tried again if we didn't.

But with him I did get pregnant! This time I went to the psychiatrist bloke alone. He sent me back to our own doctor who was very decent. He gave me stuff which caused me to have one hell of a painful period and no abortion was needed. He then put me on the Pill – and the trouble I had hiding that from my mum!

I scraped enough passes to get (in spite of my school record) into a teacher training college. Even here I am still in trouble, for I have to wear a bra and short skirt and tights to go practice-teaching. I have got into a 'group flat' and my mother can do nothing except cut off my grant money. But I got VD and had passed it on to all the boys in the flat so all the boys and girls ended up at the clinic. Now we have little sex outside our group (which is enough for anyone with three girls and five men) except rarely at a party or something special.

Certainly when I become a teacher I shall be more sympathetic towards any girl whose problems really stem, not from being anti-social, but just from being 'oversexed'! I would not encourage a girl to experiment but if she was in fact doing so I would help her overcome the accompanying worries and strains by seeing that she did plenty of finger exploring before having the real thing to avoid pain and disappointment; seeing she knew the symptoms of VD and where to get help if it ever occurred; seeing that as soon as she is having periods at all regularly she goes on the Pill and knows where to get it – the right one for her. And that she doesn't think of marriage as a solution to the sex problem – if she's young it's apt to increase it.

Miss E.C.,
Scotland

If you'd been brought up in Samoa, it would have been your mother and teachers who were thought odd, not you. Whether we like it or not, we have to face the fact that children brought up without sexual repression are likely to be as free as you

214

*were. (I admire the sense of humour and basic common sense
with which you coped with the conflicts between your sex drive
and your environment. You seem neither to have acquired any
guilt, on the one hand, nor been driven by rebellion into having
more sex than you really wanted, on the other.)*

*Perhaps the strongest argument against early sex in our cul-
ture is that it will distract the child from acquiring the education necessary for economic survival. But in your case at least
I get the impression that the attitudes of your parents and teachers were probably more of a distraction than your sexual and
emotional involvements; yet in spite of both, you got your
exams. No one, I believe, has yet studied the relationship between academic success and sexual behaviour in the pre- and
early teens. It may be that the Freudian notion of sublimation is
correct: the child with no involvements putting his excess energy into school work. But it might also turn out that highly
sexed young people work better when there are no sexual frustrations to cope with.*

*It is high time we had more fact and less opinion to guide us
in this controversial area.*

SEXUAL FREEDOM

My husband and I started as surreptitious lovers at a time
when this just wasn't done, and suffered from much needless
persecution over sex matters. We decided when we married that
this was the reason for much of the violent side of sex activity
and that we would try to bring up our children in an atmosphere of loving permissiveness.

They say that sexual freedom exists only for the very rich or
the very very poor – neither of whom really care what the world
thinks.

Although my husband did come into an unexpected windfall
of considerable proportions we are not very rich but were able
to buy a house in its own grounds and raise a big family – two
boys and three girls of our own and an adopted boy and girl – in
financial comfort.

From the start, we made a point of caressing the babies'
genitals as much as any other part of their bodies and bringing
them up to see themselves and ourselves naked when appropriate indoors and outdoors when swimming in our pool or sunbathing.

We never put on a display of the sex act for their benefit, but our bedroom is never locked and we never objected when one or more of them came in and discovered us making love. Since we make love for the joy of it we don't find it necessary to use coarse language or extremes of pressure to have orgasms, though we may sigh with pleasure or squeal with satisfaction.

Although having many rooms to choose from (and each child had his or her own den) they usually preferred to sleep with at least one other when they chose to stop sharing our room, and of course enjoyed sexual exploration and mutual comforting when appropriate. The children learned eventually not to embarrass outsiders with the sort of conversation which they regarded as normal at home and even their cousins and occasional visiting friends seemed to quickly learn that while life was enjoyable at our place, it wasn't the norm, and that to discuss it outside was profitless.

Both my sister and my husband's sister hardly approve of our way of life, but the opportunity to leave their children for a day, week or month, seemed to be more important than their approval, to judge by the number of children we often had staying.

Both our adopted children had problems of behaviour in their first years but rapidly became calm like our own.

The oldest boy found at an early age the pleasure his younger sisters could give him and they both, by nine or ten, were pleased when they could take him inside their 'ginas 'like mummy does with daddy'. They even pretended to have orgasms and were very superior when he managed to ejaculate inside them – a first sign of maturity. When he obviously began to prefer this activity with girls outside the family circle they were a little disappointed till they discovered that their cousins were more fun to screw with, and eventually boys at school even more fun. This cycle went through the whole family but always the accent was on gentleness and pleasure, not rape or making it painful as a pander to guilt.

The boys were very interested in when they would need to start using french letters (of which we always ordered a bulk supply) and when it might be safe to screw without them. The girls were very impatient to have recognizable breasts, or decent pubic hair, periods, firm nipples and underarm hair in, I think, that order. Brassieres have just never been thought about unless in jokes in our family (except when I was nursing) and the girls would never risk spoiling their boobies by wearing them.

Having money we sent them all to an expensive progressive

216

local school (as day pupils). Here dress was not formal – though they dressed more 'modestly' than at home – and sexual activity was far more frequent than the staff imagined.

The cycle is now repeating itself as my son and oldest two daughters bring their own children to our house for weekends and holidays (one daughter has a son but refuses to marry).

Our youngest two are now at college and the girl, having been on the Pill since puberty, has enjoyed a freedom her older sisters never knew. I never believed in the chemicals one has to use with the diaphragm so taught them to be aware of their cycle and use condoms – or ask their boys to do so. As a result we had one pregnancy – our oldest daughter – and she refused to have an abortion (at 19) and took a year off college to have her baby. Again, being rich made it easy! Poorer girls would have a less easy choice. But she enjoyed the experience, loves the child and is now on the Pill and having a varied love life while her younger sister is happily married to a man 10 years older than herself.

One of our girls has been quite cool (if competent) about sex. The other three could all have orgasms by about 13 or 14, either by themselves or mutually masturbating or with any boy who knew enough to bring them. The cool one has had an affair lasting four years with a medical student (the others have more hectic sex lives). Surprisingly, she is the only one who has ever had any venereal trouble. (Her student gave her a dose after their first night together to his tremendous embarrassment and her sardonic surprise.)

None of our children would make good Army material unless in defence of their children, perhaps. But all have been brought up to know sex as a friendly, expressive thing and nudity as a healthy, sometimes sensible thing. The girls all started on tampons from their first period and none has ever made much fuss or complained of pain. None of the family has become inward-looking because of masturbation or incest. None has found any satisfaction other than curiosity or temporary consolation from homosexual relationships. None has found (though they are still young) any need for experiment in any exotic forms of sex. All have found group sex a warm confidence-inspiring experience and all except one like a great deal of sex (though not all now wish a variety of partners).

In our 50s, my husband and I still enjoy frequent screwing though we don't get the thrill we used to – nor crave it.

With travel, music, sailing, to live for, and especially our families, we live very contented lives, quite proud that we can still bring each other more than once a night and often do so several nights in a week.

Mrs S.N.,
Southampton

Judging from letters to Forum, *many parents who have tried to bring their children up in sexual freedom have run into problems – to the extent that* Forum *consultants generally warn against going too far in this direction.*

Yet you appear to have been lucky; your children seem to have become warm, well-adjusted people with fulfilling sex lives but no obsessions on the subject.

There are a few hints from your letter as to how this has been achieved; though much of the secret probably lies in your own personalities and the good parental relationhip you were able to hold up as a model for your children.

First, you seem never to have forced sexual activity on the children; and they always had privacy (their own rooms) when they wanted it.

You seem neither to have encouraged nor discouraged incest. Your attitude seems both to have protected the children against guilt feelings when they found out how society views it, without promoting it to an extent that made outside relationships difficult to form.

You contrived to make your children proud of their bodies and their sexual capacities without voyeurism on your part or encouraging exhibitionism on theirs.

Most difficult of all, you managed to get across the message that home was different from outside, and that behaviour appropriate to one was not appropriate elsewhere, without causing any conflict between these different norms nor rebellion against yours in adolescence.

I still could not recommend the type of upbringing you gave your children wholesale; inhibition, guilt feelings, suppressed voyeurism or incestuous wishes can do so much harm. Children are very sensitive to 'unconscious' motives and, precisely because such feelings are unconscious, it is very difficult for a parent to be sure his or her motives are really healthy. What works for fully loving, sexually happy parents like yourselves can do much damage if applied by others with emotional and sexual hangups. Even so, your letter contains many useful pointers for parents who do wish to give it a try.

NOT READY FOR SEX

I am 15 years old and am afraid I may have a problem. I hate the thought of intercourse, and yet very often dream about it.

My father is all for my getting into intercourse, saying, 'You haven't lived until you've tried fucking'. My mother remains distant about the whole thing. She hates me even to swear, much less be around when they're telling dirty jokes.

I have tried masturbation a couple of times, and hate it. And yet, when a boy tries to feel me up, I freeze, and refuse to let him touch me again. Do you think this might hurt my chances of getting a husband? Am I frigid?

I have read *Forum* a few times (with my father's blessing) and decided you might be able to give me some sensible advice. It's not as though I feel insecure about the whole thing. I have nothing to worry about, because both mom and dad plan on getting me on the Pill soon. Unfortunately, I believe that sex belongs only in marriage; this is a belief of my own choosing. Could there be anything wrong with me?

Miss S.M.,
Address withheld by request

Assuming that your dreams about intercourse are pleasurable (since you did not indicate otherwise), I think that your fundamental attitude towards sex is probably healthy. Sometimes, those who love you the most try to either overshelter you or encourage you to get involved in things for which you are simply not prepared. Different people have varying emotional and physical capacities in coping with important developments like sexual awakening. You sound like a very sensitive young woman and it may well be that you are not quite ready to have sexual relations without a great deal of prior consideration and, perhaps, emotional maturity. Do not let anyone force you into anything prematurely. You must decide to follow your instincts at your own pace; when the time is right, you'll know it. Furthermore, regarding your anxiety about being frigid, there is no reason to make any assumptions about yourself so early in your life.

TEENAGE SEX

SWEDISH ADOLESCENCE

I was interested in the liberated lady who found the more rigid mores of the United States a frustrating problem. I myself am in some despair that I do not know how to let my own children enjoy the advantages of the liberal upbringing I myself enjoyed.

I was brought up in Sweden in a family which even by Swedish standards was liberal for its time. We spent all our holidays at my grandfather's lakeside summer house, where the loft was a den and dormitory for usually upwards of a dozen cousins and close friends aged about seven to 17, of both sexes.

In summer we not only slept, sauna'd, swam but sunbathed, sailed and often ran about quite naked. When any of the girls amongst us (rarely) wore a frock instead of unisex jeans and singlets the last thing we ever thought of was wearing knickers. They were just things you wore for a couple of days during the worst of your period. If any of us had bought a bra we would have had to learn how to fasten it!

We often went away overnight in mixed groups for fishing, camping or walking trips. I don't really remember my first experience with sex for I probably wasn't even at school, but do remember at about eight or so that my brother managed to get a finger in my vagina while I managed to tease his penis into an erection. It was certainly long before my first period that my cousin managed a penile penetration with me and I had been able to take and I think enjoy two fingers quite a bit before that.

I certainly could 'bring' my cousins and pals to some sort of climax before either they or I really reached puberty and enjoyed being able to, but never had an orgasm myself till I was about 14. I am sure some of the other girls did manage this younger.

A high spot in our sex careers was going proudly to grandfather (who was a doctor) for a diaphragm after our periods arrived. Carrying a diaphragm in one's purse gave far more satisfaction than carrying cigarettes to today's adolescents and no drugs or drink could have given us a better trip than the one we got when we learned to have orgasms.

Another high spot was the bawdy but not cruel jokes when I

walked proudly but obviously a little sorely for a couple of days when at 14 I was determined to not only accommodate but bring to a decent climax my 16-year-old cousin's pal who was noted for the size of his penis. Another was going away with two of the boys in a tiny tent for the weekend at 15. We always found an extra boy better than an extra girl if there were uneven numbers, for we had no hang-ups over privacy and girls recover quicker for more.

Sweden being notably illogical, we had all sorts of rules in spite of our apparent freedom – largely unwritten but fairly well observed.

Never have intercourse with the same partner twice running – to avoid emotional attachments too young (often broken, this one). Never take a chance in the unsafe period and always double contraception in the danger days. A terrible drag, this! Never try to force the sex scene, but never unreasonably refuse to have intercourse with someone needing it.

In spite of all this I only remember one girl, my sister, getting herself pregnant – and going promptly and without qualms to grandfather who dealt with it equally promptly and without reproach.

We indulged in little except fairly straightforward intercourse (but plenty of that) and it all took place naturally amid a hectic life of sailing, swimming, tennis, dancing, music and the rest.

We felt it just as rude to sit hiding sexual parts from our group as we would have felt it rude to needlessly display them before strangers. So that we girls never pulled our legs together when sitting down in skirts, tugged at skirts on windy days, or pulled unbuttoned blouses across our breasts, when leaning forward. Thus we never looked lewd no matter how skimpily dressed we were when going into town.

Some problems arose: my sister's frequent inflammation of the vagina made her very sad at times as did my cousin's tight foreskin, till grandfather sorted these out. A schoolfriend had a tough hymen, but she was also treated and advised to have very frequent intercourse all summer to prevent it reforming – to the delight of the boys and eventually herself, but to our slight envy!

By about 17 this promiscuity began to wane in favour of more emotional and personal attachments, so that when student life made these trips to the summer house more difficult we didn't miss them so much.

From experiments with living with someone I have progressed to marriage and having a family and am now teaching. My only worry is that here in Scotland my two girls and a boy may not grow up to experience the wonderful young way of life that I was so privileged to enjoy. Believe me, whatever some of the experts say, I cannot imagine that the free, casual acceptance of sex that I grew up with can do anything but good.

Mrs S.T.,
Aberdeen

NAUGHTY OR NORMAL?

When I was 12 I was sent to an expensive boarding school in Surrey. In no time, the nosy girls in the dorm had wormed out of me all my details and when I admitted I wasn't exactly a virgin they invited me to join the club. This was a group of about a dozen girls aged 12 to 16 who ran a sex service for the school more for fun than for money. The staff were all boring and wouldn't get a job in any decent school and either they never noticed or 'E' the oldest girl had them terrified as she had all the other girls too terrified to tell by blackmail. We had to wear a little red badge on our grotty grey jerseys which had nothing underneath, just as we wore nothing under our pleated grey non-miniskirts. And we had to be ready to oblige the boys at any time. We carried a lot of paper tissues!

For a bob it was hands up our jersey and a bash up our skirt in the classroom, common room or store cupboard. For two bob (later 10p) it was skirts and jerseys off – though we often kept our white socks on. For five bob we'd smuggle the boy into our dorm and have him in bed for the night. For ten bob we'd step down to the boys' dorm and have as many of them as wanted. We soon became very popular and quite well off and it was really quite exciting and daring. I was big but skinny and my periods didn't start till I was 14 so I was very popular for the boys didn't need the extra price of a french letter. Plenty of girls in this school were neurotic sloppy sobbers but all the girls in the Club seemed cheery types and none the worse for the fun. In fact only the hols were a drag, when we missed it a bit.

Then my parents came up here and as the school didn't cater for older pupils I went to a very snob school here and all the girls were shocked that we charged the boys for it and said no one did that any more. They are much more strict and you have to be terribly careful where you do it and where you hide the used french letters. But the girls here aren't so smart.

I soon learnt how to judge my safe period by the states of my tits and my cunt. The boys like it much more without a letter and so do I but I get two very randy spells and one is right at my danger time so I have to be very careful. The other comes right before my period and is best fun. The boys at this school are older and much better at it and I like to have it off with someone most days of the week. I go a bit off my work at my period, or if for any reason I'm not getting balled enough (which is a pity for I'm taking maths and science which calls for concentration).

As before, the real mixed-up morbid girls here are the ones who are not getting it (their own fault) and maybe the ones who are having love affairs and not continuing to mix it as I do no matter how much I fall for one of the boys here.

Miss M.J.,
Perthshire

It is always pleasing to hear from an enthusiast, but while I don't think there is anything in the least inherently improbable in what you say, clinical experience has taught me to be a little sceptical about unreservedly accepting a young adolescent girl's account of her sexual behaviour. Such girls can be very fanciful and I have no doubt that many of the stories purveyed to the press by some gynaecologists, psychiatrists and social workers with the aim of 'proving' how permissive and degenerate are today's youth, represent no more than the sex fantasies of their early and mid-adolescent female patients. I have often seen adolescents who claim all manner of activity but who are demonstrable virgins. Interestingly, too, the stories are not fabrications in the usual sense but are often sincerely believed.

However, I do agree with your general theory that women with an unsatisfactory sex life suffer. Since at least Greek times the man – or woman – in the street has assumed that this was the cause of neurotic behaviour in women. However, some of your 'neurotic sloppy sobbers' may have been so reared that they will only adjust to their heterosexual duties with difficulty or perhaps not at all. The trouble may not be so much a direct sexual one as an emotional one or a difficulty in interpersonal relations. Simply undertaking sexual activity of your type may make them worse and not better. So sex itself may not be the primary need of a neurotic woman.

What you say about your first school certainly rings true. Girls – unlike boys – tend to divide themselves into a number of separate groups and the 'naughty' ones do get together to form one of these. Usually they look down on the rest and think the other girls are backward and silly, as indeed you did.

Since you are at a boarding school, it may be that your home background has not been fully conducive to absolutely normal development. You say your behaviour with boys is devoid of emotion and so it occurs to me that really your sexual activity amounts to masturbation, just replacing your fingers and fantasies with boys and their penises. You may be more guilty about your sexuality underneath than some of the 'sloppy sobbers'. Most girls of your age at least 'play' at relationships with boys, and while they may be involved in mutual masturbation, the majority have not gone as far as intercourse. Those who have may be precocious, or over-guilty about masturbation or they may have had a disturbed relationship with their mothers or fathers when small.

Again, I am fully prepared to agree that it is sensible to have relationships with lots of boys during adolescence; but if the need to love and to be loved by one person develops in late adolescence an erstwhile 'promiscuous' girl may find she can't give up casual sex in return for commitment. Sometimes an earlier disturbance of emotional development may be the cause of the 'promiscuity' but the trouble is that 'promiscuous' behaviour in earlier adolescence may impair subsequent emotional and psycho-sexual development. At some stage in her teens, a girl must fully accept responsibility for her own personal sexuality if she is to grow up 'normally'. If she is unable to do this she may rush round after boys with the immature aim of allowing them – perhaps apparently justified by the payment of money – to give her the pleasure she is unable, due to guilt, to give herself by masturbation. This discourages 'normal' sexual development and such girls often have difficulty in obtaining orgasms later. This is a paradox since the causes of this type of 'promiscuous' behaviour are, in point of fact, excessive guilt and inhibition!

However, I don't want to sound gloomy. I know many women who behaved as you are doing and yet grew up perfectly well. The points for you to watch are the avoidance of pregnancy, efficiently learning how to 'accept' orgasms, and to pay attention to emotional development. If you can combine these with your present cheerful and cheeky attitudes you should turn into a happy woman. You must remember though *that there is more to sex than just sex if we are to obtain the fullest pleasure from it. (Consultant)*

'I JUST LIE THERE – BUT IT WORKS!'

I am 18. My fiancé and I have a fine sex life. We have had intercourse about 15 to 20 times but I have only just experienced a complete and wonderful orgasm. I feel guilty because I think I reached this climax in a selfish way during our love-making.

When the usual pumping and thrusting during intercourse speeded up, I knew my boyfriend was reaching his climax, while I wasn't near orgasm yet. I suddenly allowed my body to go completely limp, with my legs slightly spread apart and my arms thrown above my head. I lay absolutely still while he thrust furiously in and out of me. When I relaxed, his penis felt wonderfully deep inside my body – I had an incredibly strong climax! I couldn't budge for about 15 minutes!

I would love to continue achieving orgasm in this manner but is it selfish to lie so still? Also, for a good orgasm, must the clitoris always be stimulated during intercourse? While my boyfriend pumps, my clitoris is never stimulated in the missionary position. Can you suggest any other position which will cause it to be stimulated during intercourse? The only way we have been able to do this is when he manipulates me with his fingers during penetration.

Miss D.G.,
Address withheld by request

All orgasm is good orgasm! Some methods affect some women more intensely than others, but whatever turns you on during intercourse is good! You seem to respond well to both clitoral and vaginal stimulation. If totally relaxing when you know you are reaching the point of no return is stimulating for you, I see no reason for guilt or hesitation. Furthermore, your partner seems to be bringing himself off during intercourse by uninterrupted thrusting so nothing seems to be changing except that you are enjoying more effective climaxes when you relax your muscles.

There are various ways your boyfriend can stimulate your clitoris with his penis during intercourse. Placing a pillow beneath your buttocks will allow him more effective access to your clitoris as well as deeper penetration of your vagina. Just before the moment of no return, your boyfriend can brush and/or directly apply pressure to your clitoris with his penis. One of the most effective positions for penile stimulation is the female 'superior', in which the woman sits or lies astride her lover. She can manipulate his penis to her own and to his satisfaction. This way, you can do the thrusting and feel his deeper penetration. When on top you can rub his penis along the top rim of your vagina allowing for clitoral stimulation.

If your boyfriend enters you from behind, he can easily manipulate your clitoris with his fingers, or you can do it yourself.

Experiment with new positions. You don't have to fit yourself into a category, like 'I only come when I totally relax my body'. Discuss your technique, passions and problems with your lover. He might have some suggestions too!

16-YEAR-OLD'S WORRY

I am 16 years old and bisexual. I am in love with another girl, my stepsister.

When we go on double dates with guys, I envy the guy she is with. I spend a lot of time with her. I hold her hand sometimes while we are playing around, and once I danced with her. I have known her about a year and a half; my feelings for her grow stronger each day.

I think I'm more of a lesbian than bisexual, because boys turn me off. I still date them and so on, but I am very shy and won't take my clothes off. Like a boy I like to call the shots, be the aggressor.

My stepsister's friendship means a lot to me, so how do I tell her that I want her. Maybe I could kiss her when she playfully puts her arms around my neck, but would she get mad?

Miss T.R.,
North Carolina

You say that you are bisexual, then later in your letter that you are more of a lesbian. Perhaps you are not very sure just yet which way your feelings are going to settle. Lots of people have these doubts, especially at your kind of age.

Your stepsister sounds very attractive and exciting, and I am not surprised that you want more physical contact with her. I think you are wise, though, not to have tried to rush her into sex play. For one thing, it may be that she is only seriously

226

*physically interested in guys, in which case you might worry her
and embarrass yourself if you suddenly let her know just how
much you desire her. For another thing, I'm not convinced that
you have dated enough boys yet to be sure that there aren't some
who could turn you on. Perhaps the double dates are not such a
good idea if you really want to find out whether you could
respond physically to some rather special male, who would only
be in the shadow of your stepsister if you met them together.
(The right man for you might be someone who likes his women
to call the shots!)*

*Even if you do – tactfully – take your passion for your step-
sister further, and she reacts as you hope, I still think that you
ought not to label yourself lesbian for some years at least, and
not until you have had a lot more social life independently of
her. You may find that, important as these romantic feelings for
her are just now, they don't last for ever. I hope that you will
discover that you can love more than one person in a lifetime,
and that some day you will have more freedom of choice than
at present seems possible to you.*

MOTHER READS MY DIARY

I am 17 years old and still a virgin. My story started about
three years ago. I used to get on with girls very well. I did just
about everything with these girls except having sexual intercourse.

I recorded all this in my diary but my mother found the diary
and read it. My parents then began questioning me on what I
had done; they made me so ashamed and so disgusted with what
I had done and they wouldn't let me out of the house for three
months. Since then I have been very shy and I have only had
two girlfriends whom I got nowhere with. I have been to about
five dances but I just can't seem to have the courage to make a
pass at a girl any more.

This problem is so worrying; it is having a noticeable effect
on my work.

Could you please help me.

*S.H.,
Buckinghamshire*

*The very unfortunate occurrence of your parents discovering
your diary and being so critical in their attitude is one which
might well be expected to make you become a little unsure of*

yourself. But you should not now avoid situations where you might come into contact with girls because of this experience; you should continue to date them, although perhaps taking your time about carrying out loveplay with them. Try to date the girls, talk to them and become relaxed and at ease with them before making any physical advances. When you feel comfortable and confident in just chatting to them – and girls very much like being chatted to! – then go on and in a relaxed way start to hold their hands, put your arms round them, kiss them, caress them and while you are doing this, try and concentrate on the very pleasurable feeling which is associated with touching and caressing a girl . . .

At dances, you might do well first of all just to dance and make no pass. If you find that you are dancing in a relaxed way and can talk to her between dances then just continue to chat to her and get at ease before attempting to become more friendly.

By using a gradual approach you should find you very quickly regain your confidence and that you can continue and carry on the sexual explorations where you left off before the episode of the diary.

I would add that if present home conditions are unchanged then it might be a bad idea to keep another detailed diary! Clearly this is something which concerns your mother and there would not be any great advantage in increasing her anxiety.

Try not to feel guilty about what you have done, as everything you report is quite normal and the sort of thing one would expect any functioning person to do at your age. My strongest advice is to try as soon as possible to pick up where you left off and do it in the way I have outlined. Don't worry if you stay a virgin for a while – most boys your age are.

BOYFRIEND GETS LEFT BEHIND

I have a big problem and a question. I'm 17 and a virgin. When my boyfriend fondles my breasts or genitals, I have orgasms which last about one to two minutes. When I have these orgasms I shake all over and my boyfriend holds me close till I stop.

After the first orgasm all he has to do is touch me in an intimate place and I'm sent back into ecstasy. We would have had intercourse long ago if I didn't always react so violently. I want to have intercourse with him, but he spends all his time trying to calm me down. I enjoy orgasms tremendously, but I want him to enjoy some excitement too!!

I know all this sounds too wild to be true. I even counted my orgasms one night, just out of curiosity; and found I had close to 25 in little more than an hour. I need a solution. Is there any way I can delay my orgasms until the right moment so my boyfriend can enjoy our lovemaking too?

Ms J.E.,
Address withheld by request

Often – to people who are new to the experience of orgasm – the feeling of being out of control or seeing someone else out of control is frightening. However, it is nothing to fear; rather, it is an experience to be enjoyed by both partners. It seems as though the problem is not yours but your boyfriend's. I don't see why it is necessary for him to be constantly calming you down (unless you keep the neighbours awake). It would be advisable for you to tell him there is nothing to fear from your excitement and not to worry about calming you down, but to continue with the sex act while you are having your orgasms. It also might be advisable at this point in your sex life together – if you both desire to have intercourse – to refrain from any foreplay and begin immediately with penetration.

Some 14 per cent of the women Kinsey talked to claim to experience mutiple orgasm, as you do. At that time, they were not believed – but Masters and Johnson have confirmed that these repeated orgasms are indeed genuine. They write: 'If a female who is capable of having regular orgasm is properly stimulated within a short period after her first climax, she will in most instances be capable of having a second, third, fourth, and even fifth and sixth orgasm before she is fully satiated'. Indeed, they observed women who were capable, like you, of reaching full orgasm many more times than this.

CAN'T SAY NO

I read Dr Chartham's book 'Sex for Beginners' and I think it's fabulous. I've learned a lot of new things from it. But I still have this terrible problem. I'm almost 16 and I'm more on the quiet side. I've gone out twice and both the boys I went out with wanted to couple. I didn't because I feel I'm too young but I let them because I didn't want them to think of me as a prude. I don't think I have got the reputation of a prostitute, yet, but I might soon if I go on like this. The problem is that I don't know how to tell a boy to stop and if he asks me why, I don't know what to say. I admit, I'd rather be a prude than a prostitute but I'd rather be an in-between than anything. Please help.

Miss T.F.,
Address withheld by request

I must point out that sex in England is illegal until the age of 16. Believe me, you do not have a problem at all. Just as we all have a right to sexual experience, so we have an equal right to refuse a sexual experience if we don't want one.

A short time ago I asked 300 young unmarried men what they thought of female virginity. More than three-quarters said it was nonsense. A little later I asked, 'Do you want your wife to be a virgin when you marry her?' and three-fifths said, 'Yes'! How stupid can men be? If you don't want to ball – don't ball! That is your right.

Of course, the boys you say No to will say all sorts of unkind things at the time. This is natural, because they are so sexually tense. But when they calm down, they will respect you much more than the girl who always says Yes. (Robert Chartham)

GROUP SEX

I am a young girl of 19 and my life is in ruins. I was a 'Gang-bang Moll' and went out of my way to be abused by them.

I have been in six gang bangs up till now and I am the talk of the neighbourhood.

I got VD as well as the shame. I would like to warn girls like me to shy clear of these scum.

At first I thought it would be good to have eight guys make me at the one time. I was so trendy and thought I was 'with it' but looking back to the action I remember vividly one boy in my vagina, and one in my mouth and after them the others – mostly in my vagina, and the obscene language was terrible.

To be honest I enjoyed the action up to a point but the numbers sometimes became impossible like the time I was pretty drunk. I was sore as hell.

Now I have made up my mind to leave the district because of wagging tongues. I have also been threatened by older girls. Now I am alone. All I feel is shame and remorse. I hate myself completely.

I hope this warns other girls to avoid gang bangs like a plague.

Name and address withheld
by request

The story you tell is a common theme in female sexual fantasy. That some women put the fantasy into practice is only to be expected. There are many precedents for this sort of behaviour including several famous and powerful women. Usually, however, the women involved are young, emotionally immature and in contact with males who are still sufficiently adolescent to consort together in groups. Apart from these there are some professional women who 'entertain' all the members of business conferences in their hotel. Usually they work in pairs and put on a lesbian show to warm up their clients beforehand.

I think you are being very hard on yourself. What you have done does not make you a bad girl – only an unwise one. You are still young and still a year or two away from adulthood so you can't be expected to be a fount of all wisdom. Whether the moralist likes it or not, and whether most women will admit to it or not, girls of your age do have a tendency to be attracted to very many males and all have a potential for promiscuity. It is a form of learning. All you seem to have done is to concentrate your promiscuities into a few episodes. This is why you were unwise; due to the very circumstances you let too many people know of your sexual behaviour.

Girls who are known to have experience of a lot of men can have difficulty in finding a partner, since the male fears adverse comparison with others. Women, on the other hand, tend to be hostile and critical towards other females with a lot of sexual experience. This is partly inspired by jealousy, partly by fear of the possible threat to their own relationships and partly by the projection of their own guilt about their sexual fantasies on to the woman who is being criticized. In this way they can assert their own 'purity'. It is due to the projection of sex guilt that women are much harsher on each other than men are on women.

I guess you did not have a great deal of previous sexual experience before you embarked on these escapades. Paradoxically it is the sexually inhibited who are the most attracted to orgies. Your inhibitions are likely to have prevented you from acquiring as much experience as the average girl of your age. You probably suffered from above-average doses of guilt when younger. One pattern of behaviour that an inhibited girl may follow in late adolescence is to have first intercourse with a male of whom she thinks little. This is then followed by a bout of really promiscuous behaviour which lasts a few months or even a year or two. At some stage – as in your case – her conscience takes over and she is horrified at what she has done. She may become very depressed and always loses self-confidence. This can be very severe if she gets pregnant and/or VD in the process.

Helpful steps you can take are to stop condemning yourself and realize that it is our social conventions which are to blame. They are too frustrating; you did your best to obey but were overcome by natural urges. If you had been less guilty about sex you would never have found yourself in this situation but would have taken to sex more easily. In some cultures what you have done would be considered admirable!

It would be best for your own peace of mind to leave and go somewhere new. This will help restore your confidence. Stop being inhibited and learn to enjoy normal sex. Resolve not to have intercourse until you have known the man for some weeks. Instead concentrate on foreplay techniques until you are sure a relationship exists. However, don't make a thing of not having intercourse. Don't tell any future partner about these activities but don't worry that he might find out. You have been silly but there is no point in punishing yourself for life. Your life is not in ruins unless you now make it so.

One final word of advice – do try to avoid going back to these scenes in fantasy and particularly do not use them in masturbation or you might find yourself repeating the experiences.

WANTS TO BE A PRO

I get fed up with every job I try and I would like to make some money out of sex, which is the only thing I'm good at and can't get enough of.

I am 18 now but started sex young (at primary school) and now am only really happy if I come about three times in a day. I don't seem to be really able to fall in love with any fellow seriously but I get one big kick out of bringing a fellow, especially when I come myself.

I've looked after myself and I look OK without needing tons of make-up. I haven't worn a bra for years so my tits are tough enough and big enough and thrive on a lot of handling. The nipples stand out well enough to show against most shirts or jerseys. I haven't worn knickers since I was old enough to leave school, so my cunt never gives me any trouble now with discharges; once I took five blokes in one group in one night without being all that sore afterwards.

I've got a sun lamp now so I've no white marks on my tits or arse, so I think I should be able to make some money as I can bring almost any male between 14 and 60 – I know for I've tried. I can't dance for I'm no good with music. I think I could model but I prefer action. I don't want to get in with any ring or pimps or anything. I live in a flat now but it's too bad to take anyone older to.

Surely there must be some way a girl can start honestly, and give good value and enjoy her work without the pros or the pimps or the gangs busting in?

I've had to leave two jobs after the men talking when I'd had most of them, but I never charged because I liked it.

> *Miss M.P.,*
> *Sussex*

Your letter worries me. It's good for you to take a pride in your female form and your female functions, but I am less sure about the desirability of using them for income at your age.

You seem to be developing normally physically and are well adapted to your sexual role, but I think your emotional development is lagging behind. You seem to have no clear idea of what type of man suits you best; and indeed you appear to see them all as a set of genitals against which your own sexual skills can be pitted. However, from the indirect evidence in your letter it seems you probably have a preference for older men.

What worries me is that if you concentrate on earning a living from your sexuality this might well enable you to stifle emotional and personality development – which is not complete at your age – to an extent that will ultimately make it impossible for you ever to enter a satisfactory one-to-one relationship. At 18 this might not seem much of a point. As you get older it will probably be experienced as an increasing deprivation. Perhaps you really feel no man will love you, so you are already ignoring this aspect of your needs and prefer to take money from men instead.

Although three orgasms a day is by no means excessive in a

233

girl of your age, I think you are using your sexuality as an excuse to avoid facing up to emotional needs and to work. A woman, with a little organization, can easily find sex partners at places other than work so you don't really have to lose your jobs by seducing all the men.

In short the arguments you put forward to convince yourself to earn money from your sexuality do not seem very good.

A woman can earn money from sex by exhibiting her body in various ways, by using her body for directly sexual purposes, by using her personality or by using her brains. The first includes erotic modelling for photographs, fashion modelling, acting including nude or near nude posing, films, modelling for anatomy and art students, and work in strip clubs or topless establishments. Agencies exist that will obtain work for suitable girls in all or any of these forms of employment. Many such girls stick simply to this type of work but others pass into, or also indulge in, the second category and thereby become occasional prostitutes, temporary mistresses and the like in return either for cash or gifts. Others enter full time prostitution usually under encouragement from someone else.

Other forms of prostitution such as the call-girl type or hospitality-prostitution on behalf of companies and perhaps official bodies is more difficult and would, presumably, depend on establishing contacts.

The third category, which basically depends on the personality, exists in many forms. It would include escort work and hostess work in clubs. (Sometimes this is just a front for prostitution but sometimes it is not.) Forms of work which do not demand the direct sexual use of the woman's body but depend more on her personality and attractiveness such as massage establishments, 'hands-only' girls and women who flagellate men could come under this heading as could sales-girls who are employed to sell directly to men. Some highly paid personal secretaries are employed for their intelligence, looks and personality rather than any particular skills. This category merges into work for which women have a particular suitability. If you could tolerate a little discipline, you might find nursing a very satisfactory career which could solve some of your problems.

Unless you feel very compelled to enter the second category, I would advise you to postpone a decision for another year or two and then see what you think about it. In the meantime, experiment with fewer but closer relationships.

SCHOOLGIRL QUERY

When my parents were away my older sister had a party for her school and other friends. Some left early but those who stayed started strip games which they let me join in for a bit of fun. Eventually they were all in rooms or corners snogging and poking and I was left out of it and bored. I found a boy with no partner and asked him if he would like to try it with me and he agreed for he was bored too. Now I know his cock wasn't very big for he got in quite easily and I was really enjoying it till my sister came along and humiliated me and made me put my knickers on.

I often go home from school with a certain boy and we had often had a good feel of each other but now I agreed to let him in properly but he was much bigger and I was very dry or something and it was just sore and no fun. For a week I opened myself gently with vaseline on my fingers and slept with a candle up in me and can now get a boy's cock inside me easily and I think a lot of the boys at school like me because I really enjoy having my knickers off and am not always sore or discharging or menstruating like some of the other girls in our mob. But I like it only when I'm with a bunch of others and get dry and tight if I go with a bloke all by myself and try to make love. Is this just because I'm young (13), or I need a few boys and girls around to be confident?

I think my sister was 15 when our doctor put her on the Pill on the quiet and she hadn't been having periods for all that long. Should I get him to give me the Pill or wait till my periods start? I don't want to have to start buying rubbers for I like to feel the boys come all wet and warm inside me – besides they don't like them either.

I have enough tits now to show a good shape without a bra but my nipples don't show up points on my blouse or T-shirts. Does the Pill cause this or must I do exercises to get decent nipples? I haven't much hair on my fanny and think maybe the Pill makes this grow quicker. Then older boys with bigger cocks would like to have me and would maybe bring me all the way more often. I also want to do very well at school and get a decent job. I do my school work better when I'm going a lot with boys. Will the Pill make me moody and spoil my work or make me so sick I can't concentrate?

Miss A.B.,
Scotland

Letters such as yours are always very difficult to answer. I don't want to put you off your enthusiasm for sex – which is good – but your letter and general experience indicate that you are not acting in your own best long-term interests.

I am not being negative. If I could see no harm I would say so but the fact is that too early intercourse does seem to injure, at least in the case of many girls, subsequent personality development, later capacity for full sexual response and also the ability to relate to an individual male in a total manner.

It is difficult to explain why this is so. In theory, early resort to intercourse could be due to the girl possessing some disturbance in her personality derived from an 'abnormal' relationship with her parents when she was a child. If this is the case, then her sexual behaviour is but one manifestation of her disturbance and later on the other upsets I list above will also emerge. This would mean that her sexual behaviour is an effect and not a cause of subsequent troubles.

However, this is theory and in practice sex is obviously the most important way in which we relate to members of the opposite sex. Early experience is of importance and probably governs all subsequent sexual activity. In growing up – doing anything before we are ready can be harmful for this reason.

On your own admission you felt humiliated by your sister, you have had to stretch your vagina and you feel uncomfortable in circumstances other than an orgy. In fact you can't perform properly without others being present. Perhaps what it all amounts to is that you are inhibited over masturbation and are really using boys as masturbatory instruments. If so, you should concentrate on overcoming your prime inhibition rather than continuing your present activities. Masturbation, which at your age implies a real acceptance of your own sexuality, is an important way in which efficiency in intercourse is learned. Being a girl you can always accept penetration but this doesn't necessarily teach you how to accept yourself as a sexual being. In learning how to copulate, you may never learn how to have intercourse.

You can become pregnant before the periods first start but it is rare. The Pill is not the answer since it can stop you growing and until your periods start you will keep on growing. The hormones in the Pill can assist with nipple and pubic hair development, but your own hormones will eventually do the job themselves. Nipples, of course, are not usually erect except when cold or as a result of sexual excitement.

*From every point of view, the best advice is to take a step
backwards towards masturbation and, if you wish, mutual masturbation but stop copulating. Because you are at a stage of
development when your sex hormones are beginning to be produced in large quantities, your interest in sex is high. Nevertheless, your experiments at penetration, of which you are
obviously afraid, may be more due to female curiosity and a
wish to prove to yourself that you can attract male partners
than really genuine sexual desire. Your comments about your
breasts indicate that this may be so. Your ability to work better
is probably much more to do with your success as a female than
the fact that you copulate.*

*Your pleasure in showing your vulva and body to boys and
your interest in their genitals shows that you are in the petting
stage of development. Stop competing with your sister and
the other girls. Be sensible and do what is best for yourself;
remember too that you are under the age of consent
and could get your partner into serious trouble if the fact
that they had intercourse with you became known to your
teacher.*

VIRGIN BLUES

I'm a 19-year-old virgin and I'm beginning to be afraid I'll be
a virgin the rest of my life. From the way men act, you'd think
we belong to another species. Nobody, but nobody, wants to be
the first any more!

I was very shy as a young girl and in addition went to an all
girl boarding school in a small town so I didn't even start dating
until my senior year. A few of my classmates had real boyfriends but I think the majority were virgins too. It was quite a
shock when I got to college and discovered I was about the only
(female) virgin there.

When a guy took me home after a date and said 'why not?' I
would say 'I'm a virgin, I want to wait till I know you better.'
The guy would jump back as if he'd touched a leper and head
for the door!

At first I did want to know the first man well, if not love him,
but that soon faded. By the end of the year I was so tired of
petting, getting really excited and never doing anything else that
I would have slept with anybody. But anybody wouldn't sleep
with me! I still felt I had to tell whoever it was it was the first
time – otherwise if I bled or it hurt or something I might scare

him to death. The word virgin was enough to make them lose all interest.

I think men are afraid of 'deflowering' a virgin because they think she'll want to get married the next day. Or maybe they're just afraid of the responsibility of being the first and teaching someone and all that. I don't know what it is, but I want to tell all male readers of *Forum*: I would guess most virgins over 16, like me, don't want to get married for a long, long time; are quite willing to learn whatever needs to be learned from several men if any one isn't a good teacher; and just want to get that damned hymen out of the way so they can get started! So don't run away from us – help us get started.

Miss J.M.,
Address withheld by request

LAST OF THE ROMANTICS?

I have only just realized that ordinary people can write to you! By 'ordinary', I mean that I cannot tell you that I am unable to make love unless an umbrella is present, or that a pair of workman's squeaky boots sends me culminating down the High Street, as it would not be true.

I was brought up on a diet of 'men are filthy beasts'. I could never understand this. I knew that some boys at school picked their noses; the teacher even dished out pieces of clean rag to one boy – who preferred his sleeve anyway – no doubt he was a potential Midshipman! So that's what she must have meant! My 'love life' started when I was 13. I met the son of the local publican over a lemonade and a packet of crisps in the children's room. He was 14 and was one day going to be a famous boxer! Each week he gave me a quarter-pound box of chocolate and lent me his latest copy of Tarzan. After Sunday School, we'd walk through the wood which surrounded the village. He would swing from the trees, emulating his hero, and I would stand below, worshipping. And that was all. No kissing, no groping, nothing worth writing about in your magazine, but I'm glad that I lived when I did.

Since those days I have known the most wonderful love and romance and all that it entails. Forgive me, I am not being superior, but I feel so sorry for any young people who 'miss out'. But the order of the day, according to some magazines, seems to be how gymnastic one can be in bed, and how many times one should culminate. Lips and arms and legs are no longer enough, it seems. Odd shaped rubber and hard applicators can do so much more (they say).

Had these books been available when I was young, they would have made me feel so sexually inferior that by now I should have been quite frigid.

My open mind tells me that there must be a need for books like *Forum*, or they would not sell, but I must confess that I do not understand it. Perhaps my age group are the missing 'sexual' link between romantic dreams and robot masturbation?

Perhaps this is what is causing so much disturbance in the young of today. Brought up by mums who were brought up by mums like mine, and now all this is thrust at them – no wonder they are confused. I know I am – but I still believe in the old romantic bit!

Mrs A.R.,
Sussex

You don't state your age but I wonder if firstly you might not have the wrong idea about the younger generation and secondly whether you might not be a little bit jealous of what you suppose they do?

Believe it or not most 13-year-old girls today are not very different to how you were. Most of the young are not missing out and the quality of relationships between the older ones is probably increasing. They are interested and concerned about each other. Some 13-year-old girls still go to Sunday School and select older boys to admire and worship. Today's young are just as romantic as ever and possibly less shy about it. I don't think many of them are devoted to genital gymnastics and boasting, amongst boys, about their intercourse performance is decidedly rare today. Euphemisms like 'culminate' are out – which is surely an improvement – but it is true that late adolescent girls may worry and seek advice about their orgasmic responses. This too is surely sensible since it is better than proceeeding into frigid adulthood. Learning is much easier and more sure in adolescence.

I don't know to which 'applicators' you are referring but the use of objects in vaginal masturbation, at least occasionally, is widespread and always has been. It is better to use a specially designed device than to run the risk of damaging the vagina with unsuitable objects or even using ones that get 'lost' and have to be removed by a doctor. Most women, however, manage perfectly well with their fingers.

239

Again, I think more open attitudes about sex are more likely to reduce rather than increase frigidity. Most people have a fairly healthy scepticism concerning the prodigies of sexual performance about which they may read.

Your reference to 'robot masturbation' makes me wonder if you perhaps have some difficulty here? I sat listening to a male Roman Catholic virgin in his mid-20s the other day who always prefaced any reference to intercourse with the words 'cold and animal-like'. He apparently distinguished this from some other kind of intercourse which he never actually specified. He seemed to think that nearly everyone actually had 'cold and animal-like intercourse'. Why? You won't need more than one guess.

If you have enjoyed your love-life as much as you say why knock the young? They are much more sensible than their elders – average against average. Human sexuality doesn't change much but honesty about sex and emotions does. (Consultant)

LUCKY PILL GENERATION

I would almost be jealous of my husband's younger sister who stays with us and is the most likeable girl – if I hadn't married the most wonderful, kind, sexy, strong man and have a fascinating job in a local hospital which I'll only give up when my baby is born.

I'm so happy now but for years before and after my parents threw me out I was constantly becoming unhappy and all because I liked the company of boys as much as girls and get really turned on by sex. I was caught by neighbours, teachers, parents learning about my own and boys' bodies. I had to have an abortion – which was difficult five years ago here. I got VD too. I had some marvellous times with some wonderful boys but my education and my family's love were the price I paid.

Now my husband's kid sister has just as hot pants as I had and as he has (which is why we enjoy being married), but she is the happiest, kindest, cleverest girl around, sitting seven O-levels this year, playing hockey every Saturday and visiting old lonely ladies two nights a week. But then she is on the Pill which I couldn't get seven years ago; this is the difference.

I come home at six and there she is, working like a Trojan in the kitchen, making the meal in her navy school skirt and white socks like any school prefect. Only the odd movement reveals that she is braless and that her panties are in her schoolbag, because she has probably been home with her boyfriend for a quick screw after school. He is in the class above her.

At weekends she goes to stay with her old gran where she tells me she is having a very good affair with her half cousin – a few years older. There are no other men in her life but she is having a very full sex life for a girl of 16. Neither of her boy-friends has ideas of marriage nor grudges the other (in fact they know each other and are quite friendly). My husband knows all this and approves and she can talk about it and asks me about positions and oral sex, but says she doesn't care much because she usually gets a few climaxes and her boys like it missionary-style and so does she.

I think I would have been as happy at 16 as I am now if I had lived in the age of the Pill and the underwear revolution.

Some of her friends live the same sort of way but only the ones with parent trouble seem to be neurotic about it.

Mrs S.V.,
Scotland

LIBERATION

DANISH FREEDOM

I went to Denmark last summer for an archaeological dig, and entered a different world which has made me dissatisfied with my own.

At my College of Education I thought I was as with it as anyone, in attitude and dress, with a decent wardrobe and two mini-affairs behind me (with no regrets). But as I struggled off the boat at Esjberg in my platform boots and leather dress I was met by Kurt, Karl and Inge dressed in denim and with their belongings in bedrolls in the back of the wartime jeep Karl proudly owned. My enormous case filled the rest. We motored south to the site near the sea and met a dozen young Danes who promptly elected to speak only Danish. That evening at a record player 'hop' in the main hut of the camp I saw that most of the girls were dressed in simple but expensive-looking dresses but that was about all. In my jewellery, warpaint, shelf-type bra, tights (and even pantie-girdle) I felt like a visitor from outer space – complete with space-suit. Everyone was friendly and anxious to make me feel welcome. We drank a lot and I found myself sleeping with Karl – and liking it!

The work was not hard but painstaking and although only two were archaeological students, all did it conscientiously. After dinner there was often a candlelight hop or a beach party depending on the weather.

I soon discovered Danish girls don't go much for bras. From Karl's kind but personal remarks I gathered that Danish boys don't like them on their girls either, so I went braless too, trying not to walk around with my arms folded all the time till I got used to my bouncing boobs.

When the sun came out we used to swim before lunch and I soon discovered the Danes swam in the nude. Moreover, Danes on digs don't wear underwear. I had never before seen a prick that wasn't erect and suddenly realized that men could be beautiful naked and that one can be naked and delightfully relaxed.

Everyone seemed to be sleeping with someone except two beautiful girls who preferred each other most nights. It seemed natural to sleep with Kurt or Karl under the circumstances, but

I began to have a thing for Karl, and Kurt and Inge also began to swing together.

On hot days we worked topless for hours on end, the girls stripping their shirts off as unconcernedly as the boys. None of the dozens of spectators asking questions about the dig ever seemed surprised or annoyed at the braless bosoms displayed. The first time I walked topless with some others to the kiosk in the village for Cokes I felt I knew what real freedom meant. It's illegal but unpunished there! Soon my bikini patches disappeared and I no longer felt a foreigner.

On the last day we were packed and ready to leave the dig by 11.00 a.m. and had a swim followed by a party lunch in the dunes. No one bothered to dress and it all ended in a friendly, if exhausting, screw-around by way of saying goodbye. Several of the boys had obviously been keen to screw with an English girl but since I had become close with Karl no one had pressed me though all had been polite enough to suggest it. That day I joined in (even the lesbians did!).

Back home to college – and a new brand of hell. Parents, aunts and classmates criticized me for the way my boobs bobbed about and the indecent way my nipples made bumps on my shirt or sweater. But it was worse still when Karl came over for a week to stay; my parents insisted in putting him in a downstairs bedroom and expressed horror when I explained I had slept with him in his own parents' home. He was so near and yet might as well have been a 100 miles away. I cried at nights. After three nights we hired a car and a tent and blew all my grant on a four-day tour of Scotland. We were in love – deeply.

I am going to Copenhagen for Christmas, thank God! Also I should finish college this summer and hope to go and work in Denmark where life is more civilized, where sex and nudity are respectable and where you can't be called hot pants if you don't wear any. Time will tell whether two people from such different backgrounds should consider marriage but at least we already know we have a lot of fun to share – at least in Denmark.

Miss S.A.,
Bristol

FREE UPBRINGING
I was reared in a small city in northern California, one of four children in a nudist home. I must explain that my parents

and friends were not members of any sunbathing club nor did they attend naturalist camps. But they loved to be naked, were proud of their own (and each other's) bodies, and frankly also had a strong and healthy interest in sex which was never concealed from us kids. They took the 'official' nudist position that nudity is important for educating young children and preventing prudery and hangups of various kinds in later life. But their ideas went beyond that, and they never pretended, as the nudist movement in this country used to, that nudist adults were more moral than other people, or that seeing others naked removed all sexual desire or interest. On the contrary, they and their friends and relatives used their bodies to enlarge their sex activity. They were nudists because it was sex-provoking. Sexy fun.

In the summers we would spend as much time as possible at my grandfather's farm in the mountains. My grandparents, both born in Sweden, went naked casually even in the winter (indoors) and whenever they could outdoors. Both were tall, handsome people in their 50s at the time and frankly most attractive, sexually speaking, as I recall whenever I look at old photos.

From May to October we kids would be practically permanent residents up there, and our parents, uncles, aunts cousins and several friends – about 15 families in all – also stayed there. Sometimes the fathers would have to work all week and only come up weekends, but there would be anywhere from 25 to 60 or 70 of us there at one time, including kids of all ages from babies to unmarrieds and newly marrieds in their late teens and 20s. My parents and their friends were in their 30s. A few could sleep in the big house, but mostly we all shared a big communal tent-house, canvas top and roll-up sides, wooden floor and screening. Each family had its own cubicle or maybe more than one, but there were no inside doors and partitions only went up about five feet, so no privacy was possible or wanted. No husbandless woman slept alone unless she wanted to.

I can't remember ever not knowing exactly how men and women make love, from seeing the older residents, teenagers, our parents, and the other adults doing it. The grownups did it mostly at night, but not altogether by any means. The teenagers did it day and night, indoors and out, whenever the mood struck them, which was whenever any two of the opposite sex met, you might almost say. Boys wore condoms in their hat bands or in a

244

pouch around their neck, and girls also carried them, either in a pouch or a little purse strapped on one wrist. From babyhood on, we kids all knew about them, and helped pick them up with other litter whenever we found them.

I probably was first actually penetrated when I was about 8, after some years of playing at it with younger boys. Fellatio may have been first practised even younger, I'm not sure after all these years and it doesn't matter. I began to have little orgasms at about 11, had my first periods at 12 and had a marvellous surprise party and a big fuss made over me as a result. By 14 I had a moderately buxom bust and womanly curves at the hips and was interesting to fellows much older than I.

Those winters as a teenager, I naturally dated other fellows as well as my cousins, uncles, and in-laws and nudist friends. Some of my fondest memories were of the great fun I would have pretending to be a typical modest type who had to be approached very gradually and talked into even a kiss or innocent petting. Then suddenly shifting gears to become an aggressive, absolutely uninhibited sex 'maniac', to the amazement and education of my date. I would often doubledate with my brother and we both enjoyed being able to initiate less fortunate fellows and girls into acceptance of happy, healthy, unreserved sex.

Naturally, in case there is any doubt, we kids indulged in that horrible naughty-naughty practice of incest sometimes, just as our parents did. I never had sex with my father or grandfather, but certainly did with all my cousins, nephews, uncles and other relatives, as well as my brothers. Doing it with a brother was mostly a friendly, sisterly sort of thing to do when we were alone, dateless and horny. Why not? We never felt it was any more wrong than any other sex. At the farm, and around home, we kids had played with each other, slept together and been intimate in every way but sex all our lives. It was no big thing, and no more important than our parents' extramarital play. We also might do it just for the hell of it to loosen up an overly inhibited or prissy date – usually a non-nudist girl who my brother was educating, as he so delighted in doing, once he had entered her two or three times when they were alone. We also did it a few times at least to demonstrate techniques to our littlest brother or other kids in the camp who were just learning how.

OK, I don't need to give more details. The point is, there must have been hundreds of other outdoor arrangements for families and groups of friends in California and many other states as well. We've known many, many people as adults who had more or less the same exposure to sex by the encounter method, the discovery method, or whatever you call it, with parental approval (or sometimes without).

Admittedly, this isn't normal here any more than in the U.K. (or maybe not even in Denmark for all I know). But it seems to me the recent explosion of sex openness indicates definitely that millions of young adults now think sex should be open and natural because they learned about it that way at their mother's knee. I was taught that way and I am teaching my kids the same way.

Sex ought to be as natural for kids as eating hot dogs, swimming or dancing.

Mrs E.S.,
Virginia

Incest, while fairly common, is of course illegal.

Because of the individual variation and because of the prolonged periods of observation, which are necessary to obtain results, it's very difficult to compare one form of education with another. Sex education is no exception. What we would all like to see is a system which ensures that no one encounters any avoidable difficulties or failures later in life. I wonder how all of you have worked out? People I have encountered who were reared like you don't encourage me to think the issue as open and shut as you portray.

Children probably learn more by simply seeing and copying their parents than in any other way. This is the 'natural' method. The higher animals learn about sex in this manner and they can be useless – the males particularly – if they do not have the opportunity. In some human societies sexual activity is not necessarily hidden from children, though the child's own sexual behaviour may well be restrained by its elders. In Western society, at least, the oedipal risk applies (whether it is universal or a reflection of our close family system of rearing is hard to say) and so witnessing parental sex in our culture can do harm. Again, one doesn't know whether the harm is due to the sight itself or to the attendant secrecy and shame with which intercourse is normally surrounded.

The sexual instinct is a drive towards sexual gratification, but it does not of itself tell us how to do it. Everyone is to a degree incompetent at first and learning the art of sex takes time. If we are not to use 'natural' education we should certainly institute a programme of sensible and effective sex education along with a suitable research programme to assess its effectiveness.

Even more important than sexual adjustment is personality adjustment. Too early sexual experience, in many cases, can warp personality development, and one comes across sexual athletes who are incapable of having real interpersonal relationships. Of course, it may be that such disturbed people are rebels and express it by sexual behaviour a long way outside the norm. If everyone were reared as you describe, perhaps the rebels would seek self-expression by maintaining their virginity!

I agree that we are all potentially promiscuous and that sex can be a token of friendliness between men and women. Anything which reduces suspicion between the sexes and makes them more valuable to each other is to be applauded. But I really do doubt whether excess of anything is good for us.

According to your letter, you more or less had sex with anyone on the slightest whim and really seem to have been preoccupied with it. You did it with your brother out of boredom. Both of you took pleasure in more or less raping others. This seems to imply that the only aim of having anything to do with a member of the opposite sex is to jump on them. The sweetness of seduction – no matter how sham it is in reality – and the pleasure of exploring another, and not only sexually, is all lost. Your desire to make sex an issue of blank confrontation and to force your notions on others shows that you may not be as sure of yourself as you suggest.

One difficulty may be that having been reared in a fashion different to the norm makes adjustment a permanent difficulty for you and for others who have been brought up in a similar non-standard fashion. Perhaps if we were all reared the same way it would not matter.

Whether we would be managing our lives better as a result is a question which I still regard as open, in spite of your letter.

SEXUAL VARIATION

It is still an uphill struggle for our predominant-
ly heterosexual society to recognize that the
homosexual minority is as human as anyone else.
Homosexuals, lesbians and bisexuals are all
members of the same sexual spectrum. Like heterosexuals, these people also experience emotional
joys and sorrows in their social as well as their
sexual relationships.

HOMOSEXUALITY

JEKYLL AND HYDE

I am usually heterosexual but when I drink alcohol I feel extremely effeminate and can think only of homosexual acts.

At other times I feel sympathetic to homosexuals but am straight. I feel attracted to the 'butch' pictures of myself taken when sober. How come I am not able to have anything but straight relationships?

I am not transvestite but submissive to homosexual acts. This is very strange to me but doesn't worry me. Once I got drunk and was sucked off by another boy in a lavatory.

Could I be a repressed homosexual?

S.G.,
London

If you felt some homosexual desire when sober (even though you were then mainly heterosexual in your urges and entirely so in your actions) and merely found the desire for homosexual acts irresistible when drunk, you might say that your homosexuality was 'suppressed'. The distinction is not of practical importance in your case, since you seem not to mind much about your bisexual make-up.

The complete repression of an important sexual urge except when you are intoxicated must be due to powerful controls within your personality, which keep unacceptable and forbidden ideas from your conscious mind. These controls cease to operate effectively when you are drunk, so you find your sexual appetites changed. You may feel that homosexual desires are not unacceptable by you even when you are sober, and this would mean that the controls (repressive 'superego' forces) have unconscious roots which you do not recognize. Alcohol diminishes the restraints of conscience and in doing so not uncommonly alters sexual preferences in bisexual people. But it does not generate impulses or urges which are not already present.

I am interested to learn that you find butch photographs of yourself attractive when you are intoxicated. My impression is that men can get easily stimulated by sketches or photographs of their own genitals, but that sexual arousal by portraits or photographs in normal clothes is fairly unusual.

HOMOSEXUAL HAPPINESS

My reason for writing to you is that I thought my long experience as a full-time homosexual may be of some use to others who have written to you on the subject. Particularly young people who have become, or are becoming, aware of the fact that all is not quite normal.

Try though I may, I cannot remember when I first accepted the fact that I was definitely sure of my homosexuality. Perhaps this is because I never gave the matter a thought until I lost Michael.

I grew up with Michael, and we learned the art of making love at a very early age. As the years passed by I doubt whether either of us gave the matter a thought, for to us everything seemed so natural and our association was totally satisfying . . . or *we* thought so.

Of course we knew at a very early age that two males should not have any sexual contact with each other, and without any suggestion being made, it just so happened that our association was always kept completely private.

In the process of growing up we became top-class athletes, in due course we became fairly expert at our trade, at no stage did we live together, at no stage did we seek the friendship of other homosexuals, at no time did we frequent or in fact even visit any place where homosexuals gathered, and the only time we were together for any length of time was on a working holiday overseas. We did plan weekends together and we did plan a get-together whenever time and distance allowed. In between times masturbation sufficed, but there *were* the occasions when a homosexual relationship came out of the blue and with someone we were associated with in some way or another. I never remember an association with a stranger.

Having Michael, and being able to satisfy one's sexual urges in a way we considered perfection, it never dawned on us that there were many problems connected with homosexuality. In this regard I am not concerning myself with the attitude of society, but more with the personal problems one has. True it is that society does not accept us and never will. Having seen many countries where homosexual acts are legal I can say that, though Parliaments pass acts legalizing such, this does not mean that society accepts the homosexual.

A true love affair, whether a homosexual or a heterosexual affair, is a pretty wonderful thing when one is young. I say young for, when young, one's sex episodes are somewhat animalistic and uninhibited and I can assure any doubting heterosexual that homosexual love is just as wonderful, perhaps even more so, than other forms, for one can go for one's life knowing there will be no unwanted result.

For me there were no problems of any kind ... not until I lost Michael and then the awful truth dawned. Suddenly one realizes there is no one, no one who understands, suddenly there is no one to laugh with, cry with, nor a shoulder to lean on.

I said there were no problems. Maybe I was a bit too emphatic. My parents wanted a daughter-in-law and grandchildren and there were many times when the thought occurred to me that I would like children, a thought which came to me later rather than sooner. There were questions to be answered in this regard which were not that easy to cope with. At the same time such matters cropped up only on infrequent occasions and were quickly, if inadequately, disposed of.

On not one occasion have I had cause to think that anyone has thought of me as a homosexual. On the surface I believe I have lived a fairly normal life, I enjoyed dances, I enjoyed taking girls out, I enjoyed mixed company of any kind. Perhaps in my youth the male/female relationship was far more staid than it is today. Sex was a dirty word and unmentionable in polite society. The unmarried mother was an outcast and, where possible, pregnant daughters were packed off to Europe or some other place to get lost till the *all clear* sign was given.

As is the case today, young males frequented brothels, and I paid my respects on a number of occasions only to be totally disappointed and disillusioned.

I have many times wondered what the circumstances would have been had I not been 'married' to Michael. Would I have been homosexual? Would I in fact have made the success of things as I have done if it had not been for the encouragement handed out to me by Michael? Such encouragement, of course, was not one-sided.

I know there are many forms of homosexuality, including the effeminate type, and I would suggest that anyone in doubt should first of all give profound consideration to intercourse with the opposite sex ... intercourse over and over again until one is convinced that the heterosexual world just isn't on. Let me say that on every count I would recommend that every endeavour be made to be hetero rather than homo. Sure, I was lucky, but I may have been of a small minority. And in any case am I so lucky now? Is there a place in society for the middle-aged homosexual?

If having proved conclusively that you are a homosexual, and having exhausted every avenue in an attempt to change the scene, I can only suggest that, having accepted the fact, you find a mate with whom you can share your life in a true give-and-take fashion. This is being done, it is a common enough practice the world over and, as was the case with me, it is a wonderfully rewarding and satisfying existence.

I would say beware of those on the beat, those in search of a one-night stand, and the kinky stuff. But that's me. I can appreciate the feelings of those interested in those things, just as I expect others to appreciate my whims and fancies. Some would refer to oral sex as kinky, but to me it's the greatest. Let me put it this way. I consider my private life very, very private.

P.D.,
Australia

ELECTRIC SHOCK

I am 19 and I have always been homosexually inclined.

For about seven months now I have been friendly with a man who is 42 who is also a homosexual. To have sex with him I have been paid £3 to £5 a night. I visit him at the most twice a week, but normally it is only once a week.

Since my first visit I have been asked to undress, sometimes he likes to be allowed to do the stripping. On a number of occasions he has been naked too. He asked how old I was and I told him I was nearly 22 as I didn't want to lose him. But although I am only 19 I look older.

I have indulged in most homosexual acts with him and have done almost everything he asked, to the extent of being photographed with and without erection and masturbating myself: some of his photos show close-ups of ejaculation.

But what worries me is that, since last October, I have been asked to let him tie me spreadeagled on the bed and be brought off by electric shock treatment. This is his own invention and he made it for himself. The instrument uses reduced power so as to make it safe. The sensation on the penis is a tingling feeling like pins and needles and it can be increased by means of a volume control which he operates.

I have experienced orgasms with this I never knew existed. But I am a bit concerned about how safe this instrument is and

253

about what harm it could do to the penis as, when on maximum power, the penis is rigid. It is such an intense orgasm that I have experienced great heights of ecstasy.

As I mentioned earlier, he has been paying me. At first I refused, but as he wanted me to take the money, I have accepted all he has offered me.

I would like very much to have advice on the points I mentioned about the electric shock treatment and about my obsession for this, especially the relationship I am having with this man. I have given every encouragement to him, because I don't want to lose his friendship and the delights of sex with him.

Please understand how I feel. I have never felt for girls the way I feel when in the company of boys. I live in constant fear of being found out by my parents as I have always kept my homosexual tendencies from them. I would really like to go and live with this man. Please advise.

D.H.,
Glasgow

In spite of what several books say and in spite of the special pleadings of various interested organizations, I do not think you should too readily accept at your age that you are in fact a homosexual. If you have attempted to form a number of affectionate and intimate relations with girls and got nothing out of it, then well and good; but many late adolescent males fail to give girls a chance due to their conscious and unconscious fears of the emotional and sexual aspects of women. Males take a long time to develop their sexuality properly and the law, in recognition of the fact, tries to protect them from homosexual seduction by older men until they are 21 years old.

Your fears may be based upon your relationship with your mother when you were young and your concern about keeping your behaviour from your parents may be of special significance. Perhaps, too, without realizing it you find the friendship and regard of your partner a substitute for the affection and esteem you perhaps felt you lacked from your father when young. Your initial refusal of money from your friend indicates that this could be so and your subsequent acceptance of it may mean that you regard it as a mark of love. Although accepting the money makes you a 'prostitute', it is obvious that the man's friendship is of far greater importance to you than either the money or the sex. In fact, you are rather nervous about the sex side of the relationship and to some extent you participate in order to retain the man's interest in you.

I am not really sure the man is worthy of the warm feelings you have towards him and I hope he never causes you a great deal of grief. I would suspect he may be manipulating you. Tying you down and inflicting electric shocks on you, no matter in what form, is motivated by sadism. I feel no happier than you about it and would like to know what he has done to other people and how extreme his sadistic fantasies are before advising you. You should proceed with great caution and ensure that you are never made totally helpless. If you have a friend you can trust you could tell him all you know about your partner and let your partner know you have told someone about him.

If his device is plugged into the mains then again you should be very careful since even factory-made, let alone home-made, electrical equipment can often be defective. It would be wise to test it out at full power on him first on every occasion. The very minimum precaution would be to try it on your hands.

All manner of electrical devices have been tried on the penis in order to help with impotence. None work reliably, so the assumption would be that their stimulating effect is largely psychological and that any physical benefit is akin to the stimulation that can be achieved by other means.

Perhaps the reason you find the pleasure so intense is a degree of masochism in yourself. It may be that at full power the shock is painful and this helps to release your full response. It is not impossible that, without realizing it, you have encouraged him to be sadistic to you. However, there are safer ways of indulgence than electric shocks.

GAY TODAY

After reading a recent issue of *Forum*, as a homosexual I feel I must raise my own small voice of protest through your letters column. Every time someone has mentioned the word homosexual, you tell your readers how hard life is for homosexuals, and this time you have gone too far by saying 'unless you're very tough, the homosexual life can be difficult'. Perhaps you will let me, as a homosexual, enlighten you on what life is like today for gay people of Britain?

It certainly is not as gloomy a picture as you paint it, and I suggest that you stop printing inaccurate accounts of what homosexuality is all about. I can assure you that public attitudes are more enlightened these days and 'gay' has come to be accepted as a 'variation from normal', rather than as something abnormal, to be sneered at or condemned.

A great deal of the oppression you speak of is in the minds of a minority of homosexuals and if there are some who have just cause for complaint, perhaps they deserve it. My boyfriend and I have been together now for five years, and we still live only for each other. My employer and colleagues all know about our relationship, and I am pleased to say we are totally accepted by everyone.

We have never made any secret of our true feelings. I have never heard anyone say anything condemning homosexuality. Homosexuals now have more freedom, and in fact society has put its stamp of approval on it by legalizing homosexual acts in 1967.

Today in 1974 the 'gay scene' looks very good. No one is interfering in the way we want to live, so what more do we want? We now have 'Gay News', Europe's largest newspaper for homosexuals, printed fortnightly in London. We are also allowed to advertise to meet other 'gays' if we want to, openly. This was not possible until very recently. Sweeping reforms are now also being put forward by the Sexual Law Reform Society, to eliminate all remaining legal discrimination against homosexual as opposed to heterosexual behaviour. We now have Gay Switchboards all over the country with up-to-date information on the 'Gay Communities'. We have a choice of 13 'Gay Discos' in London alone, where we can dance openly together, and the police are giving their support in granting licences.

It is also encouraging to see what is done for the continental homosexuals, especially in Holland where the age of consent is already fixed at 16 for gays. The Dutch now are to allow sexual relations between people of any age, both homosexual and heterosexual. My boyfriend and I hope to be married in Amsterdam next month, as Dutch law now accepts gay marriages. There, indecent exposure laws have also been abolished, and hard core pornography is on sale in supermarkets, as well as in most shops everywhere. This includes homosexual pornography. The Dutch have discovered that by making sex as open and as ordinary as eating or drinking they have reduced its mystery and have at the same time reduced sex crimes.

In England, that vociferous minority group, Lord Longford and Mrs Mary Whitehouse, are seeking to tighten the Victorian corsets which already threaten to strangle our freedom to read, see and hear what we want. But there is one consoling thought: if Holland is the leading country in a forward and uninhibited way of life, then we who follow can learn by their mistakes and know only the better qualities of such a society.

I hope you print this letter, if only to show that homosexuals have everything going for them. Ignorance is the enemy, and old ingrained attitudes which throw up stereotyped, often inaccurate visions of what homosexuality is all about.

Your magazine could do a great deal, by helping the taboos surrounding this subject to disappear, and by giving your readers up-to-date facts of gayness in Britain today. I feel that the time has come for us to accept each other for what we are. Society is doing so in accepting us.

To all gays I would like to say, throw that chip off your shoulder, as it is up to us to show others that being gay is just a way of life. I hope I will not read any more stories of society persecuting or discriminating against us, as personally I find it to be quite the opposite.

According to the American sex researcher Kinsey, about one person in seven is homosexual. All authorities accept that the number of homosexual men in this country is, at a modest estimate, one person in every 15. And yet, despite this high proportion, there persists a great deal of misunderstanding and ignorance about the homosexual. I hope that all men and women, whatever their sexual preference, can work together towards a situation in which any form of discrimination, legal, civil, social or medical ... ceases to exist.

P.P.,
Berkshire

No quarrel – your aims are our aims, although we feel you underestimate the strength of British SMAGS – the Sex Misery and Guilt-Spreaders! (Ed.)

GOING GAY

I am 27 years old and I live alone. I have been dating the same beautiful girl for four years. We still are not ready for marriage. One day I went to see her after work and her brother was visiting. We had a few drinks, ate supper and then drank some more. I was feeling slightly high and I was feeling sexually excited so I suggested that we have a threesome. We all went into the bedroom and everything was great until my girlfriend's brother reached over and grabbed my penis. Before I knew what was happening, he was sucking my penis and doing a fantastic job of it. I came in his mouth and it was the best fellatio I have ever experienced. I tried to push him off but it was useless. When he was about to come he covered my body with kisses and whispered to me that he loved me very much. I was dumbfounded and lay on the bed numb from the whole experience. After he had left, my girlfriend told me that her brother was bisexual although he preferred having sexual relations with men.

All this happened about a year ago and since that time I have been unable to get an erection when I am with my girlfriend. She has tried everything to stimulate me but nothing has worked. If I look at photographs of naked men I can get an erection but my girlfriend gets terribly upset when I do it.

Now, I certainly do not classify myself as a homosexual just because of that one incident. That was the first time in my life I shared a bed with another man. However, all I have to do is walk down the street and see an attractive male with a bulge in his pants and I get a massive erection. Please tell me, am I turning out to be a homosexual? If so what can I do to prevent this from happening? I am terribly shook up and upset about the whole situation.

> *Name withheld by request,*
> *Canada*

All human beings are potentially bisexual, but cultural conditioning supports heterosexual expression, and oppresses homosexual expression. The experience you had with your girlfriend's brother, while homosexual, does not automatically classify you as a fixed homosexual. In many ways, it's obvious you were not prepared for or looking for this kind of sexual expression. Nevertheless, it happened and you are left with trying to work out the consequent feelings associated with homosexuality in your mind.

First let me say it's important for you to accept your sexual feelings, whether you see them as heterosexual, homosexual or bisexual. Whatever society thinks, you are closest to your own sexuality, and you alone can decide what is good sexually for you. Apparently, you feel strongly attracted to men now, but cannot bring yourself to 'come out' homosexually and act on your feelings. No doubt, it's difficult for your girlfriend to support you in this action, since she feels she will be rejected. As it presently stands, you cannot relate to her sexually because you are putting so much energy into repressing your sexual feelings towards men. I suspect that were you to get support for relating sexually to other men and able to feel good about this, you would find that gradually you would also be sexually attracted to your girlfriend. The reason for this is that when we deny strong sexual feelings in a certain direction, we block off sexual feelings in every direction.

I suggest you and your girlfriend separate for a period of time to allow you to work out your sexuality in a free space. You might consider therapy with a counsellor who is sympathetic to diverse sexual expression, or perhaps join a men's group made up of both gay and straight men working out their sexuality. Your discovery of gay feelings need not be looked upon as a problem, but can be viewed as an opportunity to further explore your sexuality. Your girlfriend needs to understand that your separating from her is not so much rejection, as time and space to discover yourself and your new sexual feelings. Trying to be with her as before will not solve the issue; only dealing with your feelings honestly and with courage will reveal your true sexual orientation. Once you have discovered this, your next task will be to accept yourself with this orientation. Your struggle to discover your own sexual nature and to accept it links you with other men and women around the world who share this struggle with you.

LESBIANISM

LESBIAN LOVEMAKING

I am 18 years of age and I am having a lesbian affair with a girl of 23. We are very much in love but we can't satisfy one another.

When we make love she will only let me suck her breasts for a few seconds, even though this turns me on immensely. When masturbating herself she can get a great deal of pleasure but she never reaches a climax. When I masturbate her she gets some pleasure from it but not much. When I enter her she hardly feels a thing. Her vagina is very big and my fingers cannot reach the top of her womb. Could this be why she cannot climax?

I myself get some feeling from our lovemaking, but not much. Can you help?

Miss L.N.,
Yorkshire

Let's clear two things out of the way at once. First, the fact that you cannot reach the neck of your friend's womb with your fingers has nothing at all to do with her inability to reach climax. Second, while most women are sexually roused by manual and oral caresses of the nipples, there are quite a number who aren't. In fact, some find them so painful they are completely turned off.

All lovemaking, whether heterosexual or homosexual, makes one basic requirement of both partners: that each should know the sensitive zones of the other's body and the response of each zone to this or that caress. This also means each must know his/her own sexual responses, where caresses are most arousing and which caress is most effective in each spot. For one partner to discover the other's body, there must be exploration and experimentation, and this is greatly helped when the partner whose body is being explored can guide and direct the other's hands and mouth.

On the other hand, there are certain general observations about the location of the sensitive zones that can be made, and which serve as a useful guide, provided you always remember that the type of caress to which we most respond at such and such a spot may be quite different from anyone else's. Thus your friend does not like having her nipples sucked, while you yourself may be turned on like crazy while she sucks your nipples.

Generally speaking, the sensitive zones are: first and foremost, the clitoris, followed by the inner lips and vaginal entrance. Some women are roused by rapid and heavy strokes of the clitoral head with the finger-tips, while others are put off by this, but do respond easily to long, light strokes of the clitoral shaft. Some women who do not respond at all to finger stimulation of the clitoral head come off in a couple of minutes or so of stroking it with the tongue-tip or sucking it.

The next most responsive zone is usually the breasts and nipples (though not in the case of your friend) and they, too, will react to a variety of caresses. Next are the lips and inside of the mouth, which is explored by the tongue, then the throat, the nape of the neck, behind the ears, the lobes, all the length of the spine and the buttocks, and the insides of the thighs.

I would suggest that you get a good sex manual like Robert Chartham's Mainly for Women *and study those parts of chapters 2 and 7 which apply to women. These will give you the basic knowledge, and then it's up to each of you to explore the other's body. I suggest you would also find a battery operated vibrator useful for stimulating the clitoris until you have both acquired a certain ease in reaching climax.*

What you need is the practice of regular lovemaking, so don't worry if things don't come right straight away.

MARRIED LESBIANS

I am 20, a student living away from home in London with another girl with whom I am deeply in love. We've known each other over two years and have had a lesbian relationship for very nearly 18 months.

I'm worried now since I've been told by two close friends that something we have done is illegal and all sorts of an offence. We got married at a Registry Office – it was ever so simple. All I want to know is, have we committed a crime?

It was simple. My partner is boyish and I'm a very feminine girl. Several months ago after we had realized that the feelings which had drawn us together were so very deep we moved into a flat together and lived, as many lesbians do, a very full and happy life. Then after we had made love one night my friend asked me to marry her. 'How could we?' I asked. Simple! She 'dragged-up' in some of her most boyish clothes and she looked the part of a bridegroom!

For the wedding her hair was cropped fairly short and I kept mine very long. Off we went – me in white, she in a trouser suit. We were married and still live in the same flat as we intend to live together for the rest of our lives. But what began as a token gesture now may be liable to get us into trouble – if anyone finds out. Have we broken the law?

Miss L.F.,
London

I wish I could offer you a few crumbs of reassurance, but it seems that both your friend and yourself have committed offences. And serious ones at that.

The law is clear. Any person who knowingly makes a false declaration to procure a marriage certificate risks penalties of up to seven years' imprisonment, or a fine. Or both. Surprisingly, this rule springs not from the loins of the 1949 Marriage Act but has shuffled down through the years to us from the Perjury Act of 1911.

Your friend broke the law by posing as a man. Whether you yourself committed an offence will depend on precisely what you said and did during your 'marriage ceremony'. Even if you did not directly make a false declaration you could still fall foul of the law of conspiracy, for when two people agree to do an unlawful act they 'conspire' and this is in itself a crime.

Attempts at unisex marriages are no novelty. In a classic case in the 50s an official at a Registry of Marriages uncovered a feminine duo masquerading as boy and girl. Like your friend the 'boy' donned male garb and described herself as a bachelor. But she gave an assumed name. Pleading guilty to making a false declaration to obtain a marriage certificate she told the magistrate she wanted a sex change and to marry legally. She received a £25 fine with an alternative of three months' imprisonment.

Difficult to assess what the same court would give today. In that case the girl had had mental treatment and the magistrate took this into account. Presumably neither your friend nor yourself could or would even want to claim such an excuse. On the credit side, though, attitudes to offences of this kind have relaxed markedly in the last two decades and a magistrate hearing the facts of your case today might well treat you with equal leniency.

I can't even offer you the consolation of knowing that the law will recognize your relationship or your attempt to legalize it. A valid marriage can only take place between two persons of the opposite sex. Generations of judges stretching back to the 18th century have asserted this principle over and over again. It runs like a fiery scar through the poignant case of April Ashley. It was vigorously reaffirmed by a divorce judge as recently as 1967 when a wife asked him to annul her marriage. She'd gone through a ceremony believing her spouse to be a man. The truth quickly emerged but she continued to live with her 'husband' for several months. The judge ruled that no marriage existed.

The Nullity of Marriage Act 1971 has erased any remaining doubts. A marriage will not be valid unless the parties are respectively male and female.

I urge you to see a solicitor. There is a defence to the Perjury Act which may apply to you.

SAPPHO

To counteract the social ostracism of gay women, eventually to eradicate it, I'd like to use your columns to tell readers about the magazine *Sappho*.

Sappho started as a magazine when a parent paper, *Arena 3*, folded. Unlike *Arena 3*, there was no lack of cohesion, enthusiasm or leadership – only money and material. The first issue was quite a struggle, scrounging for articles, subscriptions and advertisements. Since then the magazine has more than doubled in size and its concerns have widened tremendously. Regular meetings certainly account for much of their success, for the editorial board and subscribers meet twice a month. One meeting is for subscribers only, though a guest may be signed in, while the other is for subscribers as well as newcomers – straight or gay. Being female is the only entrance requirement!

Although both male and female homosexuals seem to face similar problems when dealing with the outside world, men actually have it easier – witness the large male membership and domination of such groups as CHE, Gaysocs, GLF.

The meetings provide the greatest source of relief to the lonely and isolated lesbian. Here is one of the few places she needn't be afraid. though she may be very shy. There's little fear that such a social get-together would result in her being picked up by someone totally disagreeable. The meetings are held in an orderly fashion: *Sappho*'s editor Jacqueline Forster will begin with a few words on *Sappho* happenings and related gay scenes for those who can participate. She then introduces a speaker – the topics vary from Women's Lib concerns to poverty – and the audience breaks into smaller groups to discuss whatever subject is closest to them.

The magazine itself is of course the prime means of lessening isolation. Articles usually come from subscribers, letters proliferate and even poetry is found a place. In addition, *Sappho* gives mention to any gay movement, meeting, disco and whatnot whenever possible.

Sappho's main object as a magazine is to rid the lesbian of her frequent fear of being a freak. There is nothing wrong with being gay – it can be a beautiful experience once the hangups are overcome. 'Coming out' is another issue. No gay girl can be totally happy until she has faced up to this problem.

Sappho has another, more tangible, objective; a Centre. This would serve as a permanent home for the meetings which are still held above pubs where drinks can be costly. Literature would be available to inform both gay and straight women about being female, about being gay. Of course *all* women are encouraged to come. *Sappho* feels that the social image of the 'lecherous lesbian' needs a great deal of revision. Once straight and gay women begin to socialize together, the straights might eventually learn that there is little reason to fear a gay girl. In fact, they might even come to like each other. And the Sappho Centre, like *Sappho* itself, would open its doors to the bisexuals, who are accepted by neither straights nor gays, as well as to those girls who are in doubt about themselves, who can find no acceptable place for experimenting but are continually tortured in themselves through doubt and indecision.

Sappho's address for articles and all correspondence is SAPPHO, 39 Wardour Street, London W1.

J.A.,
London

COFFEE AND COMFORT

About two years ago I was extremely frustrated sexually. I had been married for over four years, but my husband was (and still is) most ambitious, and he devoted all his energies to becoming a successful business man. The result was that, when he was at home, which was rarely, he was too exhausted to think of sex. I naturally sought relief in masturbation, but though this

264

was physically satisfying it left me emotionally empty. I began seriously to think of leaving my husband.

Then another couple came to live near us. Soon the wife and myself became quite friendly and we would meet each other for coffee at home. She was a remarkably beautiful woman, the kind one sees in the adverts in glossy magazines. It was the time when mini-skirts were in fashion and she certainly knew how to wear one with maximum effect. She would sit in a chair with her legs sprawled wide apart.

I should explain that I had never had any physical attachment for another woman, and I regarded those who did as freaks. Even so, I found something strangely exciting about the way she displayed her body. One morning, I noticed when she spread her legs even wider than usual that she was not wearing any pants. I must confess I found this tremendously exciting.

She was not difficult to talk to and when the subject came round to sex, I found myself telling her everything about my sexual relations with my husband. She was very comforting and tried to console me and when she left, she put her arms around me and gave me a warm, friendly kiss. I was so aroused by the sight of her private parts that, when she had gone, I went to the bedroom and had the most gratifying 'toss-off' of my life.

When I next visited her flat, I found myself looking casually to see whether she was wearing pants or not, but this time she sat with her legs crossed and I could only see her thighs. She brought up the question of sex again and remarked that she had noticed me looking up her skirt and wondered whether it was to see whether she was wearing pants. I was most embarrassed and tried to pass the whole thing off as a joke.

To my astonishment, she stood up, raised her skirt and took off her pants. She walked over to me and pressed her tummy against my face. I could feel myself becoming excited, but I had no idea what to do, which must have been obvious to her. She proceeded to undress me with great tenderness and led me to the couch. She introduced me to oral sex and I experienced what I can only describe as a triple-strength orgasm.

Since then, we have enjoyed each other's body regularly at least once a week. We are as abandoned as we wish and have no sexual secrets from one another. The result is that I am a far happier and healthier woman, something which even my friends have noticed. I now masturbate less frequently, but more effectively in the emotional sense, and my relationship with my husband has improved enormously. I can now accept his tiredness without getting upset, because I know that the next morning I can always have my 'coffee and comfort' session, as we call it. Moreover, I also feel less inhibited which means that I can be more patient and helpful with my husband and I am not afraid to make the first move.

Mrs B.B.,
London

BISEXUALITY

CASUALTY

I am 24 and I wish to pass on to you an incident that happened to me last year which not only had all the staff of the Royal Brisbane Hospital talking, but also made me a laughing stock of the Gay scene. (I later learned they were not laughing at me but with me.)

I am bisexual and have at times had to take the passive role in bed. I found that this used to hurt considerably and would affect the zest of my sex play with my partners. So I thought I should do something about it, and I purchased a vibrator. I felt that I should put it to use to probe my anus and find out why I had so much trouble with anal intercourse. I started, but at this particular time I was so frustrated that I ended up pushing it right in and closed my legs and masturbated. To my surprise and shock, the vibrator travelled by itself (at this point I had it switched off) and landed at the base of my spine and somewhere behind my stomach. I tried to pass it out in the toilet, but to no avail, and I couldn't grip it with my fingers.

I told myself not to panic as it could make things worse (heaven only knows how much worse). At this point I knew that I had to be honest with myself and go find a doctor, although my heart was beating hard and fast with fear and embarrassment. I walked carefully to the doctor's office and found it locked up so I waited on the street corner wondering what should be done. To my surprise an ambulance stopped, on the way from a call which had been a false alarm. I asked the driver if he could take me to the hospital, and he said 'What's the matter?' I didn't quite know what to say, but I told him that 'I was playing around with this thing, um, and, um, it's still in me,' so he took me to the casualty department.

I was instructed to lie down on my side with my legs pressed against my chest and to wait till a doctor arrived. Five doctors turned up, all young, and one smiled at me and told me not to worry as they were all broad-minded at this hospital. They probed around for some time, with much pain to me, but they couldn't get it out.

One of the doctors told me that he was going to admit me into a ward for an operation so I was wheeled off. After a short rest in the ward of about 10 minutes, the curtains were drawn around me and the hospital barber came in to my cubicle, and asked me to lie with my backside in the air, resting on my arms and knees. He started shaving me and half-way through stopped and asked me what had happened, and I told him I would rather not talk about it. He left my bedside, and the next thing I heard the nurses laughing, and he came back, finished the job and patted my bum and before leaving said 'Watch out for falling objects!'

To cut the story short, when I came to after the operation, the first thing I wondered was whether they'd cut me or did it come out the way it went in. I quickly looked under my blankets. No scars – a sigh of relief – they took it out of the anus. The next day I was discharged and I had a word with the head sister of the ward and she told me that they didn't mind helping me out, but to try not to do it again. Then she asked me if I wanted my vibrator, or what was left of it, back!

Well, that was it, a true and strange incident that I hope will never happen to me again. I learned to laugh it off when I was sent up about it. I hope my story may prevent the same thing happening to someone else.

K.G.,
Australia

BISEXUAL BLUES

Although I have never considered myself the least bit bi-sexual, a recent incident has disturbed me very much and I would appreciate your advice.

It all took place about three weeks ago at a beach club where I bathe. I was changing into my suit in one of the cabanas when I heard a low moaning sound coming from the other side of the wall. A tremor of excitement passed through me and I did something I have never done before or even imagined doing; I dropped to my knees and peered through a small crack in the wall.

Though the light was dim, I could plainly see a young woman on the bench facing me. She was nude from the waist down facing my direction with her legs spread apart and she was slowly masturbating with her left hand. I had never seen another woman masturbate although I have occasionally watched myself in the mirror, and the sight of an attractive, well-built woman playing with herself so uninhibitedly drove me wild. My hand stole down between my legs and I began to masturbate following her rhythm, speeding up as she did until I felt myself nearing an absolutely marvellous climax. At that moment the door to my cabana burst open and a woman of about my age, 26, stood in the doorway. Though I was absolutely mortified at being caught peeping, let alone masturbating, she did not seem the least nonplussed.

Instead of stammering out an apology and running off, she came in and locked the door securely, staring at me all the while. I felt sick and terrified, but for some reason I continued to masturbate. I guess I just couldn't stop. When she had undressed completely she dropped her hand between her legs and herself began to masturbate. Then she slowly walked over to me, placed my hand on her pubic area which was wringing wet and placed her hand on me. Without a word we began to masturbate each other and in less than a minute we both climaxed. I had never before experienced such an intense orgasm. As we lay on the floor exhausted, I couldn't keep my eyes off her body, particularly that lovely moist spot between her legs. When we had both recuperated a little, we began to masturbate again, this time doing it to ourselves and watching the other with intense interest. After about half an hour we both dressed and she left.

Since that day I have never seen the woman, nor do I want to. The incident was immensely pleasurable, both at the time and as I relived it later in my masturbation fantasies. But then all of a sudden it began to trouble me. What came over me?

Is it normal for a woman to respond as I did, or am I a lesbian? Until this incident I had never had a homosexual experience, not since girlhood exploration anyway, or even homosexual fantasies. Just lately I've begun to accept the notion that people are naturally bisexual or homosexual and only social mores and the lack of opportunity account for the fact that most people remain strictly heterosexual. However, I'd be interested in your opinion and in the opinions of your readers, male and female, who have had similar experiences.

Name and address withheld
by request

To answer your question directly, judging from your own statements, no, you are not a lesbian. What's more, your reaction to the bathhouse incident can certainly be considered 'normal', since that's the word you chose to use. But let's consider the circumstances and the immediate situation, to provide you with a better understanding of your own behaviour.

Being at a beach club, in a bathing suit, in the presence of other semi-nude men and women is erotic in itself, and watching someone masturbate is undeniably exciting and certainly something few people will turn away from. As to your masturbatory play with an attractive woman of your own age, I don't think you've any reason to get upset or consider yourself abnormal. Narcissism is part of all of us, and the sight and touch of an attractive member of one's own sex can gratify important (though not necessarily sexual) needs, while providing a bit of reassurance that all of us can profit from.

I'm sure that when your letter appears, some of our readers will write in to share similar experiences, but in the meantime, I'd like to reassure you that isolated incidents of homosexual activity are quite common to all sexually liberated people.

BEAUTIFUL BISEX

I am 26, married to a beautiful woman and a graduate student as well as being blissfully and beautifully bisexual.

Being bisexual, I feel, removes a lot of anxiety surrounding one's sexuality.

My earliest recollections of sex are about playing doctor. The thrill of touching the first woman in my young life has stayed with me to this day. My mother had a beautiful garden and her yellow roses provided 'needles' for the shots which were given below the waist. I would get on all fours and my young playmate would plunge my small erect penis into a peony. The delicious feeling of all those little cool petals made my head sing and of course I obliged her with similar treatment much to her delight.

The mother of a schoolfriend provided me with my first full act of sexual intercourse at the age of 16. I adore that beautiful woman, her skill and understanding made a man of me. I was invited to use her pool for the summer and I got used to seeing her and enjoyed her conversation and her company. One day I blurted out that I loved her and she took my hands in hers and asked me if what I really meant was that I wanted to make love to her. I nodded yes and she led me upstairs closing the French doors behind her as we entered the bedroom. After unhitching my tennis shorts and removing my shirt, she caressed my chest and my legs. When she touched my penis it was more than I could bear and I spilled out all over her chest. She scolded me gently and told me I should have waited for the real thing. This raised my anger and we began to wrestle. Soon she had me nestled in between her thighs and we made love. Her cries of delight taught me the sheer joy in pleasuring a woman.

My first homosexual experience came at school. Being on the hockey and football teams I was required to put in extra hours of practice after classes. One particular guy and I stayed after the others left and after an extra hour's workout we headed for the showers. The conversation sooned turned to sex and we related our most recent adventures to each other. We both got erections and my friend said that he was going to masturbate before he got dressed. Soon he was masturbating me and then he fellated me. I had a really fantastic orgasm and I returned the favour.

I have not mentioned my sex life with my wife because I assume you understand that we have a great horny love affair going on between us. We lived together for three years and married when we were 23. We have a small son of nearly three and my wife is expecting another child. I have another young son aged six by another woman and he lives with us. Our life is very quiet now except for a few weekend parties.

My wife has read (and got very turned on, I might add) and helped write this letter and although she has no deep homosexual feelings herself, she has given it the 'Bi is best' seal of approval. We feel our life has been and is typical of many young bisexual couples.

E.W.H.,
Canada

SECRET BISEXUAL

My husband and I are in our mid-40s and have been married 20 years. We have four wonderful children. Our sexual relationship was very good until after the fourth child. Then, because of fear of pregnancy, our sexual sessions fell off considerably. About two years ago I talked my husband into having a vasectomy, to eliminate the pregnancy fear and improve our relations. It has. In fact, our relations now are much more satisfying than when we were first married.

But, several years ago (quite by accident) among my husband's things I found a 'gay' book, listing 'gay' restaurants and cocktail lounges all over the country. At that time I was upset but decided to say nothing about it. Recently my suspicion has been confirmed – my husband is bisexual – since I've found (also quite by accident since I'm not a snooping woman) pamphlets with male nudes pictured in all kinds of positions, evidence of ordering male sex films, vaseline and even a vibrator. There is also a book with phone numbers, listing men's first names only.

Let me assure you that our marriage has been wonderful. I love my husband very much. He's been a considerate husband and a marvellous father to our children.

Should I bring this out in the open and have a frank discussion with him? Since my discovery, I am not sleeping and my nerves are about to crack.

Name withheld by request,
Maryland

I don't think you are being fair to yourself by bearing this anxiety alone. Only you can decide how to bring up this subject. You may want to consult a marriage counsellor or a therapist before you speak to your husband. However, I do suggest that you make it quite clear to him that you are not prying into his affairs. You can legitimately claim that his homosexuality is seriously affecting the stability of your marriage, if you are sure this is so.

As you have not noticed any apparent difference in your relationship or your love life (except that it has improved) since your husband had the vasectomy, it is unlikely that the operation could have been the impetus to his homosexuality. These inclinations (which you have not even confirmed as yet) may be merely a fantasy or a part of his past.

It seems to me that you have not really considered the effect of his activities on your personal life. Have you felt yourself repudiated? If you consider this state of affairs something which he should feel embarrassed or ashamed of, that is one matter. To reveal your pain and confusion is another.

If your marriage remains as successful as you describe, I see no reason why anything should have to change between you. But, for your own peace of mind, I think it is only fair to discuss this matter with him. It may well be that his apparent homosexuality is quite secondary to his love for you. I suggest you find out directly from him.

COPENHAGEN EXPERIENCE

I have just returned from a business trip in Copenhagen where my firm sent me for a computer conference. Luckily the conference finished each day at 6 pm and in the evenings I was free to explore the most liberated city in Europe.

Well I did all the expected things and saw all the obvious shows and indulged in all the experiences I had planned to indulge in. I won't write of those because presumably you know about them all. But on my last night I had the mostest in experience, and it was so unexpected that I couldn't believe I was really enjoying it until the next day on my flight back to London when I relived it all in my mind.

I have, to the best of my knowledge, always been heterosexual and never even thought about homosexuality since the days when, at 17, a friend and I measured each other's pricks with enjoyment!

In the bar of my hotel that last evening I got talking to a Dane of about my age (I'm in my late 20s) and after chatting for a while he asked me outright if I'd be interested in being photographed for the porn market. I was a little taken aback, but thoughts of doing exciting things with a gorgeous Danish blonde were too much to be resisted. I visualized the porn pictures I'd been looking at for five days and imagined myself in the role of the strong silent male while nude and lovely birds surrounded me. I said yes without another moment's thought.

Off we went to his studio where there was another young man fiddling about with camera equipment and lights. My new found friend bade me to strip. 'Where are the girls?' I said. 'No girls' came the answer, just like that, and he too began taking off his clothes. It appeared that these particular porn pictures were to be 'men only' studies; when I protested he insisted that it was quite normal and OK for two hetero men to indulge in this sort of thing without another thought, and told me that the vast majority of gay porn was made by straight guys! Well it took me five minutes to adjust to that fact, and to my disappointment, but two schnapps later I was lying on a divan with legs apart being sucked off by the fellow, and not wondering any longer if I could get it up for a male! Because what became clear to me at that point was that only a man knows what a man likes – what he feels, and how he is going to react.

Probably the most exciting bit was when we were in an extraordinary sort of 69 position with me prone and him kneeling over me with his prick in my mouth and my nose almost up his backside. I didn't know if I was getting more out of my own prick, which I couldn't see, or his, which was obscuring the view of anything else. Somehow having the photographer there, calmly snapping away, made it all better and more exciting.

There was absolutely nothing between us except our bodily lust – indeed I doubt if I would recognize him if I met him in the street – yet after the long, long session, he dropped me back at my hotel and casually asked if I'd like to continue. Would I! He came back up to my room and we fucked and sucked and screwed in 20 different ways for the rest of the night, with absolutely no personal attachment whatsoever. In fact we haven't even swapped addresses, and I don't know his surname.

On arrival home I spent the evening with my girl. Not only had I lost nothing, but she complimented me on my enthusiasm!

So my question is, what am I? And don't say bisexual, because I hear that bisexuals always imagine males in their masturbation fantasies, and I certainly do not – girls girls girls all the time!!

J.P.,
London

I am sorry to contradict you, but you are clearly bisexual. What you have heard about the masturbation fantasies of male bisexuals is a myth. Some bisexuals, it is true, do fantasize male images, but, in my experience, more fantasize female images.

Don't reject bisexuality. I am in the process of making a study in depth of it, because for some time now, it has been becoming clearer and clearer to me that there are more bisexuals of both sexes about than we have previously imagined. The Forum Survey asked people to rate themselves on this; 63% of men and 77% of women describe themselves as entirely heterosexual; 24% of men and 17·5% of women said they had some homosexual leanings, and about 3% said they were completely bisexual. In fact, I believe that all of us have bisexual tendencies, and that those who do not engage in homosexual activities, are those who suppress the homosexual side of their sexuality; in the same way that while it is certain that all of us have exhibitionistic and voyeuristic tendencies (most certainly the latter) most of us do not seek to satisfy these tendencies by deliberately turning ourselves into 'flashers' or Peeping Toms.

The whole subject is a fascinating one, not because of the fact that bisexuals enjoy physical homosexual activity as much as they enjoy physical heterosexual activity, but because of the emotional response to both kinds of partner. The emotional response between two men can include love, which is just as valid an experience as love between a man and a woman. In particular, however, the responses are different in nature. I do not feel ready yet to define these differences in detail, but all those with whom I have discussed this point so far assure me that they need both kinds of relationship in order to feel fully fulfilled as human beings.

What I have just said is somewhat contrary to your experience, J.P., when you stress that you spent the night in sexual activity 'with absolutely no personal attachment whatsoever'. But couldn't exactly the same thing happen with a girl 'pickup'? I believe that if you were ever to develop a more permanent relationship with another man, you would find that a personal attachment, with satisfying emotional involvement, would also develop, without necessarily interfering with your capacity to love a woman subsequently or even at the same time. (Robert Chartham)

PROMISCUOUS BISEXUAL

There are three reasons for writing this letter. The first is a technique my wife and I have worked out which may be of value to your other readers.

I am a happily married 52 year old, blessed with a very powerful sex drive. I am still coming seven or eight times a week, sometimes as much as 14 times. After we have been making love to each other for 20 minutes or so, I get over my wife in the usual position, except that her legs are closed, or close together, and then fuck very slowly (so as not to come myself), rubbing my cock up and down in the lips of her cunt. This means that my knob is rubbing against her clitoris. She finds this much more satisfactory than when I use a finger, which tends to make her sore.

I wait till she makes it, and then either go into her and fuck fast till I come myself, or just carry on (if I am very excited) and either come on her belly or between her legs. She isn't strongly sexed like me, and usually only comes about twice a week; but I can nearly always make her come using this method. Sometimes she will come again as she feels my cock thrusting into her fast, or when she feels my spunk spurting in.

275

The second reason is this. When I married, I started doing it twice a day for about the first six months, and then slowed down gradually till I was doing it about once a day. After that, I slowed down very gradually (at exactly the same rate that Kinsey describes), till I was down to about three a week. But then I had an experience which made me speed up again. I was staying with my brother-in-law, and was having a sexy dream in the morning. He brought me a cup of tea just before I came! I didn't get home till 16 hours after this, and spent the whole day feeling frustrated and sexy. I made up for it at the weekend, and suddenly realized that I was still perfectly capable of doing it every day. So since then, (this was when I was 46) I have kept up seven or eight a week without any trouble.

As I mentioned, my wife is not strongly sexed, and she found this a bit much to start with. But she is a wonderful wife, and is bearing with me. She never refuses me sex when I want it.

The third reason for this letter is this. I am bisexual, probably basically homosexual. Virtually all my contacts before my marriage were men and boys. I spend a couple of days every week away from home, having to travel on business, so there are plenty of opportunities for me to make safe contacts with males who don't know me and are never likely to see me again, and I have had hundreds in the last 20 years. I make a note of their marital status (I also note how many times I come – and how), and 66 per cent of these contacts are married men. I am drawing about 50 per cent of my outlet from my wife; 30 per cent from men contacts, and the rest from masturbation. I used to worry about my homosexual relations when I was first married, but the urge was too strong to resist, and I have gradually come to accept it. However, I get a bigger thrill from fucking my wife than anything else I do.

I know that a very large number of married men have these homosexual contacts, and I would like to know what their wives think about them. I would like to tell mine all about it, but I am afraid it might damage our marriage. Though broadminded about many things, I doubt if she could take this information in her stride. I have told her many times not to mind if I pick up a girl and fuck her when I am away, and that there would be nothing more in it than sheer physical relief for me – just like having a pee, or eating or sleeping. But she doesn't see it this way, thinking it would always be a breach of trust, which she considers one of the bases of marriage.

From my experience, I know that there will be many of your

readers in the same boat. Some of them must have told their wives – or been found out. I would be very interested to learn what their wives' reaction has been. I want mine to know about it – I want her to share all my secrets. But I am a bit afraid she just couldn't stomach my real self.

E.B.,
Wales

Although many readers will understand what you say, many more will be surprised that such a heterosexually vigorous chap as yourself should also enjoy homosexual contacts.

You are, of course, 'promiscuous' but seem to be luckier than most such people in that you have managed to establish and maintain what seems to be a good and even loving relationship with your wife. As judged from your letter, the chief value you seem to place on her is sexual – but this conclusion could be unfair to you. You are concerned about both her orgasms and her possible reaction to your infidelity and this is a sign you really do have love for her.

Promiscuous people are ones who undertake prompt connections at short notice and basically wish to avoid more entangled relationships. What you say about there being no risk of seeing your male partners again is typical – you can only fully enjoy them in this way. Probably the same is true of your female ones too. Very promiscuous men are very closely related, psychologically, to homosexual ones and are frequently bisexual.

Your inhibition may also show up in your use of four-letter words – perhaps you still think it naughty to use them, and they probably still excite you. I think, too, your method of intercourse is a way of 'excusing' yourself from using the vagina on as many occasions as possible. Unconsciously you still fear the vagina or feel that penetrating a woman is a bad thing to do. However, since your wife likes the method all is well. As a preliminary to penetration many women might enjoy it since the vulva is so much more sensitive than the vagina.

Your wife, too, may be a bit inhibited and possibly feels that being masturbated by hand is rude whereas contact with the penis is acceptable. From what you say about her libido and orgasms it sounds as if this is possible but it is also possible that without either of you realizing it you have dictated the pattern of her response, since you could not stand a more passionate one from a woman you love. Since you enjoy intercourse with her.

277

more than anything else this fact is of no practical consequence.

I presume that your reason for saying you think you are homosexual is that your masturbation fantasies are homosexual? Possibly, too, you fantasize a homosexual scene during heterosexual intercourse?

I see no real value in you telling your wife about your homosexuality unless you feel so guilty you must have absolution from her or because you essentially want her permission to continue. I think the best advice is to get on with it and keep quiet.

Everything you say fits together. You have been very fortunate that it has all worked out so well in practice so my advice to you would be to alter nothing. Otherwise, troubles you don't anticipate might take you by surprise.

SPECIALITY SEX

Some of the more unusual and unfamiliar sex practices bring a light-hearted aspect to the serious subject of 'making love'.

ARM FETISH

Since I was a youngster I have always been fascinated sexually by bare arms. I was incapable of intercourse until my partner had bared her arms. I would push my sleeves up to my shoulders and link our bare arms, rubbing our upper arms together.

I loved to have women handling my arms, gripping them, and even caning them, until they were well marked with weals.

I also like to flaunt my bare arms in front of women; when out in my car, if I saw a girl walking along, I would stop and get out, pretending to look at the tyres, preferably with my back to them, and plump my arms out so that they could have a good look.

I could, and can still, masturbate whilst looking at a woman's bare arm. The more receptive girls in my office will grip my bare arms whilst I masturbate, and I often prefer that to intercourse.

Up to the last three or four years – I am 28 years of age now – women interested me most, but I have now had a homosexual experience or two and find myself just as much fascinated by male arms. As they enjoy my naked body, I beg my homosexual partners to grip my upper arms 'as hard and brutally as you like', and this they do when climaxing inside me. That is why I always take a passive role in these experiences – and that is why I spend endless time and money on beautifying my bare arms.

I am now courting a girl and we are deeply in love. Naturally, I haven't told her any of this, and indeed, when I am with her my arms don't seem to play such a big part; but I think my reticence is more out of love and respect than because the arm fetish is waning. My fiancée has very nice plump white arms and I have to control my demanding desire when I caress them.

What do you advise?

A.T.,
Liverpool

What is your fiancée going to say if and when she discovers your sexual predilections? Will she throw up her hands in horror and send you packing, or will she understand and accept you for what you are? Clearly, these are very important questions which need to be looked at before you set the date.

If you feel reasonably confident that you can hold your

'desires' in check, or alternatively that with marriage these will lose some of their savour and thereby become less obsessive, then I wouldn't bring the subject up for discussion. If, on the other hand, you doubt your capacity to exercise self-control, or you think she would be sympathetic and understanding anyway, then I would certainly talk the matter over with your fiancée. Although in these circumstances you clearly run the risk of being jilted I think it is far better to broach the matter before rather than after marriage.

It is always possible, but only remotely so I fear, that your fiancée will have like sexual preferences. If this is so you are fortunate indeed since your sexual pleasure will be shared.

Should you desire treatment to lessen your obsession – unnecessary, I think, unless it threatens to disrupt areas of your life you value more – a psychiatrist may be able to help. Therapy is chancy, however, and success cannot be guaranteed.

BOOTS, BOOTS, BOOTS

I am a boot fetishist. A sex dictionary defines a boot fetishist as a person who makes love to boots, particularly to women's boots. In my case, that is essentially correct. For a long time I thought I was the only guy in the world who had such an attraction to boots, but apparently, there are a number of similar fetishists around, according to my studies on the rather vague subject.

I am 20 years old and live with my parents out in the country. There aren't any girls around and I have had this attraction to boots since I was about six or so. I have developed many techniques to satisfy myself.

One of my favourite methods is to put on a pair of leather hip boots and then a wet suit, with a hood over this. I put a hot water bottle, filled with air pressure, into the crotch of my pants so it presses against my penis. This makes me sweat all over and in a little while I slide around in my wet suit and it feels heavenly, like I'm in a bathtub full of butter. I put a gas mask over my face with two air hoses running into my hip boots so I can breathe the hot vapour seeping from my boots. This smells so fantastic as I breathe it into my lungs deeply. I lie on my bed and masturbate against the rubber hot water bottle. I put the tube of the hot water bottle into my anus with a syringe. Just before I ejaculate, I release the pressure and let the air rush up my anus.

This is really fun and relaxing. Don't knock it if you haven't tried it!

M.A.,
Address withheld by request

There is a danger in placing air in the anus. This of course depends upon the amount of air used and the pressure under which it is applied.

Air is used in X-ray studies of the intestines. It is used to help increase the contrast effect of the study on the X-ray film. When used in this manner it produces intestinal cramps.

It is important to be aware that whenever air is placed in the human body the potential danger exists that the air might enter the general body circulation which can result in death. Since one must compare the potential dangers against the benefits obtained by any procedure done to the human body, I would discourage the use of this means of gratification. (Consultant)

'WHICH?' GUIDE TO CORRECTION

Like many of your readers, I am interested in what the news-agents' window cards call 'correction and discipline'. But I cannot afford to waste money on following up these ads at random and so have taken to making a preliminary visit to inspect the 'model' and her equipment before committing myself to a session.

I think readers may be interested in the insights into the 'discipline business' I have obtained so far by inspecting four such establishments advertised in a Mayfair newsagents.

The first was a top-floor flat not far from Green Park underground station. The model was described on the phone as 22 years old and 34-23-35. She was extremely attactive with an Irish accent, and looked even younger than 22.

The place was slightly seedy although the 'maid' was quite friendly. Despite the prominence of 'correction' in the advertisement the only discipline equipment was one whip, fairly good, and one cane which was light but swishy. There was a very limited amount of rubberwear including a wigan (rubber-surfaced) hooded cape, also some latex pants and a vest.

My questions revealed that she had really very little idea about discipline, and she didn't appear well equipped for bondage and restraint, a point which would preclude any serious operation in this field. She was, however, friendly and would not accept any money for showing me her facilities. In this she was unique.

On then to Earls Court and two establishments in Warwick Road. The first was disappointing.

The premises were dirty as was the equipment, and the model was far from attractive. The equipment included a moderate selection of whips, canes and tawses, some of which were quite powerful. A none too strong whipping frame and a rather rickety pair of stocks were available, and some of the gear was obviously home-made. There was very little rubberwear and what there was was very dirty and worn. A rather disappointing visit.

The second place was much better, a clean, good-class establishment with an attractive model probably not much older than 22 but much more mature than the girl at my first port of call. She seemed to know what whipping was all about.

She had a wide variety of whips, canes, tawses and straps, some capable of providing considerable punishment. Restraint was possible in several ways including a large sturdy whipping frame with padded cord restraints for wrists and ankles. The cords could be applied. A padded neck restraint was equipped with a chain although it was uncertain how this was secured. (It would clearly be dangerous to apply much tension here, and indeed there appeared to be no provision for so doing.) Stout cords were also provided on a large double bed, and they were also fitted to a single bed in another (smaller) room, and these provided very secure and effective bondage.

The large wardrobe of PVC and rubberwear was impressive. Wigan coats and rubber lined satin macs were available as was a long red rubber lined satin dress with a zip-up front. Various drawers claimed to contain numerous other articles including nurses' uniforms, ropes, hoods, gags, rubber sheeting and more. A vast collection of shoes was housed in a large shoe rack and many pairs of boots – long and short, in rubber and PVC – lined one of the walls.

This was, then, an impressive establishment and reasonably priced – a whipping being offered for five guineas (plus a tip for the maid!).

The final place on my list was near Knightsbridge. The girl here, although not quite so young or attractive as in the previous case, had a strong personality and was the friendliest I encountered. She talked freely and showed me all her equip-

283

ment, and although I have not yet availed myself of her services she gave the impression of skill and competence.

She had a moderate selection of canes, straps and tawses. Although she had what she called a 'stretch rack', which was a vertical whipping frame of uncertain strength, her pièce-de résistance was undoubtedly her 'whipping chair'. This was a very sturdy apparatus with provision for straps to secure various parts of the body, and which was arranged to hinge backwards in such a way that the naked bottom of the subject was presented at a convenient angle for chastisement. The rubber and PVC collection, though not large, had some good items including a heavy rubber lined mac with zip-up front, wigan and PVC macs etc.

Although uncertain what to expect, I cannot claim to be surprised at the wide differences in the standards encountered at different places. This could be a crucial factor to a beginner, such as myself, choosing a telephone number at random from a display cabinet and just turning up. An unfortunate choice could result in great embarrassment and unpleasantness, probably putting off the daunted adventurer from conducting any further exploits. A preliminary visit could save a great deal of trouble.

At the same time the operators should realize that there is some relatively effortless income to be made by simply exhibiting their collections to interested visitors. A suitable fee would be around two to three pounds (but with no hidden extras) possibly with a discount against a subsequent full service. This has clearly not occurred to these shrewd business ladies as was obvious from the hesitation occasioned by my request for a look round, and the unease which I detected at most places during my visit.

A final word of warning to the beginner: a curious form of gazumping takes place with such questions as 'How much do you have with you?', 'How much do you want to spend? After all £5 is only the basic price.' On occasions of this nature I rarely exhibit skill in bargaining and very quickly find myself forced up to £10. After the price is agreed, there is often a 'tip for the maid' who always keeps the change.

To conclude, I'd like to describe a slightly amusing observation I made, although I did not tumble to its significance until I had completed my visits. I came away with a hazy impression that business must have been pretty brisk. This somehow didn't square with two other observations, firstly that all the operators were happy for me to arrive at any time with no need to make an appointment, additionally that no one else ever called when I was there. I eventually realized that everywhere I had been I had heard the 'maid' answering telephone queries. I also realized, on reflection, that I always seemed to have interrupted such a call by my arrival, and that none of the telephones actually rang at all.

An interesting set of coincidences!

A.H.,
Yorkshire

LIMPING ADDICTION

My wife and I have been reading *Forum* regularly for over two years. But we have never seen any reference to something which really turns me on, the sight of an attractive girl who walks with a limp especially if she has a calliper on one leg.

Some weeks ago I was walking down the road behind a very attractive, well dressed, blonde girl with a calliper on her right leg and I became so aroused that I developed a very strong erection.

Is my addiction unique or do other readers have similar feelings?

J.R.,
Hertfordshire

Physical defects are as capable of becoming turn-ons for some men as specific physical attractions are for others. A fascination with limping women is not at all unique, and cases have been described by sex researchers from Krafft-Ebing onwards. Similarly, there are men who are excited by partners who squint, or have had a limb amputated, or are grossly fat.

Technically, as you know, these unusual turn-ons are called fetishes. They seem to originate in childhood experiences, and in extreme cases can interfere seriously with the establishment of satisfying relationships. But few people are completely without any predilection for some sex object apart from the 'normal' ones – even women, who seem less prone than men to extreme forms of fetishism, often find themselves particularly attracted by, for instance, moustaches, and unable to really enjoy making love to a man who has not got one. The fact that your mild fetish is an uncommon one should not worry you in the slightest.

SEX IS DIRTY

The several times that I have read your magazine I was particularly interested in the letters. There's somehow safety in numbers and I keep hoping to find a comrade who shares my fetish.

I am a happily married man of 28. My wife is a petite, lovely little blonde whom I love very much. Yet there's a certain aspect of my sexual desires she can't satisfy, though I couldn't possibly tell her about it.

I have this thing for ugly, fat, trashy women. Most men are turned off by the reject types who hang out in bars longing to be picked up, yet the scum variety excites me unreasonably. I prowl for some dog who's not a hooker, just lonely and horny, and say such things to her that Shakespeare would note were he alive to hear them. I'm rather good looking and I have no problem getting quickly involved sexually with these women. I buy them obscenely sexy lace garter belts and crotchless panties with matching bras with cut-out nipples. I am repulsed and in heaven all at once and make love to these women in a heat of passion that I've never experienced with even the most beautiful and sexy regular girls I've ever been to bed with. Some of these gals are so fat they need help getting out of a chair. Others have rotted teeth, severe acne or an abnormal amount of facial hair. Many pay very little attention to hygiene, and yet I beg them to let their bodies smell natural and sensuously earthy. The majority wear so much cheap make-up you'd need a palette knife to ever see their actual skin, but I'm terribly aroused by the slutty air it lends.

It all sounds neurotic, even to myself. I keep justifying it by saying these women have probably never been courted so grandly in their lives. I treat them as intensely desirable females, and they are starved for it. I've had this fetish ever since I was a teenager but of course was unable to establish any long term relationship with this sort of woman because of social pressure. I felt I had to marry the kind of girl my parents and friends felt was in my league. I love my wife, and she's everything any man would want – except she's not stupid, ugly, fat and cheap enough to please my hidden desires.

I would honestly like your opinion as to whether this is just a harmless fetish or a serious maladjustment.

J.S.,
Address withheld by request

You're in good company! The double image of women in our culture is centuries old and still very much current today. Women are Madonnas – virgin mothers – or whores; and clearly there are things one can do with the latter that one wouldn't envisage with the former. Sometimes the two types of women are divided by class – thus the English public-school dictum that women fall into two categories, the ones you can screw and your friends' sisters.

Given that the notion that 'nice girls don't' is still widespread, what makes it take on such importance in a particular case? Very many men will go further with prostitutes or casual pickups than they would with their wives, or dream longingly for years about things they simply couldn't ask decent women like their wives to do – without actually seeking repulsive partners.

Clearly, you despise and fear your sexual nature. You fear that to reveal your true depth of sexuality to a 'good' woman like your wife would make her think you trashy (in fact she might be delighted!).

The women you can go with are women who, because they're lonely 'rejects', will feel grateful for your attentions, far from holding them in contempt – and they're also women whose opinion of you doesn't matter a damn. Your sex urge, you think, is so dirty that only a dirty woman is a fit partner.

I hope you treat your pickups with kindness and consideration – they have feelings just as you do. If this is so, one might say that things can happily go on as they are provided you are discreet. But naturally you would be happier, and your marriage richer, if you were able to express your sexual nature fully with your wife. This will be easier if she too has hidden sexual depths; more than likely, though she may outwardly be inhibited. You could try very gradually to get her to express more interest; bring a copy of Forum *or the 'Sensuous Woman' or the 'Sensuous Couple' home, saying you found it in a bar or something.*

On your side, try to accept emotionally what you already know intellectually – that women, all women, are at least as sexy as men if not more so; that sex is good, the 'social glue' without which human culture would never have begun; that anything two people do lovingly together is fine; that some highly respectable women have cut-out bras and crotchless panties tucked away and are no whit the less good mothers, good wives, and pillars of the community.

Therapy may help you come to terms with your sexual nature and also help you be yourself. At the moment, you are obviously over-influenced by social pressure to conform and social status; this is an important factor in your problem.

NOSTALGIE DE BOUE

I feel, due to the broad-mindedness of your magazine, that I can speak of my long-silenced problem.

For over a year now I have had a strong urge to make it with old men like tramps and drooling drunks. In fact the more sordid and disgusting the situation, the more aroused I become.

At first I thought this was just a natural fantasy and did not let it disturb me. But recently I have found that I cannot reach a satisfactory climax without first imagining it. I did not let this worry me as I found it most enjoyable.

But now I feel I have let it go too far, as recently as I was walking home late at night I found myself being followed by a lecherous street-prowler who was making his intentions quite obvious. Much to my disgust I was not afraid; I found the whole situation exceedingly exciting and took great joy in provoking him.

This stimulated me to such an extent that eventually I let him have intercourse with me, whilst making the pretence of fighting and struggling against it, to heighten my own ecstatic enjoyment.

As a result, I now cannot face having sex with anyone as I feel so disgusted with myself. Sometimes I feel that everyone knows and is looking at me. I have begun to think that I really am very abnormal and just don't know where to look for help, as I don't think that I could speak to anyone face to face about it. Please could you help me, before I go mad with worry.

Miss J.L.,
Surrey

It is not easy to write a full reply to your letter without knowing more about you. For example, you do not say how old you are, or what sort of social and sexual life you had prior to this difficult last year. But I can offer the following comments.

Firstly, your fantasies and experiments are a little unusual but in no way shocking. Most of us have quite complicated attitudes to sexual activity, and view it with mixed feelings. There are deeply rooted psychological reasons why this is so. At times we think of sex and love as being linked with 'higher' attributes of ourselves and other humans: at others, it is the primitive and animal aspects of sexual behaviour which impress us. We may 'split' our sex drive or libido by allowing ourselves to feel only tender, non-genital emotions towards one person while directing our physical desires or lust at another.

Perhaps you have had some special difficulty in feeling sexual interest in socially eligible men and have felt an urge to go as far as possible in testing out your physical instincts in a situation which is totally out of keeping with the rest of your social life and habits. Perhaps (again, I can only speculate) you are mildly masochistic, and the repulsion which you feel when you think of having sex in squalid circumstances carries excitement because it brings a sense of degradation or self-punishment. Your feigned struggle with the lecherous street walker somewhat supports this explanation. A great many normal women have mild masochistic tendencies.

Whatever the precise reason for your recent thoughts and actions, I am quite sure that no damage has been done. The guilt which you describe is understandable but unnecessary. If your general health is alright and the rest of your life reasonably satisfactory there is no reason why you should not soon return to the more conventional sort of sex life which you presumably had in the past.

If, on the other hand, you have any reason to think that your general nervous health is disturbed (for example if you are sleeping badly, or if the mistaken idea that everyone is looking at you persists) then it would be a wise precaution to consult your doctor.

ROCKING HORSE JOYS

I have just found a really exciting masturbation technique, and would like to share my discovery with your female readers.

I was playing a game with my young son which involved my riding his rocking horse. This is a large horse which has been in the family for many years and will take the weight of an adult quite easily. I got on and started to ride it, whooping like an Indian, while he was the cowboy.

But as I rocked back and forth I was aware that it was exerting a pleasant pressure on my clitorus. As soon as he was in bed (my husband was on night work) I got on the horse again and started rocking again. After a few minutes I was feeling just about as randy as I have ever been; I took off all my clothes and really rode in earnest! At first I was content with the gentle friction of the saddle but as my excitement mounted, I rode faster and faster until I had one of the most violent orgasms I have ever experienced.

Now, nearly every day, I go for my 'ride'. You can't beat the old toys for new pleasures!

Mrs G.H.,
Berkshire

LOVE IN THE SADDLE

I am 28, single, and an only child. I was brought up in a small town, on the outskirts of which live an aunt and uncle who own a farm. Our home is within easy walking distance, so from the age of nine I often went there on my own, to help my uncle with the animals. He kept horses, too, and this is where my story really begins.

At that early age I developed a great liking for horses, would watch them at their romps in the fields and also became quite accustomed to seeing a stallion mount a mare. I enjoyed watching the stallion's huge lump of flesh entering the mare; I used to wait eagerly for this to happen; and when it did, would get as close as possible to witness it. Not being able to restrain my curiosity any longer I asked my uncle why they were doing it, and received the reply that 'he was giving her a baby'. I was even allowed to be present at the birth of a foal and it was then my young mind began to wonder: if horses do that to make their young, do humans do similar things? I became more and more interested in the lump of flesh between the stallion's legs, noticed there were times when it would lengthen (up to a foot or more) and also became fascinated by the knowledge that it also used it to pee through. Such observations seemed to hold me spellbound.

I continued visiting the farm and at the age of 15 my interests reached their peak. My uncle had a particularly fine stallion, whom I christened Bobby. I made a fuss of him, fed him, and we became good friends. I had learned to ride and had many good trips around the fields on Bobby's back. It was on one afternoon when I had dismounted and was opening the gate for us to cross into another field, that I noticed Bobby peeing. After that his 'thing' started to lengthen and get stiff. It was then my desires got the better of me. I had always longed to touch the intimate parts of a horse. So leading Bobby through the gate and into the next field, we stopped behind some trees. I stroked his head, face, back and under his belly, and moving my hand backwards got hold of his weapon. I cannot explain the tremendous thrill it gave me to masturbate him.

When going to bed that night my thoughts were on what I had done to Bobby, and they excited me to the point of playing with myself. Bobby's place in the stable was at the far end, thus when knowing when nobody would be around to disturb me I would make excuses to go there and see how he was. If he showed signs of excitement I would attend to him until he came.

At 16 I got myself a boyfriend and one day while together in the woods, hugging and kissing, he got sexually excited. He took out his penis, put my hand there and asked me to rub it for him. The feeling of such a tiny thing in my hand was almost laughable, considering I had been accustomed to handling a horse's. However I rubbed him off and him fingering me gave the moment added pleasure. At 18 I had my first sexual intercourse with another boy but the feeling of his penis inside me didn't seem to give much satisfaction. I have tried it with other males since, but experienced the same unsatisfactory results. If they played with my breasts or fingered me I enjoyed it; but when it came to penetration, the size of the penis has never brought me to orgasm. I have even had them do it to me in the rear-entry position; but that too has failed. My sexual practices with horses have now ceased although I still masturbate myself while thinking about them. Your comments could help.

Miss J.A.,
Lancashire

The problem which you face is that, because you did not have any notion of other forms of sexual outlet when your interest in horses first began, you have used the fantasy of a stallion's penis as your masturbatory excitement. Now, at least in regard to penis size, men cannot match up.

You could try to readjust this fantasy by becoming excited by thoughts of horses, then, when you are about to have an orgasm, imagine a man's penis, either being held, rubbed, or inside you, and come while thinking of this. Gradually, you will find that you can use the image of a man's penis earlier and earlier in the fantasy until you are only using that.

As far as your sexual relationships with men are concerned –

I am not surprised that your orgasm is not affected or triggered by the size of penis. That is the case for virtually all *women! What matters most is the degree of clitoral stimulation you get (by moving the genitals together while making love, or by using the fingers and tongue of the man) while lovemaking. Don't worry about your partner's penis size – get him to rub your clitoris like you do when you masturbate and you* will *get satisfactory results!*

THE EROTIC ENEMA

A month or two ago, during a spell in hospital, I had to have an enema. I found this extremely embarrassing; for when, at the nurse's request, my pyjama trousers were removed, a very erect penis was revealed.

Nothing was said by the nurse as she inserted the nozzle of the enema and commenced syringeing me. But I became possessed with an insane desire to put my hand up her clothes and although I naturally did not do so, I am afraid I lost control and 'came off'.

I was handed a towel to wipe up the mess, and I very sheepishly offered my apologies to the nurse, who however, seemed quite unperturbed. She said that men patients sometimes reacted in this way when being syringed.

I was given several more enemas and on each occasion the same thing happened causing the nurse to ask if the syringeing gave me pleasure. And I had to confess that it did.

This was not all however, for having realized the sensitiveness of my anal opening, on being released from hospital, I bought myself an enema syringe which I now use quite frequently. The results are still the same, a powerful erection and an almost violent ejaculation at some time during the syringeing, often without any stimulation from my hand.

Please tell me, is it a normal thing for some men to react in this way to an enema or am I some kind of freak? I am 50 years old.

My sex life with my wife does not appear to have been affected although, of course, I have not told her about the enemas.

I do have a very happy recollection of being syringed in this way by my mother during my boyhood. Can there be any connection?

J.T.,
Birmingham

As regular readers will know, erotic reactions to enemas are quite common. The anus has nervous connections with the rest of the genitals and everybody, probably, has some degree of sexual sensitivity there.

When adults take to enemas as eagerly as you have, however, one generally finds some childhood history of receiving enemas. At the time when you were a child, 'inner cleanliness' was all the rage and constipation thought to have serious consequences. Laxatives and purgatives were in great demand. The result is that many people have been left with some degree of fixation on enemas. Fortunately, self-administration of enemas – provided reasonable common sense is used – is harmless (though medically unnecessary). A number of nurses offer their services in the classified columns of some papers and magazines to those for whom self-administration is not enough.

Try persuading your wife to manipulate your rectum during intercourse, as a common and acceptable way of incorporating your anal eroticism into your ordinary lovemaking.

SHOWING HER OFF

I am 40 years old and have been in love with the same woman for more than a decade. Last year we got involved in a three-way encounter with another man. I found that I become tremendously excited and stimulated when I undress my sweetheart in full view of others and I love seeing her fondled and fucked by other men. I have never experienced such profound pleasure or felt more capable than during this encounter when I watched her being eaten by another man.

Lately, I find that whenever possible, I start undressing my wife in front of other men. As she is very beautiful, I have never found other men unwilling to watch or participate. She knows that she is not obligated to do any of this and if she desires she can do anything she wants with me, the other man, or both simultaneously. However, no homosexual activities have or ever will take place as I cannot even stand the thought of making love to another man.

My question regarding my relations with my wife is whether or not this is normal behaviour. When we are alone our lovemaking is fantastic too. She has always cooperated willingly and enjoyed herself, so she must derive as much pleasure as I do. However, I think she sometimes wonders if she is allowing herself to become a 'lesser' person. I only love her more for wanting to be everything I could ever ask for.

P.D.,
Address withheld by request

I sense from your letter that you are as unconvinced of your wife's feelings as you are about the normality of your acts and desires regarding exhibitionism. You may be treating her unfairly. She may not feel comfortable being undressed by her husband in front of other men or being shared with other male partners. Perhaps the only reason she has not objected is because she is worried you may lose interest in her or because she feels intimidated by you and does not have the courage to voice her disapproval. On the other hand, she may enjoy being displayed in this manner as much as you enjoy exposing her.

Most men find the idea of displaying their wives to an appreciative audience very erotic and egotistically reinforcing. In a ménage à trois, watching two people make love can be as stimulating as participating. Exhibitionist tendencies are really quite common, although few people admit to it. However, I think you may be carrying this beyond the range of normality. You seem to constantly want gratification from the covetous eyes of strangers, a kind of approval that reasserts your wife's sexual attraction. You want to continually affirm that you 'possess' a beautiful wife.

Two men might very well be better than one, but I think you should discuss this with your wife. She may not want anyone but you. Perhaps she has reluctantly been submitting to the gratification of your fantasies. If you discover she does not really enjoy this mode of lovemaking, then you should make other arrangements. Your desires are not all that's involved here. You must take your wife's opinions into consideration, so find out how she feels.

PLEASURES OF SPANKING

I have always felt intolerant towards homosexuals and believed that they should be publicly whipped.

Shortly after I was married, I went to a party on my own. Someone started an argument about homosexuals and I was soon on my pet subject. Whether it was mixing drinks or because somone doped me, I woke in a strange bed the next day and was perturbed when another naked body started to maul me. I hopped out and took a look at my bedmate, a huge hairy fellow. When fully awake, he said he had enjoyed me immensely. I was the best 'girl' he had ever had.

I am smooth with hardly any body hair and am rather plump. My breasts are rather big for a male. When he had convinced me he had really used me, I attacked him. With a grin, he grabbed me and putting me across his knee, gave me a spanking. When he released me, I was almost in tears.

My wife had the 'no speaks' because I had stayed out all night. What was worse was that I had become temporarily impotent. Though in bed for three nights she made no attempt to make love, I knew if she did, I would not have been able to make it.

Finally on the fourth day, fortified with a few stiff whiskies, I began haltingly to confess. At first she showed complete indifference, but once she understood that there was no other woman involved, she seemed to show amused interest. When I told her of the spanking, she nodded her approval. The further I got with my confession, the more I seemed to be not a husband but a small boy confessing to Mam knowing he is going to get his bottom smacked.

That is what I wanted then so I asked her what she would have done to me for staying out all night had I been her son instead of her husband. She said no problem: over her knee and my pants down. Rather foolishly, I suggested pretending that I was a boy. She seemed quite enthusiastic about the idea. I stripped off and she took me across her knee spanking me with a long handled clothes brush. It was extremely painful but sexually exciting. When it was over, we made love on the bed; it was lovely, never had it seemed better.

'Mam' took complete control of me from then on with at least one spanking a week and the occasional caning.

For rudeness to her mother who stayed with us for a period, I was spanked. When her mother found out, she approved believing that men were only little boys grown up.

Spanking sexually excites me. To my wife it is a serious business. I love her more now than I did at first. My wife is a very understanding woman and after a number of years, I would not have our relationship any different.

Would you say I was a freak?

J.S.,
Australia

*No, not a freak, but somebody with some awareness of a long-
term personality problem. Your partial awareness relating the
boyhood spanking with some of the present desires has a ring of
truth and all goes well for your taking the next step. That step
would lead you to link the spanking that you now enjoy as a
preliminary to sexual excitement with your wife. Your homosexual preoccupation and subsequent involvement presents
further complications that you could consider latent. If you
really want to face up to the matter, it will mean hard, intensive
and prolonged work on your part with a psychoanalyst. Yet if
you and your wife are content with the feature of your present
relationship that you mentioned, there is no need for you to
change your behaviour. Unless that were the case, you would
not be sufficiently motivated to begin and continue the rigours
of lengthy emotional treatment.*

THE SMELLS OF LOVE

As a woman I am very interested to read letters on sexual
smells and people's reactions to them.

I must admit that smells of this type neither encourage nor
discourage me in lovemaking, but my husband is very much
affected by vaginal odours. When smells emanate from my
body, my husband's sexual reactions are completely different
than when there are none.

After a bath, when all the natural smells have been washed
away, we have sex in the usual way. But when my husband
makes love to me before my bath, and the normal vaginal
odours are present, his lovemaking is quite different. Like a dog,
he sniffs around until he finds the source, between my legs, and
then he licks and sucks me orally until we both climax (he
usually comes off over my feet).

Strangely, he only reacts like this when I smell womanly, and
if I use vaginal deodorants, or perfume, he only wants straightforward intercourse.

He also finds the smell during menstruation offensive, and
during this period I usually fellate him.

Because he is so affected by smells I am able to choose whatever lovemaking method I like, just by deciding whether to
bathe or not.

My husband is 42 and we have been married for 16 years. He
is extremely virile and likes to have sex every night, but it is I
who decide how.

I was very interested to read a letter in which the writer, Mrs. M.M., describes her husband's reactions when she peed in him during oral sex. I had never ever considered doing this before, but that encouraged me to try the same experiment.

I did, at the first opportunity, and discovered that my husband's reactions were the same as hers. He loved it and it made a very pleasant and new thrill for both of us to enjoy. I would certainly recommend your women readers whose husbands enjoy cunnilingus to give it a try and see their husbands' reactions. I was very surprised, like Mrs. M.M., by discovering that in fact my husband really enjoys the taste of my urine, and I have repeated it twice since.

I would also like to hear the results from any readers who try this, and their menfolk's reactions.

Mrs. M.O'D.,
Kent

EXCITING ODOURS

I have found little in *Forum* about a particular 'thing' I have about sexual odours.

I am 39, and have been happily married for 13 years, with two lovely children. My wife and I enjoy a full sex life, and we have been in a well organized swapping circle with five or six other couples for nearly a year. But there is always something missing for me in these sessions. All the women seem to bathe beforehand.

I can explain better what I mean by divulging an experience I had at work a few weeks ago. I am an assistant manager in a concern which manufactures domestic electrical items, and for some time I had been keen on a packer. She is about 30, short, blonde and has a sturdy but shapely figure. In my imagination I always started by kneeling before her, pulling off her panties and burying my nose in between her legs.

(In fact, this has always been in my thoughts whatever girl I fancied. My wife is very particular about hygiene, and washes and perfumes her vagina and anus before we make love. I wish she wouldn't do this, but somehow cannot bring myself to broach the subject.)

To cut the story, I made good progress with the packer. I heard on the grapevine she was a randy piece, and she obviously knew why I wanted to see her in my office after working hours.

We had a couple of drinks and a smoke and then a passionate

kissing session. Then I was down before her, and peeling a pair of black frilly panties from her heavy buttocks. She wanted to lead me to a thick rug before the fire, but I held her back and drew her towards me. She pulled away a little, and said she had not 'washed' for three days. This, in fact, made me more excited, and I buried my face in her crotch. The smell was very heavy and pungent, but it made me quite overcome with lust. I even spun her round and, pulling her buttocks apart, put my nose hard against her anus. We had normal intercourse on the rug later and I went at her like a mad animal. We both came together with a most satisfying climax. The following week she left the company, much to my annoyance, and we didn't meet again.

Now, every time I see a female I fancy, I imagine her unwashed and with a strong, sweaty, pungent but sweet odour in her pubic hair. I even, on visiting other flats or houses, sneak off and look for a dirty pair of panties or tights to smell. If successful, I am twice the man and am complimented in our swapping games.

Is my desire dangerously unhygienic, and am I warped to be this way? It does worry me, so please advise me.

B.D.,
Essex

Odours make a very important contribution to sexuality, especially in the lower animals. They help to distinguish, identify and locate the sexes, to reveal the sexual receptivity of the female and to encourage the male to pay attention to the vulva including stimulating it with his tongue and mouth. Your interest in and arousal by odour is therefore normal and is part of our animal inheritance.

With humans, however, the effect of odour is variable due to the attitudes we are given about it during rearing. Many children are told not to touch or enjoy the smell of excreted material because it is 'dirty'. Later they are told not to touch their genitals because it is 'dirty'. This over-emphasizes the connection between excretion and sex; also it explains why sex is seen as a 'dirty' subject by many people.

Thus it comes about that many women really regard the vulva and vagina as being like drains or sewers and so dislike the odour and genital secretions. They dislike touching their genitals, worry about the smell, hate menstruation and reject cunnilingus as a 'filthy' procedure. It was probably because she

298

*had allowed you to smell her that your blonde left – she was
ashamed of herself and couldn't face you again. Some men also
have the same attitudes towards the vulva and they are usually
inhibited over sex to an above average degree.*

*The vulva has special 'scent' glands and the perfume they
produce is largely responsible for the characteristic odour of the
area. To most men this is exciting and smelling it enhances their
arousal. However, if the vulva is not cleansed regularly the
accumulated secretions begin to decompose due to bacteria
which are present and the odour ceases to be subtle and
becomes pungent and offensive. It seems that when a woman is
in this condition she is maximally arousing to you. It is difficult
to say why this should be so. Perhaps you have a poor sense of
smell and so need a real 'pong' before you perceive it or perhaps
there are marked masochistic features in your sexuality which
make you enjoy being humiliated by the odour. On the other
hand you are possibly sadistic and like to humiliate the woman
by making her uncomfortable by smelling her when she feels
unclean.*

*Since the vulva and vagina are 'septic' areas of the body, ie
there are many bacteria present, the practice of cunnilingus is
unhygienic. But so is kissing the lips! In consequence there is
no great need to worry about it unless the woman has gonorrhoea, when you could infect your tonsils with the germ. Cunnilingus is common but acute mouth and lip diseases are
relatively rare.*

COLD SEX

Do any other readers get sexual excitement from jumping
into sea or river when it's freezing cold? Better to be pushed,
better still to be wearing a rubber mac, best of all to have
shared a whipping first.

It started when I was 13. At my grammar school we were sent
swimming in the river all through the summer term. It was a
couple of fields away, and though we were allowed to wear
practically nothing in the water, decorum in the 1930s demanded that on the way down we covered it with a mac after
changing at school. There was a knotted rope hanging from a
tree, on which you could swing out over the water and back to
land unless someone else stopped you with his foot or joined
you, which meant an eventual forced immersion.

In October, the beginning of my second year, I discovered

299

that a number of boys were voluntarily continuing to swim after school hours. I joined in; I'd already got hooked on the cold showers my parents thought 'good for me' since I was 10. Numbers dropped as it got colder, and the first snow reduced us to five, who swore never to surrender.

It was then that one boy, a year older, whom I admired, remarked that we all came down in the same kind of mac. Single-texture rubber wasn't uncommon for boys before the war, but many people thought them a bit thin for winter, so it was a sign of toughness I suppose. My mum thought them 'healthy', but they were also cheap, which was important when you grew out of things every year or so. I'd worn them for years and thought nothing of it, yet I was electrified when my friend went on to say they were a good thing to have because it wouldn't hurt them if we happened to fall in.

I knew by instinct that this was what he did want and so did I. It took only a moment to dare him on to the rope before he'd undressed and then join him there. In the moment of suspense before we dropped I could feel his horn against mine, and in the icy water I had my first real orgasm.

We repeated the process other days (the rest didn't seem to find it odd) but said nothing to one another until one day he said casually it was time he got himself caned again. When I looked surprised he said it was better than the rope, and why didn't I join him? I forget now what we did, probably got ourselves caught smoking cigarettes. Caning was rare at the school, but they took it seriously. We turned up in the gym after school, dressed as for swimming, in slips that left most of one bare, and the young gym master cheerfully informed us that he'd try to hurt as much as he could.

My friend kept his mac on to the last moment, then spread it on the 'horse' over which he was bent. Looking from the side I could see his hard, and feel my own growing as I watched the cane cutting raw welts into his bottom. Oddly, that was the worst; when my own turn came I enjoyed it, though it hurt like hell. Without a word we ran as hard as we could to the river and came like volcanoes in it.

Rubber and cane seem to be common enough stimulants, but I don't often hear of a cold dip in this connection, yet I suppose there must be others like me, as in every other matter.

L.B.,
London

300

WIFE AN EXHIBITIONIST

I'm 31 and my wife is 28. We have been married for six years. My wife is very beautiful, and in the past year she has become an established exhibitionist. She has certain ways that she exposes herself, whether we're in the supermarket, theatre, or wherever we are. Because she has a tremendous body anyway, men are constantly looking at her, but when she manages to expose a breast, thigh, or even her pubic area in a public place, the men really go crazy.

She seldom wears anything more than bra and panties around the house, and I have come home many times unexpectedly to find her washing dishes or doing some other household chore in the nude. As in all homes there is the constant flow of salesmen, the postman and of course the paperboy. When I asked her what she did when they came to the door she said, 'Nothing, I answer the door no matter what I'm not wearing'. Because of this we have salesmen calling all day long, since word has got around about my wife. I've tried everything to get her to stop exhibiting her body to everyone, but she says, 'I'm not doing anything wrong, only allowing other men to see what you see every day, and I enjoy letting other men see me in the nude'.

What do you suggest I do to get her to stop?

Name withheld by request,
New York NY

Does your wife have a healthy appreciation of her own body? It may be that her chronic need for attention is indicative of lack of self-esteem or even hostility towards men. If, however, she does seem genuinely at ease in the nude, you might explore with her at least four issues.

1. Other men may see her as you see her, ie, nude, but you also have the privilege and pleasure of physical intimacy whereas other men may simply become angry at a 'cockteaser'.

2. There is potential danger to her by frustrated and angry males who are 'turned on' while she is alone in the house.

3. Her behaviour may draw stares, but it may also be drawing the laughter of ridicule.

4. She may be exposing herself to arrest or legal problems.

You seem rather cold in your appraisal of your wife's vital statistics. Do you value her as a person? Perhaps patience and authentic affection on your part will support her in exhibiting her nudity in a more joyful and less compulsive context. And are you sure that the life she leads gives her enough opportunities to express herself in other ways? If she has some frustrated talents or abilities, encourage her to use them in study or work – perhaps modelling – this would give her some other way of self-validation besides the sexual. You can impress people, achieve status (needs we all share) through your career. Your wife has only housewifery as an outlet. She may well be one of the very many women for whom this is not enough.

FEMALE EXHIBITIONISM

Several recent letters to *Forum* concerning female exhibitionism have given me the courage to reveal my own sexual hang-up, which I have never admitted to anyone.

Although I live in a fairly populated area I generally keep late hours and so do not bother to close the curtains at night when I undress for bed. One night several months ago when I had taken off all my clothes and was about to turn out my light, I noticed that the curtains in a flat across the street were slightly parted and that a fairly young man was watching me and (I could tell by the movements of his hand) masturbating.

Though I have had no little sexual experience myself – I am 24, unmarried, and considered good-looking – my first reaction was one of horror and I rushed to close the curtains, unthinkingly, I'm afraid, since this provided him with a closer view of my nakedness. I could see his hand moving very rapidly. The knowledge that I could see him did not disturb him in the least; on the contrary, it seemed to stimulate him all the more and, as I stood transfixed for a moment, I saw him ejaculate into a handkerchief.

Needless to say, I was quite shaken by the experience and for the next few nights made quite sure that my curtains were closed. Still, I could not get the picture of him out of my mind. At work my mind would wander to what I had seen and I would grow so excited that I would be forced to go to the ladies room to relieve myself by hand, something I had not done with any frequency since my adolescence. By the end of five or six days I was masturbating several times daily with the most intense climaxes of my life. Each time I fantasized how he had looked, and my deepest desire, though I fought it constantly, was to repeat the experience.

About 10 days later I did. I left my curtain open and made a point of walking around the room totally nude, finding frequent excuses to pass before the window and even (though I am ashamed to say it) to finger my clitoris in what must have been his view. After several minutes of this, he appeared at his window, nude, his penis erect, his right hand slowly stroking it. I could not move from the window, nor could I control my behaviour. I began to masturbate, first slowly and almost as if in a state of hypnotism, then more rapidly and wildly, until I came as I never have come before, all the time watching his hand and penis and face. When my climax subsided, I felt sick and cried myself to sleep. I had never been so thoroughly disgusted with myself.

You might expect that I have never repeated the experience but I have, several times in fact, each time with the same uncontrollable excitement and afterwards with the same guilt. It is as though I cannot help myself. My exhibitionism has even extended to other outlets. For example, I have taken to going without panties and sitting with my legs uncrossed in buses, restaurants, and even at work. I derive tremendous excitement from the effect of this upon men. I can see their erections rise through their pants, and several times (as in restaurants) when they have risen to go to the men's room I like to think that they have gone to masturbate, as I too often do after such incidents. Since I do not compromise myself as much in these situations, I do not suffer the guilt I do from my more blatant exhibitionism.

I realize that I represent an extreme of female exhibitionism, but the letters I have read in *Forum* have greatly eased my anxiety. I find I am unable to give up my habit. The next best thing, I imagine, is to reconcile myself to it. I would be interested in hearing whether other women have had similar experience and, if so, how they have coped with them.

Miss S.C.,
Address withheld by request

Although you emphasize your exhibitionism, I am struck by the amount of excitement which you get from seeing or imagining male genitals. Your interest in tumescent penises, etc, is voyeuristic, although I appreciate that it is heightened by the thought that these men are reacting especially to you.

The wish to exhibit the female body and thereby stimulate male interest and excitement is perfectly normal. Your own desire to display the genital area to strangers in everyday situations is less usual.

Males and females tend to differ from each other in the value which they place on looking at their genitals. Men have to expose, see and handle their penises several times daily while urinating. They grow up familiar with the sight of their penises, each able to recognize his own by its unique details.

By contrast, most women take little interest in the shape of their own vulvas. To get a good view requires undressing, acrobatics, and a mirror. Some women cannot be bothered to inspect themselves in this way, others feel inhibited from doing so, and few become any more familiar with the sight of what they have 'down below' than men do with that of their own anuses.

Hence the female genital exhibitionist can have little confidence in the precise appearance of what she is exhibiting, and (as you may have discovered) she is also handicapped by the difficulty of doing so without effort and contortion.

Again, one theory of exhibitionism in the male assumes that it is based on infantile fears of castration, and a desire to demonstrate that the penis is still there. The same theory postulates that the female unconsciously regards herself as a castrated male – hence female genitals are things to be concealed rather than exhibited!

Whatever the reason, deliberate genital exhibitionism in females is quite rare, and very few criminal charges have ever been brought on account of it. By contrast, deliberate general body exposure, with hiding of the genitals and (when legally necessary) nipples, is an almost universally approved social activity.

Returning to your own experiences, I see no reason why you should not be able to integrate both your voyeurism and your exhibitionism into a more shared personal sex life. I would regard your recent activities as an experimental phase.

PAIN/PLEASURE

Frequent recent correspondence on punishment and spanking prove such activities popular enough in thought if not in deed. Many of the letters seem pure wishful fantasy. Chance would be a fine thing!

There have been five episodes of 'violence' in my relationships with women, spanning a period of over 30 years.

The first was in 1944, when 20 years old and billeted ashore in an East coast of England port when my ship was mined. I had a room of my own in a house and got friendly with an army corporal in the ATS (the British Army's women's service). She was a lovely girl some seven years older than I, who frequently reminded me she was a married woman with a husband overseas. She only allowed mild petting, so I packed her in for more willing partners.

However, she was often in my room on my return from an evening out. I always tried to seduce her, without success, trying harder each time until our sessions became wrestling matches. I did not push it to the limit, being no natural rapist, but she always returned for more – sometimes waiting until I returned very late after sex with other women.

I came back one night after drinking and it struck me she *wanted* me to rape her. This could have led to trouble but I took the chance. Let me say that for over an hour we struggled and sweated, grunted and groaned, until I was about ready to quit. Her defence was most strenuous, but I never would have prevented her leaving the room – nor did she attempt to at any time. At last I had her below me on the bed in a considerable state of undress: tie removed and shirt wide open, bra removed and breasts out, khaki pants and skirt pulled off. Her legs were forced apart by my knees and both of us were quite exhausted and gasping for air.

Believe me, rape's not worth the effort for amateurs. In the grappling I'd lost any erection I had, but regained one by kissing her mouth and breasts while holding her spreadeagled arms down by the wrists. Penetration followed and she gradually began to convulse and orgasm strongly, all the time pleading 'No, no, please, no,' while evidently unable to prevent arousal. Indeed she gripped me so tightly and locked her legs around me in the latter stages that I feared impregnating her.

On her final subsidence, I withdrew and heaved myself up to come over her breasts. She then began sobbing and abused me for 'taking' her like that, though I suspected she was relieved I had not ejaculated into her. I could only imagine she wanted it without appearing casually unfaithful to her husband. I took her out a few times after that to dances and cinemas, but refused to be drawn into her charade although she came to my room and lolled on my bed. Too much like hard work.

Over 20 years later, in the late 1960s while working in Africa, I became intimate with a young Scottish secretary less than half my age. We lived in her cottage and it was marvellous sex for me with such a cuddly partner not long out of secretarial college. We indulged in all the variations and well satisfied she seemed from the paroxysms displayed in multiple climaxes. It became obvious she was a kinky lass.

She had an African housegirl who served us tea in bed each morning around seven, when my girl would cuddle up sensuously. This of course led to me being astride her, being fellated or performing cunnilingus when the servant came in with the tray. My partner would grunt, groan and writhe and orgasm fantastically. The housegirl, by the way, thought nothing of it except perhaps that it was a little odd.

My young lover liked to flirt outrageously with boys at parties and dances, for which I did not blame her one bit. I was only too thankful for what I had received and quite resigned to losing her. She however began to nag me for allowing such freedom, sulking after such incidents. It penetrated my dull brain she wanted a strict master. To appear more possessive I got into a fight with a young admirer and being an old ex-seagoing scrapper beat him severely. I was 46 at the time and the youth was the son of a colleague, so imagine how *my* name was bandied about the white community.

Following this we began to argue. One night in bed it turned into a shouting match and ended in a physical fight. I left the bedroom half-wrecked, my nose bleeding, and her eye blacked and body pummelled. For all that I pulled my punches. We made night-long love afterwards, and she was so sweet and demure it was evident I had soared in her estimation. She wore her black eye and bruises with pride at the tennis club and swimming pool. Me? I got out. My wife was coming out for an extended holiday anyway! Looking back, I regret not smacking that young lady's bottom. I'm sure she would have loved it. Of course, not so much was written about that activity in those days, and I have to admit the thought not even remotely crossed my mind.

About a year later, my wife absent again attending to business in the UK, I met a handsome Scandinavian woman of my age, one of a wealthy group on a round-the-world junket. We danced and smooched at a party in her tour hotel, then she missed out on the game parks visits, arranged to move in with me for a week or two before rejoining her tour. This lady was as insatiable as you can get, and one morning when I was ready to sleep, after a fair night's loving, she wanted more and suggested discipline was required.

I go along with anything for experience, so let her 'discipline' me. This consisted of pinching and nipping me sharply on the chest and shoulders. As I obviously wasn't being turned on we both ended up laughing uproariously. I had no idea what her procedure would have led to, she was evidently following some ritual that would have got more sadistic and sophisticated and I must admit I've often wondered. Suffice to say I was left with black and blue shoulders – not my idea of being aroused. We went on with more conventional methods – her lips and mouth doing the necessary. A chance to learn was lost here, I fear.

My next adventure was with another overseas secretary, a bespectacled Englishwoman in her late 30s, unmarried, not too experienced but dead keen. After some time living together she suggested spanking after reading about it in a book called 'A Spy in the Family', which must have impressed her. I lay across the bed naked with legs on the floor while she took my belt from my trousers and doubled it, holding the buckle and the other end in her hand and laying into my upraised bottom with the middle bit. It should have turned me on, I suppose, for looking over my shoulder as I lay prostrate, there she was wielding the strap with full swinging breasts displayed.

I only felt bloody silly and it hurt like hell!

I stuck it as long as I could. Fair's fair, she was allowing me all sorts of liberties like applying enemas and masturbating herself on my request, but at length I had to protest. Thinking this was all part of the fun she increased her flogging, so I stood up and said to stop, enough being enough.

Again in retrospect I wish I had put her across my knee for a bottom spanking, although she never suggested it by word or deed. I think she would have gone along – she was very uninhibited once we had been together a while.

Returning home to England I was informed by a friend (a jealous bastard undoubtedly), that my wife had had an affair in my absence. I knew this, she had written to tell me of it. The man concerned was a large type in all departments evidently, over six feet tall and some years younger. I dismissed the episode without rancour as one of those things, but resented the man, I suppose, as sometimes in a teasing mood my wife would refer to his huge equipment (although she always orgasms with me and enjoys our regular intercourse), and how she had loved seeing it erect, handling it, sucking it, or taking it in her vagina.

At a party we attended the man was present. My wife drank too much, flirted with him openly, and at one stage vanished upstairs with him for a spell long enough to have the other guests winking and sniggering. I didn't mind for myself – I've had my share and I knew that with drink and his presence she had been unable to resist – I was thinking of her own reputation and how she'd rue her impetuosity in the light of day.

Back in our own home later and in bed she rambled on rather drunkenly about how randy the thought of his huge penis had made her, and that she could have lain down in the middle of the crowded room to take it. I threatened her with a beating, at which she laughed as I'd never laid a hand on her, and prattled on non-stop, even recounting a few past affairs, until I threw back the covers, lifted her nightgown, baring her bottom. I then thrashed her soundly on both cheeks with my palm. At first she struggled to turn over, but I held her down.

Then she lay clenching and withdrawing her buttocks at each expected blow as I was fairly rhythmic. She cried out but did not cry. When I had done she slipped out of bed and put on the light to inspect her reddened bottom in the wardrobe mirror.

She complained, but not angrily, and when she returned to bed was surprisingly contrite and chastened. She also cuddled against me, which led to lovemaking and sex. A few days later in my garden a neighbour came to my fence, giving me the thumbs-up sign and, regarding me with approval, congratulated me on 'giving her what for'. When I asked how the devil he knew about the spanking, he told me my wife had quite proudly imparted the information to a few women friends at a coffee morning, one of them his wife, who in turn told him. It was plain he approved because he would have liked to have done the same to his wife.

However, if I thought it was to be a regular feature of our life I was mistaken. In cold blood my wife finds spanking as silly as I used to, and doesn't go along. No doubt the conditions have to be exactly right, and it never has been since, more's the pity. Of course I could take her by force, but I couldn't bring myself to do that nor do I think she'd appreciate it.

Whatever others have done or do, or fantasize about in the smacking and punishment syndrome, the above is a true and not at all exaggerated account of one man's experience in that field. I hasten to add I find no desire to pay a female to spank; that surely must be an artificial enactment.

D.S.,
Warwickshire

BREAST MAN

I am 24 years old and have been married for four years. I should like to share an experience that I had not long ago. To begin with, my husband is a 'breast man'. I kid him greatly about this, but secretly I'm flattered because I happen to be well endowed with a size 40 D cup. I love to go without a bra as often as possible, especially when my man is around the house. This always makes him very playful; he's forever grabbing and stroking my breasts, pinching my nipples, and generally arousing me to the point where he knows I'll attack him.

Two years ago I became pregnant. Since my husband is so fascinated by big breasts, he watched with great interest as mine began to get larger and larger with each passing month. After the first several months my nipples began to change colour, from a barely visible pink to a much darker shade, and by the sixth month, I had outgrown all my bras by many inches. It was just as well because bras were rather uncomfortable to wear at that stage, as my breasts felt terrible heavy and sore. I went out in public infrequently during the last months of my pregnancy but on those few occasions, I never wore a bra. The thin cloth of my maternity top rubbed on my bare and sensitive nipples as my bloated boobies rolled gently back and forth across my tummy. I found it really arousing especially because I was in a public place. More than once I began to feel myself getting wet as I noticed some man staring at me.

My husband was the most interested spectator during my pregnancy.

He loved to comment on how big I was getting week by week. He seemed really interested in my nipples and aureoles which had swollen to twice their normal size. My doctor had given me some lotion to help keep my breasts from becoming too sore, and my husband faithfully helped me rub it in every night. He knew this aroused me, and this in turn aroused him. Sex was not really pleasurable under these conditions (I was in my seventh month), but my husband would get so aroused that I had to do something. I rubbed some of the lotion on his penis, gently stroking up and down until he erupted with a huge ejaculation. He continued to rub my breasts with the lotion while I was working on him. Eventually during this sex play, my nipples expanded to the size of thimbles and I was crying out for relief. My husband was happy to accommodate me, performing cunnilingus on me while I knelt on the bed with pillows under my tummy.

After our son was born, my interest in sex seemed to increase rather than diminish. This was due, in part, to the fact that I was breastfeeding my little son. Doing this aroused intense sexual feelings in me, and I loved to watch my nipples swell and finally begin to dribble streams of warm milk over my fingers as I stimulated each breast. Usually, I was unable to suppress my feelings of arousal and by the time my baby was in his crib, my panties were soaked. I'd unzip my panties and work my fingers over my throbbing clitoris until I had an explosive orgasm.

One night when my husband arrived home early, while I was still nursing, he decided to get into the act. I could see he had become terribly aroused and I quickly reached into my blouse and pulled out my other breast. My husband encircled the nipple with his mouth, and soon I could feel my milk being sucked from both breasts. The sensation was unlike anything I had ever felt before, and I had a violent and exhausting orgasm sitting right in my chair.

Since then we have modified our lovemaking techniques. Before we are ready to have sex, my husband stretches out naked on the bed while I undress and get out my bottle of lotion. I rub it all over each boob and then, using a pulling motion, I begin to stroke each breast from top to bottom towards the nipple. Soon I begin to feel a pressure building up at the tips of my breasts. When my nipples are heavy and swollen, I kneel over my husband and begin to squirt small streams of milk all over his body. The first jet may shoot six to 12 inches. Needless to say, this drives my husband wild. I try to cover as much of his body as I can before he ejaculates violently.

Name withheld by request
Wisconsin

BREASTFEEDING ADULT STYLE

I married soon after the war. My young wife had an excellent bosom, later producing an abundance of milk for five babies and enough spare to soak all her dresses daily.

One morning I discovered her squeezing off the excess by hand, her nipples taut and painful, dribbling the glut into a jug. I took over gently, and did the same when our other children were on the breast and her milk came in floods over the years. She found it highly erotic to feed me, and orgasmed strongly several times during any intercourse following such foreplay.

Even nowadays she holds her nipples up to my mouth when we make love and begs or orders me to 'milk' her according to her mood. Happily too her breasts have remained beautifully shapely, large and firm despite or because of all my ministrations. She wears low-cut gowns if we are partying, and it pleases me to know men eye her with approval. At 50 that can't be bad.

One could well say I must have a strong sucking complex or compulsion which might well manifest itself in a desire to perform fellatio. The idea doesn't appeal to me, although I have nothing against it for those who like the scene. I certainly love cunnilingus and go the whole hog. As a boy at sea I witnessed homosexual acts, and on occasion as a change from masturbating allowed a few of the more 'attractive' ones to go down on me. Very expert they were, and very good it was at the time (perhaps off Greenland in a gale!). One fair-skinned young man, a sensitive navigating officer, fancied me enough to get me half-drunk and into his bunk on a few occasions. His kisses were as sweet as any girl's, and aroused me enough to quite frankly use him as a girl several times over. I have never indulged since, undoubtedly because real females have been available.

I became a civil engineer, a consultant, which shows I must have other things in my mind. I've often thought I should have specialized in dairy machinery! So I travelled around and sucked milk from a Malayan in Singapore, a Chinese in Hong Kong, a doll-like Japanese lady (in Rome – busy little businessmen these Nipponese husbands), and a young unmarried mother I met in London. I set her up in a flat and my financial position was such for a while I maintained two homes and had the best of both worlds.

However, I was more than delighted when she met and married a young man who took over her child like an intelligent human and has since given her two more. The girl and I remain old friends and lovers (with his knowledge), and I 'milked' her over several years when there was plenty. This girl has lovely elongated breasts that droop delightfully under their own weight, with nipples like 'thumbs' that make sucking a privilege. A real milk-producing machine, she referred to her magnificent boobs as the 'United Dairies' with good cause.

I thought all good things must come to an end, but no, my talents for what they are worth were needed in developing nations this past year or two. My first day in Africa I was back on an old stamping ground, and went to buy a pair of sandals in a small shoe shop. The customer before me was a very young mother, black as coal but beautiful, clear-eyed, white of teeth, statuesque and magnificent of figure. She unconcernedly fed an infant boy with a breast as round as an association football, the purplish nipple big as a huge blackberry, dripping greyish fluid like a leaky tap.

She seemed to have a job finding enough to pay for the plastic flip-flops she'd chosen, diving to the bottom of her purse for the few coppers. I paid the assistant for her, and hurried out, not wishing to embarrass such a proud beauty. Later in the street she came up to me offering my change, which I waved aside. I asked her if she needed a lift, for apart from her two year old tied to her back she carried a basket of sweet potatoes and had a bunch of bananas balanced on her headscarf.

She spoke some English and with my rusty Swahili I made out she took a ramshackle bus to her village. I gave her a ride in my UN emblazoned car and baby fell asleep on the back seat. I asked her nicely if she had much milk (the understatement of the year) and she laughed quite delightedly, easing her soaked dress from her mammoth breasts, saying proudly, 'Too much!' She was faintly surprised at my following suggestion but only momentarily. Like all properly brought up African girls she was only too happy to please a man and completely uninhibited with it.

Moments later we were pulled up off the track, warm thick milk running down my chin as I gorged myself, she sighing with relief and giving little moans of pleasure as my hands roamed. It ended with a splendid fuck, during which she convulsed and orgasmed mightily, crying out 'Mama, oh Mama!' loudly enough to set the monkeys screeching in the trees and birds to take wing – not to mention cultivators who came running out of the bush thinking murder was being committed. Like so many African girls there was no evident husband in her life, and she lived with struggling parents.

I got a bungalow and she moved in to be my housekeeper, leaving her son with her mother. She took to my sucking her breasts like a duck to water, producing a tit at all times they felt swollen or hard. It even got a bit much! Sometimes after a party, quite full of whisky, she would take my head and push a nipple to my mouth. I would suck dutifully until I had to stagger from the bed to the toilet to be sick. Talk about Black Power! On my return, groaning with a head like two, she would be sitting up grinning with her beautiful teeth, magnificent bosom jutting for my attention, and I would be grabbed and put back on the nipple. I had mother's milk for breakfast, dinner, tea.

This happy state of affairs went on for almost a year. I believe she loved me; she was certainly faithful and attentive, caring, fondly affectionate. I would have married her in a moment if I hadn't already a most excellent mate – heaven would have been to have both under my roof. As to my wife in my absence, as in all my absences I suspect, she quite rightly took the chance to flirt around a little to try a new partner – one of whom moved in for a few months, and another was a mere lad, a German medical student she met at the hospital where she works part-time as a nursing sister. She's a most attractive woman, smart in figure and dress, kindly; it would be a miracle if nobody fancied her and she didn't return the compliment occasionally.

This is a true testament to my long and devouring passion, and it does my heart good to know of kindly and kindred souls like your correspondent, Mrs G.W. of Derbyshire. Long may her lovely nipples be sucked for her, and all who desire giving their surplus milk to suckers like me. For the record, I weigh the same as I did at 22 (11 stone exactly), have my hair, teeth, good eyesight, clear skin, and can function sexually better than ever. It's the good life.

For those who disbelieve, think on. You accept mass murderers, so what's so terrible about a mass nipple sucker? As a working class lad I set out to travel and make things happen to me, without moaning about lack of chances or education. I may have only succeeded to my own satisfaction, but I harmed no one and may have done a bit of good. At the end of it all, as my wife informed me the other night: my dog and my grandchildren think I'm a great guy anyway! I would like to think one day everyone will be as lucky as I and succeed in whatever they do to their satisfaction.

D.S.,
Warwickshire

BIRD WATCHING

Ever since I was a small boy I have been keen on ornithology, and have spent many hours in my youth patiently watching the behaviour of birds both rare and common. I have

313

a general interest in natural history and so watch squirrels, otters, etc. I have always been fascinated by the behaviour of human beings and have often gazed at children playing or family groups on the beach – without in any way spying on them.

In the past few years this interest in human behaviour has grown, so much so that I am far more interested in watching humans than birds. It would be hypocritical of me to pretend that I had no interest in what might broadly be classified as sexual behaviour, but that is only part of my interest. From what I have read of the subject, it seems that I am likely to be classified as a voyeurist and possibly charged with being a 'Peeping Tom'. I should like to know how the law stands on this matter. One reads of men being prosecuted by the police as peeping toms and yet in contrast one reads of members of the Royal Family and other famous people being hounded by photographers with their telescopic lenses peeping and prying into their private lives in order to obtain an intimate photo for some continental magazine, and there is very little that can be done about it. There appears to be a contradiction here, can you explain?

May I give you just three examples of my own activities and ask you to comment on their legality? I live in a third-floor flat overlooking a busy street, so the first of my examples refers to watching people in the street. My apparatus consists of a portable tape recorder, a pair of binoculars, a camera with telephoto lens and a pencil and paper. I assign myself different projects (or combination of projects) on a particular day. For example I might concentrate on pedestrians – do they cross the road in a safe manner? Are children properly supervised by parents? Are boys worse behaved than girls in the street? Are mothers firmer with them than fathers? And so on.

My second example concerns the flats opposite. If I move my head a few degrees, instead of the street I see into bedrooms and living rooms of the flats opposite. I am prepared to accept that it may be in bad taste to stare into other people's homes, but unless they live behind permanently drawn curtains or I never look out of my window, it would be virtually impossible not to catch at least glimpses of what was happening across the road. It would be ridiculous for me not to look out of my window and several of the people opposite appear to think that drawing of curtains is unnecessary.

Admittedly some may believe that their half-length net

314

curtains may confer adequate privacy, but viewed from my high flat they are ineffective (at least on lower floors). The following are daily occurrences which I often view and sometimes photograph (depending on the light).

Every morning a young married woman, whose husband goes off to work very early, draws back her bedroom curtains and stands at the window in an orange towelling négligée. After an interval she moves back a little from the window, slips off the négligée and stands there completely naked. Sometimes she brushes her hair while still nude, on other occasions she will put on bra and knickers, and possibly a petticoat, first.

There is no question of her posing or putting on an act and I really believe she thinks she can't be seen when she's not close to the window.

In another flat, three children (a boy and two girls of school age) share a bedroom with an au-pair girl of about 19. In the morning their mother comes in to wake them. All four strip naked and go to the bathroom in turns. The au-pair helps the kids to dress or find clean clothes: usually she's in bra and panties but more than once I've seen her tying the boy's tie when she was completely naked. I am not consciously attracted to these or any other children in a sexual way but I am absolutely fascinated by how they act and react in these and many other circumstances in the home.

You will note that in this activity I occupy exactly the same position (except for the direction of my gaze) as I do when watching people in the street. Can one be legal and not the other?

In the third activity I may be on more dangerous ground since my observations are made 'in the field' and tend to be concentrated on more specifically sexual events.

In the country some miles from where I live, there is an old partially ruined castle. It is near to a village where there is a housing estate. On one of my genuine ornithological expeditions, I was sitting very quietly waiting to catch a glimpse of an owl on a nest, when I began to hear excited whispers from one of the rooms below me – looking through a crevice I could discern two boys about 12 years old engrossed in masturbating each other. I watched them climax in turn but remained hidden and undetected.

I soon discovered that the castle is a favourite place for the locals at various stages of their sexual development and both sexes. From different vantage points I can see and hear a lot, and I go very early before anyone else arrives and have built a few hideouts in such a way that I can get in and then virtually shut the door by piling up stones, etc. From where I sit I can just as easily watch kestrels and owls as adolescent children – I suppose it must be voyeurism but is it illegal and if so why?

From reading *Forum*, it is very apparent that if one individual has a peculiarity he can be quite sure that it will be shared by many others. I therefore justify this long letter on the grounds that if you answer it, you will help many besides me.

Name and address withheld
by request

English law gives scant protection to the right to privacy. Believe it or not, officially we don't have one. Nothing in our legal system entitles us to be left alone.

The Levy–Lambton debacle brought matters to a head when lawyers woke up to the fact that although a national newspaper arranged for snaps to be taken of the hapless Lord Lambton in a compromising sexual position no offence had been committed. Legal journals bemoaned the absence of curbs on snoopers and clamoured for the introduction of a Law of Privacy.

At about the same time lawyers became increasingly concerned over the number of new listening and watching gimmicks available and called for Parliament to discourage their use by giving remedies to the victims. The Law Society itself urged control of surreptitious surveillance devices though it accepted that it would be undesirable to restrict ordinary cameras, binoculars or tape recorders.

No specific law makes voyeurism illegal or even refers to 'peeping toms'. But in practice when a peeper gets caught redhanded, the police try to prosecute the culprit under regulations originally designed to ensnare other crimes. The precise charges will depend on the circumstances.

Take your escapades in the ruined castle for example. If someone surprised you in your hideout the authorities might just slap a burglar charge on you under the Theft Act. A person who enters a building as a trespasser with intent to take anything or cause damage commits this crime. Of course the prosecution would have their work cut out to convict you. Nevertheless if you remove anything or accidentally cause any appreciable damage you could lay yourself open to an embarrassing trial and, just possibly, a conviction.

In all probability, though, the police would stick with one of the time honoured methods of dealing with the voyeur. Section 4 of the Vagrancy Act 1824 labels as 'rogues and vagabonds' any persons who go on premises for an unlawful purpose or who loiter about a place of public resort with intent to commit an arrestable offence. A court will more readily infer unlawful intentions for this relatively minor offence. The police, moreover, need not even prove an accused has actually done an act which shows such intent. Rogues and vagabonds risk three months' imprisonment or a fine up to £100.

When you stay in the snug cocoon of your own flat the legal position alters. I would think it most unlikely that anyone would complain – never mind prosecute you – for spying on their activities in the street even if you do use binoculars and a telephoto lens.

But when your vigils take on an overt sexual overtone – as when you watch the young housewife dressing or the naked au pair – or if your peeping becomes so open and persistent as to aggravate a neighbour, then one of the oldest surviving statutes in English law – the Justices of the Peace Act 1361 – could be used. Magistrates can require anyone who disturbs the peace or who behaves in a way 'likely to cause a breach of it' to give a surety for his good behaviour. The complainant doesn't even have to show that any incident of violence has occurred. This act has applied to eavesdroppers and nightwalkers and quite recently when some girls accused a man of peering into their window the police charged him with causing a breach of the peace.

A recent case has raised a storm of controversy in legal circles. A private detective on a divorce investigation tapped the wife's phone. Leeds CID revived another ancient offence – causing a public mischief. The private eye pleaded guilty and the CID promptly dubbed him 'Britain's first convicted phone tapper'. Public Mischief covers acts which endanger the comfort of the public or obstruct the public in the exercise or enjoyment of its rights. You can see that this offence could easily fit your behaviour, especially when you use watching and listening devices.

A very similar offence of causing a Public Nuisance could also apply as it seeks to curtail any 'interference with public comfort and convenience' which affects a public place. And quite apart from the police any person aggrieved by your peeking could sue you for damages in the civil courts if he feels it amounts to a private nuisance.

The greatest penalty you can suffer, though, is the ignominy of being caught. The tone of your letter when you say that sexual behaviour forms only a part of your interest gives an impression of honesty and candour. I may believe you. But would the police? Or the court?

Another consultant comments: To spend much time observing neighbours and strangers through binoculars is unusual and in a sense eccentric. To watch wild birds and animals in this way is to observe relatively unfamiliar things and activities, inaccessible to any other method of study, and full of opportunities for learning and discovery. Even the novice at birdwatching may soon notice something worth recording in a naturalists' journal.

By contrast, the observer at random of human life in his immediate locality is extremely unlikely to make any such discovery. Human behaviour has been studied so extensively and in so much depth for so many reasons that a vast amount of work is required to make observations of the minutest scientific value. Such work is useless unless it sets out systematically to answer specific questions precisely formulated.

The isolated, stationary observer of distant human beings can do no more than feed his own fantasies, or load his mind with useless and unrelated impressions. To have this as a main recreation is likely to be symptomatic of great difficulty in making personal friends, of power-seeking fantasies or voyeurism.

Other considerations apart, the observer may find himself observed, and (especially when juvenile sexual behaviour is in any way concerned) this can lead to embarrassing misunderstandings.

Press photographers who hound celebrities with telecameras do so in order to earn a living. This is their motivation and they know it. What is yours?

MALE CIRCUMCISION

THE REAL BENEFITS OF CIRCUMCISION

When I read the latest letters to *Forum* describing negative and positive reactions to circumcision, it occurred to me that my experience might interest readers. I submitted to this operation voluntarily in my early 40s, a couple of decades ago.

For most of the years preceding the decisive event, I had lived in environments where circumcision was mentioned merely as one of the Jewish religious rites. I was approaching 40 when, in a tropical country, I saw circumcised boys and men for the first time and learned that this treatment of the male organ was, in fact, quite common in various parts of the world, notably North America.

I was impressed at once by the pleasing aspect of circumcised penises with the firm, well-shaped, symmetrical head so clearly exposed, whereas uncircumcised organs like my own at that time ended with an ugly, soft, shapeless, and raggy skin bag.

Since my marriage, some 15 years earlier, my foreskin had annoyed me in my sexual relations. True, the moist penis head could be propelled with one quick thrust from under its hood right into my wife – an act that excited us both – but then came the painful task of making the penis shaft follow with the wrinked loose skin on it doggedly resisting until, very gradually, its natural lubrication became complete (my wife is allergic to vaseline and the like). During subsequent coital thrusting, moreover, the loose skin was sliding much better over my penis shaft and head than over my wife's inner linings so that my growing excitement and orgasm were mainly the result of friction within my own 'equipment', always reminding me of masturbation, while my wife's sensations were much less acute. However, we put up with this imperfect kind of coupling, as we didn't know any better.

I also had perpetual hygienic worries. While a reasonable degree of cleanliness wasn't too difficult to achieve when it was cool, I had to fight daily battles against smegma and smell when it was warm or sultry. When I lived in the humid tropics, these battles became yet more exasperating, and recurring irritations by fungus growths further aggravated my troubles.

After three years in the tropics, I finally realized that only circumcision would effectively improve my hygienic problems and that, in my situation, its advantages would, more likely than not, outweigh any possible negative consequences. So I got a doctor's consent and had the operation done while my wife was away for a while. (Incidentally, she had once suggested this cure to me herself, long before I was ready to consider it seriously.) I was circumcised by a GP in a small tropical hospital after application of a local anaesthetic so that I could watch – curiosity turning to satisfaction – as my organ was given its new shape.

Along with my foreskin, all molestations by smegma and smell were gone for good, to my great relief. The surface membrane of the liberated penis head soon became tougher, always stayed dry, and it could now be cleaned as speedily as the other parts of my body. After a number of weeks, however, when the tissues had adapted themselves fully to the new situation, some of the loose skin again tended to cover a part of the head, and eventually, I got a new massive fungus invasion underneath this residual overfold. A second operation, performed by a specialist, then liberated me of the remaining ring of superfluous skin, thus eliminating the last source of hygienic trouble.

Both my operations were painless. The cuts and stitches did hurt somewhat, but only for a few days and less than burst blisters on hands or feet. The organ could be used again for sex after about two weeks. Never since the operations have I experienced trouble due to my penis head having lost its natural protective shield. Neither friction against my clothes (I rather like that gentle, tickling sensation) nor sudden chance contacts with objects have ever done any harm to my bared penis head. Earlier, on the contrary, my clothes had often disagreeably pinched, pulled, shifted, or twisted my foreskin so that I had to adjust it time and again when nobody was looking. (All attempts at making it stay retracted behind the ridge of the head ended in failure.)

After the first operation, I resumed sexual activity with apprehension, but it gave way quickly to feelings of relief and heightened pleasure. Intromission of the dry penis head into my wife's vagina did, of course, meet with a somewhat increased resistance, but the penis shaft, now covered with a smooth and tight skin with much decreased mobility, could be pushed forward with an ease never experienced before. Subsequent coital thrusts resulted in greatly increased direct friction and in much improved, delightful sensations for us both. If there was any decrease in my sensitivity, it was slight and had no noticeable effect on my sexual pleasures.

Now, more than 20 years later, I am still very pleased with the positive results of my circumcision. There weren't any negative ones to bother about. I only regret that my foreskin had not been cut off long before I got married. Because of the gratifying results of my 'experiment', my wife and I also had our three sons circumcised, the older ones at ages 16 and six and with their consent, the third just after his birth. All three, now adults, seem to be as pleased as myself.

J.H.,
Canada

WANTS HIM CUT

I have always been fascinated by the male body and in particular the penis. But until last year I was unaware that boys were circumcised other than on religious grounds, and had never seen a circumcised penis.

Recently a friend of my husband called when he was out. I invited him to stay for a drink, and he succeeded in getting me to bed the same evening. I was stunned when I saw his penis. It was not much longer than my husband's, but the tip was naked and there was no excess skin sliding up and down the shaft. I found that he had been circumcised in infancy.

Since he and my husband played football and showered together he knew my husband was uncircumcised and asked which I preferred. I had to admit that a penis without a foreskin was far more exciting; after all, this was the first time I had seen a knob fully uncovered. I was surprised to notice that the glans was larger in a flaccid state than my husband's when erect. I sampled his penis in my mouth (the very first time in my life) and, despite some misgivings, actually enjoyed swallowing his semen.

Following this new discovery I tried to persuade my husband to let me roll his foreskin right back. When I pull it back it forms a tight red ring behind the glans, which turns a dark purple, and he finds it uncomfortable. Several times I have washed his penis carefully with the skin fully retracted, intending to make oral love afterwards. But I am repelled by the sight of his rolled back foreskin and I am unable to explain to him why I can't suck his penis.

Am I alone in this obsession with circumcised penises or are

321

there other females who share my views? Do you think I am reasonable in persuading my husband to be circumcised? Would he not gain some advantage from it?

Mrs M.J.,
Cornwall

You are by no means alone in your preference for the circumcised penis; most women prefer it for fellatio.

But no, it's not reasonable to persuade your husband to be circumcised against his own wish. Surgeons are very wary of performing medically unnecessary operations on the genitals, since if the man is not entirely secure and 'well-motivated', sexual difficulties may result. Most of the ill-effects reported after vasectomy, for instance, occur in men who subconsciously were unsure of their manhood or thought of the operation as a mutilation. If your husband is keen to be circumcised himself, there should be no problem; but you could both be in trouble if he gave in to your persuasion against his own real inclinations.

As for advantages for him – apart from your being willing to fellate him there would probably be none, apart, possibly, from a slight increase in the time taken to reach orgasm. (The Forum Survey has shown that there is absolutely no difference in length of intercourse between circumcised and uncircumcised men, but the great majority of respondents of course have been circumcised in infancy. Men who have had it done as adults often report a lowering of sensitivity ... which makes them last longer.)

CIRCUMCISION

I have read nearly all the articles in print on circumcision of which I am a victim.

I do not agree that the foreskin is useful for only a short time in infancy. I am sure it is a desirable aid to masturbation in youth. A correct or short foreskin must aid gentle masturbation, which in some way has just got to be better for the glans than the palm of the hand.

Complete circumcision is therefore too drastic a measure to enforce upon us. It is clear to me that if our sons are to be tampered with (and tamper it is), a compromise is the solution. The Plastibell method should be the only one allowed since it is cosmetically good, and it could be designed to remove only half the foreskin, so that the corona and frenum are saved from the rubbing of clothes – a thing I find annoying with no protection whatever.

A half circumcision I could tolerate but definitely not complete removal. Why is the Plastibell method not used in later circumcisions? When is some research going to be done by plastic surgeons into a suitable method of providing a short cover for the emotionally upset circumcised man who frantically desires a foreskin?

B.B.,
Address withheld by request

This is one more example of the circumcision/no circumcision controversy. Those who have been wish they hadn't and vice versa. This is such an emotionally loaded subject that no rational or logical explanation can be accepted by the 'victim' whether he be with or without a prepuce.

In this country no circumcision is done (by and large) under the NHS for other than medical reasons, and for practical purposes this means a foreskin so tight that it obstructs the flow of urine or results in repeated infection. I would not regard this as 'tampering'.

If a parent desires a circumcision for personal, religious, cosmetic, philosophical, ethical or other reasons private arrangements must be made and then the whole responsibility for the operation of the type of circumcision performed rests clearly on the shoulder of the person who authorizes the procedure – the father.

Other countries and cultures have other systems in force.

The Plastibell method is not commonly used in this country because most surgeons find it unsatisfactory. It is not suitable for abnormal foreskins, and hence would not do for the vast majority of circumcision operations carried out in Britain. Moreover the exact size is critical and too small a size can lead to serious complications. Most people feel its use is best limited to the removal of normal or near normal foreskins.

There are routine plastic procedures which can be used to recover the glans of a circumcised penis but they are tedious, difficult, and very expensive procedures, and the end result cannot be regarded as indistinguishable from the real thing. Hence men who undergo this sort of cosmetic surgery, on account of the emotional instability which made them embark upon it, remain dissatisfied and disgruntled.

The trouble is more in the mind than in the penis – a thank-

less message to give, as 'victims' are not emotionally mature enough to accept this or even discuss it on a rational basis.

Many circumcised men delude themselves by thinking that all their troubles are due to this – and vice versa.

Z-PLASTY

Several of your readers seem interested in the restoration of the foreskin after circumcision. I read an American article some years ago describing an American technique for doing this. The surgeon made a Z shape by incision on three sides of the penis. When the Z is pulled out straight and its edges re-approximated a considerable degree of lengthening is attained.

Is this operation available in Britain?

H.M.,
Glamorgan

'Z-plasty', as this manoeuvre is called, is a standard plastic surgical procedure used to produce skin in one place by sliding it from another nearby.

It is in constant use for reconstructive surgery, to relieve tension in scars produced after a severe burn etc.

There are half a dozen different techniques available to restore the prepuce. Almost all such operations are performed privately on the continent and in the USA.

The tendency in this country is to investigate the reason for the desire for such reconstructions. This belongs to the realm of the psychiatrist and few cases reach the surgeon. In this country only the very rare case, where some reconstruction or adjustment following a complication after circumcision is required, arrives at the operating table.

Many people are routinely circumcised at birth for religious or social reasons. Such people appear quite content and do not seek reconstruction of the prepuce. Those who, having been circumcised, desire such surgery require careful psychological investigation as the desire is often found to be emotional in nature and there is no physical reason to undergo rather intricate and so expensive surgery.

Conversely there are many others who spend their lives trying to find someone somewhere who will do a circumcision for no medical reason.

The controversy – to be circumcised, or to be uncircumcised – will probably continue for ever. Which side you take will depend upon purely personal factors such as religion, race, up-bringing, social contacts, teachings and subconscious factors. Freud had a lot to say about the death wish, and the desire for castration and mutilation in this connection.

Every operation has some risk, every operation can have complications, and not everyone will be satisfied with the end result. Hence the more experienced the surgeon, the more cautious he becomes when considering non-essential surgery – non-essential as far as physical health is concerned! If the operation is for psychological health, then a psychiatric opinion will be regarded as an essential pre-requisite by most surgeons – at least in this country.

FEMALE CIRCUMCISION

ORIGIN OF FEMALE CIRCUMCISION

A recent mention of female circumcision in your columns reminds me of the sexual customs I learned about many years ago in the Middle East.

One day I had to go to check on the progress of a work gang in the desert and sheltered from the tropical sun under the shade of the only tree for as far as the eye could see. Sidareen, the head woman of the gangs working nearby, came over to meet me; I asked her to come and sit in the shade as she made her report. But she shuffled her feet and told me she preferred the sun, which I knew was blatantly untrue because I had seen her sheltering under an umbrella as I rode up. I scented a story, and after careful questioning I got it.

She was afraid that if she sat under that tree a snake would crawl into her cunt! Rational argument was useless, she was adamant. Eventually I got to the bottom of the matter, but not without being reprimanded for not knowing my Bible.

That tree (and I was stupid not to notice that no one was under it when I arrived) was the same sort of tree that Eve had slept under in one of her wanderings outside the Garden of Eden. While she had slept she had dreamed of Adam, and consequently her vagina had opened as all women's do on such occasions. But the Devil happened to be passing by, and he noticed Eve's open hole.

Immediately he saw it as the chance he had been waiting for – to smuggle himself into the Garden unobserved by the guardian angels at the gate who were there expressly to keep him out. So he changed himself into a serpent and wriggled himself tail first into Eve's open cunt. To keep from falling out when Eve stood up and walked, he took some of her pubic hair between his teeth.

In time, Eve awoke and set off back to the Garden. As the guards opened the gate for her they noticed what they thought to be her clitoris protruding through her pubic hair, but as they had often seen it before and taken it as evidence of her eagerness to meet Adam they were casual in their regard. And that is how the Devil got into the Garden of Eden.

I was not told, but left to assume, that Adam was angry when he saw that what he thought to be Eve's erect clitoris was in fact the devil in the form of a serpent.

What I was told, was that Adam insisted that in future Eve pluck out all her pubic hair. She did so and showed Adam how she now looked. Her now flaccid clitoris however still protruded from her slit and this displeased Adam as a possible stalking horse for another serpent; so catching it between finger and thumb he pulled it out to its full length and cut it off at the root with a sliver of bamboo. And so from that day to this every woman is similarly de-clitorized and depilated.

Sidareen herself? Of course! Had she not been, her parents could never have got a husband for her. No, a husband could not be deceived for custom demanded that *every time* he had need of her she present her open hole for his inspection, and he, as he looked inside her, would pray for success in his venture into the unknown. (What he was looking into his wife for was to see that the devil was not already in residence!)

Had the mutilation been painful? Of course! It was intended that it should be, and to keep girls virgin they were told that defloration was worse. Was it? Sidareen said she did not know because, as was the custom, before breaking her in to the penis her husband thrashed her with his mule whip and nothing was as bad as that. What had she done wrong that he had done that? Nothing, it was the custom. Did she know it would happen? No. Had she told her own daughter it would happen? No. Why not? Because a good beating before she was first fucked would make her a good wife!

In the Middle East, it seems, women are still paying for Eve's original sin.

O.A.,
Wales

FEMALE CIRCUMCISION – THE MALE POINT OF VIEW

I was very interested to read the recent letters on female circumcision.

I have lived for over 20 years in a number of Middle East countries. As I am a bachelor, my 'jemadar' or head servant invariably engaged a couple of female servants whose sole job was to look after the bedroom and its 'comforts'. Many, but not all, had been circumcised. Their ages ranged from 15 to 30, and

I accepted or rejected their engagement into the house purely on their figures and looks.

It was quite noticeable that the circumcised girls had very much firmer and better shaped breasts and far more prominent and erect nipples. With uncircumcised women (particularly the Western races) nipple erection vanishes at a certain stage of foreplay and continuation of nipple caressing is rejected. With the circumcised girl intense manual and oral caressing of the nipples is carried on right up to orgasm.

Some letters have suggested the labia minora were also removed. I never found this to be the case with women I knew and cunnilingus on the labia was a 'must', especially with the younger girls who derived intense pleasure from full length stroking with the tongue. This was very easy to do because there is always complete depilation.

Nature has compensated for clitoral loss by giving the circumcised woman a very sensitive vagina and fantastic vaginal muscle control, and it is in these women that you get real vaginal orgasms of great intensity. The man places the head of his penis just within the vaginal entrance and the vaginal muscles slowly draw him in. Lying quite still, you can feel the muscles rippling up and down the full length of the penis.

In fucking, the male is not worried about the necessity for clitoral contact, whether manual or penile (probably a basic cause of female sexual frustration) and he can concentrate entirely on his thrusting technique and nipple caressing. The female orgasm is intense.

The only positions which seem to be unsatisfactory from the circumcised girl's point of view are on the side or from the rear.

This need for a full vagina in the circumcised women probably accounts for the importance attached to penis size in the Middle East countries.

J.F.,
Southampton

The term female circumcision covers operations which range all the way from removing the prepuce (foreskin) of the clitoris to the removal of the whole vulva leaving a massive scar with a pinhole for urine and menstrual blood to escape. The actual nature of the operation varies according to the locality and religious fanaticism of the family. So circumcision in the female takes many different forms and therefore has many different consequences.

The women with whom you had intercourse had suffered Sunna circumcision, which involves removal of the prepuce alone or of the prepuce and part or whole of the clitoris, and perhaps also the top ends of the labia minora. Your women had presumably endured removal of the clitoris. (The more severe forms of circumcision are classified as Pharaonic.)

Removal of a part of the clitoris does not seem necessarily to prevent intense sexual pleasure being experienced in the area or orgasms being induced from it. Presumably this state of affairs reflects different degrees of surgical and psychical injury to the woman.

I would be prepared to believe that after Sunna circumcision the nipples and the vaginal entrance acquire an enhanced sensitivity, which may be psychologically caused, to compensate for the loss of the clitoris. About half of all women obtain a lot of arousal from the breasts anyway. Sexual and emotional feelings do influence the breasts and the differences you noticed in the breasts of your partners could reflect the changes that the operation had brought about in their hierarchy of sexual pleasure.

Female circumcision as practised in Africa and elsewhere is usually carried out without an anaesthetic and the girl's appalling distress is said to give great pleasure to the operator and witnesses.

Whatever the benefits alleged, whether to the man, the woman or society, circumcision is a monstrously wicked imposition on the girl regardless of the fanciful or religious reasons for which it is carried out. Many girls die from Pharaonic circumcision and a similar fate inflicted on their parents might be no more than just. A few such examples would no doubt help to stamp the practice out more rapidly than is being achieved in those backward and barbaric countries that still fail to prohibit it effectively. The Christian Church has an admirable record of opposing these hideous tortures.

Having said this one must concede that a desire to interfere with the sexuality of others appears to be universal, and is common even in my own profession of medicine. In Western countries the law and 'morality' possibly do more total harm to individuals than does ritual circumcision in more primitive ones. The harm is all the worse for being psychic rather than physical. Again, too, it is not so long ago that the Christian Church, having first made everyone neurotically guilty about sex, then declared the more disturbed adolescent girls to be witches and burned them alive. They did away with thousands of them and I don't suppose that the female circumcisers have killed off anything like the same numbers.

It all leaves one just desperately wishing that the circumcisers, the moralists, some priests, some politicians, some lawyers and all those who seek to interfere with other peoples' sexuality on a compulsory basis would just simply bugger off and leave all 'normal' people to enjoy sex in peace.

If we also sent those who are always pushing sex down our throats to join them, the millenium would be at hand. What a vision! (Consultant)

FIRST PERSON ACCOUNT

I hope that you will forgive me all the faults and errors in my English because I have not been writing in English for many years.

I am a married woman, born in Syria, where I spent my childhood. I live now with my husband in Paris, but before I was for 15 years in Egypt, where I attended girls' school and university.

My husband showed me some time ago a copy of *Forum* in which one of the readers was asking about what he called 'female circumcision'. I think that it is worthwhile to write about this custom because it is a very important thing in the life of every Moslem girl born in Egypt, Syria or Sudan and probably other Moslem countries as well. I myself and my sisters were all circumcised so I know what it is about from my own, quite painful, experience.

The operation is a part of Moslem tradition, though it is said that it was practised by the Old Egyptians. The Arabic word for it means 'cleansing' or 'purification', and young girls on whom it is done are always told that the circumcision will remove a blemish from their bodies, with which nobody will marry them.

When my mother died I was seven. My father then moved to Egypt and married again. My new mother was a very good woman but traditional in her ways. One day I was called by my mother to her room and found there an old woman, who was a midwife. There were two other women, friends of my stepmother. I was grabbed, laid on the table and my legs were spread wide. I already had heard of the operation from my older sister, but as she was not operated on we did not know

330

what it would be like. The women when asked always said, 'They will cut your little cock, it will not hurt at all'.

But it was not the operation after all, only a sort of investigation. The midwife had cold hands and it was the first time that somebody had touched my private parts. (I used sometimes to touch myself but was sharply told off if somebody caught me. I remember that I used to do it during the night with my hands or I just rubbed my legs together.)

My older sister was then called and was investigated in the same way.

Then we were told that we would become women a week later. When the day came we were dressed like little brides, with new clothes, henna rubbed into our hands, eyes made up with kohl. I got big and heavy earrings from my aunt.

I was first called and told to undress. There were many women, but no man, because he would bring misfortune. I was firmly held by one woman while another was tying my wrists behind my neck. Then I was laid on the table with my legs flexed and outstretched so that my sex was easily accessible. I couldn't see anything because two women were holding me and only felt a stinging feeling when the midwife rubbed in some spirit to disinfect the skin.

Then she suddenly pulled the most sensitive part of my sex. I thought that she was trying to pull it out completely but then came another horrible pain. A moment later came the sharp, terrifying pain which I still remember, fresh as yesterday. I thought that she was trying to split me open and cried loudly but to no avail. There was more to suffer but the following pains were less severe or I already was only half conscious.

I later learned when I myself witnessed the same operation, done to my younger sister, that the midwife passed a safety pin through my clitoris and pulled it as far as possible so that she could amputate it at the root. It causes a lot of bleeding; the older the girl the more the bleeding. Also the inner lips were cut out.

My older sister was operated next but I don't remember her cries. I was in pain for five days and the wound didn't heal for four weeks. I could walk after a week but it was very painful.

After the operation I received many little gifts from my neighbours and some jewellery from my aunts.

The reason for this very painful experience is to prevent a girl and later a woman from seeking pleasure in sex. In Moslem society, virginity before marriage is more important than anything else. Circumcision makes a girl associate pain rather than pleasure with sex and also reduces the danger that she become sexually excited by tight clothes rubbing on her crotch or even by men who may try to caress her.

I must admit that after the circumcision I never could arouse myself, there was nothing left to play with. I wouldn't dare to put my fingers inside me, afraid of tearing the seal of virginity. Some girls sometimes try to masturbate by putting something inside and my mother warned me that a thread or wire is drawn through the genitals of such girls to prevent them from breaking the seal. I never did anything so there was no need to do this to me.

I believe that the result of the operation is similar in all girls – you don't get much from sex and have no sex feelings before marriage.

I myself never had an orgasm, but sometimes the sex was quite pleasant anyway. I love my husband for the love he is giving me, for his attention and understanding. Sometimes, however, I regret bitterly what has been done to me.

Arab girls, who were circumcised, were probably spared the dangers of virginity lost before the wedding night, at least in most cases. As the conditions of life are changing and Arab girls get a much better education, the circumcision may become unnecessary. The fact nevertheless remains that men prefer circumcised wives because man's pleasure is not changed. The woman during intercourse is obliged to do what her husband asks for, willy nilly, whether she enjoys it or not. The Arab male thus gets what he wants and if the female has no enjoyment it is better for him; he feels more secure and his masculinity is never challenged.

During my stay in the boarding school and in the University dormitory I met many girls. As far as I know all, apart from Europeans, were circumcised and had the same sort of experience. One of them was operated on by a woman doctor in the hospital. The girl suffered less during the operation but the result was even more thorough: her private parts were made completely numb forever.

New laws in Egypt were supposed to abolish circumcision but instead drove it underground.

The operation will come into disuse when the social conditions change so it will not be demanded by men. In the meantime millions of girls like me and my sisters will have to suffer the knife of the midwife. Let us hope that ours is the last generation of mutilated creatures deprived of what Allah meant to be the greatest of human joys.

Name and address withheld
by request

THE SENSUAL SCOTS

Forum's most uninhibited readers appear to come from Scotland. What is it about a Scottish upbringing that induces such liberal and appealing behaviour?

A NATURAL GIRL

My problem is that my girl comes from Orkney where they lead a very Scandinavian way of life.

She is very young and very beautiful and very experienced and came to college here this year. I desperately wish her to come and live in my flat – but she won't, and for a very unusual reason.

Her equally pretty sister and she live in her sister's boyfriend's flat.

She is very sexy in a natural way. I've never seen her wear make-up or a bra and any time we've undressed she has not been wearing knickers. But she seems to be afraid to go to bed alone with a fellow.

We made love first time I met her, at a party at her sister's place where a lot of us ended up undressed for a game. She obviously enjoyed it.

One night at my place with her sister and my friend we had a session on the carpet in front of the fire, changing partners afterwards. She had several orgasms.

She started very young but her sister says she did too, and only recently enjoyed going to bed along with an older person – and in fact is now very much going off the group scene. She says my girl will soon do this too – it is part of growing up!

We go sailing, visit motor racing, go to dances, read poetry – the lot, and get on great. But she doesn't drink and can never relax enough to stay the night alone with me in the flat.

I don't want to lose her even if it takes a couple of years or so for her to mature. I understand she needs the security in sex she always had at home for she is otherwise a very balanced personality. Am I fighting an impossible battle or should I persevere?

J.E.,
Edinburgh

You don't mention your girlfriend's age but what you say about her attitudes seems to be both explicable and comprehensible.

However, it is a bit difficult to explain. As a general background comment I think it is important to realize that whereas genuine sexual excitement is necessary in order for a man to perform this is not the case in a woman. She may, for example, have intercourse because she wants to distract the man from studying her personality, because she wants his non-sexual love, because she is curious, because she wants to be delinquent, because she wants money or favours from the man and so on. The point I am driving at is that a woman's sexual behaviour is no sure guide to her real sexuality. For example, many promiscuous girls are relatively sexless and incapable of orgasm. A man with an equivalent disability would quite probably be impotent. We can thus distinguish between sexually motivated and non-sexually motivated sexual behaviour in women.

Much of the sexual behaviour of the adolescent female is basically non-sexual. I don't mean to imply that she doesn't necessarily enjoy it in a sexual sense – but her prime aim is not sexual, although it may appear so due to the influence of conventions which require a girl to love the man with whom she has intercourse. Many mid-adolescents live up to this theme, but its transparency is revealed by the ease with which they can quickly find a replacement after the loss of a partner!

Your girl seems to be much more natural than this and to behave as she feels. She is immature, or her behaviour is immature, and is not over-laid by the apparently sexual but basically non-sexual behaviour found in less natural and more 'sophisticated' girls.

Although such girls may stick – for a spell – to one boy, their fantasies are about many boys and about orgies. Their behaviour is not maturely sexual but is often impelled by a desire to spite the mother, a desire to attach a boy to herself in order to show him off to other girls, by curiosity and by guilt about self-masturbation. Your girlfriend is still in the stage of orgies and sex games. She is not ready for a one-to-one relationship and cannot establish a make-believe one as other girls might. She is probably still uncertainly copying her sister but is deriving the same sort of pleasure from group nudity and sex games as she did when younger. What she did with you she could probably do with any boy she liked. Its significance resides within her own evolving sexuality and not in the relationship with the male. It is, in a sense, autosexual.

When she develops further her sexual feelings and emotions will turn outwards and she will then begin to abandon the present pattern of behaviour and will both need and seek an object for her love and sexual needs. Her behaviour will become genuinely heterosexual and will acquire a more compulsive character. She will begin to enjoy it much more. If you are still around, you may become the object but it is impossible to make a prediction. Choice, ultimately, is, or should be, based on personality and not simply sexual characteristics. Even if you es-

tablished a real heterosexual relationship, as opposed to the present friendly one, either of you might subsequently mature in a manner which would be just as likely to drive you apart as draw you closer together.

Whether she is worth waiting for only you can decide but from what you say I think it would certainly be prudent to keep at least an eye on her! However, you might still have to go through a period of disappointment since even when she does mature to the next stage of psychosexual development she might still wish to try out several males before she makes a final choice. In fact, she will do so if she is half as sensible as she sounds. Indeed, though, so might you.

SEX IN COMMUNES

After some months of confusion and introspection I am again as near as I'll ever get to being happy.

My tutors tell me my piano playing has recovered and is better than ever, my girlfriends say I'm not nearly so bitchy and my parents – when I see them – seem more able to talk to me.

I've gone to live in this sort of commune. It's not a real commune – we don't live off the land or anything like that. It's just a huge old flat with big rooms and a grotty bathroom in the student quarter in Glasgow. But we all – students and non-students – chuck in a fiver a week and Hamish who is older, organizes us into buying groceries, cooking, painting, etc. There are four girls beside me and nine fellows besides Hamish.

The attic flat is divided into rooms – cubicles more like – where you can be alone if you wish. If you close the door no one disturbs you but the large downstairs room all psycho-decorated has loads of mattresses and blankets and we usually doss there if we don't want to be solitary. The birds are fairly stable – only one has left since I came, but about once a month a man disappears and another takes his place. Myself, I really communicate with Hamish, Doug and Willie – and the girls.

Fiona is five months preggers. I never thought you could be preggers and beautiful but she's got a thing about pressures and prefers to go around starkers whenever possible. Her only worry is it's getting difficult to fuck now and soon may have to give it a miss.

Jean and Tillie go for each other a lot. They're the only ones who really dig a lesbian situation and only sleep with a fellow

338

once or twice a week or so. Funnily enough they are also the only ones who go for bras and knickers – and wear miniskirts and boots most of the time. They also have to spend hours in the bathroom.

I've never worn knickers since a terrible month with thrush shortly after I went on the Pill and got through a fortune in tissues and tampons; still, tights would cost more.

Lizzy is fairly new and goes a bundle on every sort of sex – oral, anal, anything.

Myself, I'm an old-fashioned girl and have all the kicks I need from cunt sex.

I haven't much pubic hair but my clit always shows and causes a lot of interest. Not that I really enjoy the licking and fiddling; I prefer to rub it hard on the base of a really big man.

Hamish is big and really makes me feel good. If I come in and no one is around and doss down in the big room I love to be wakened by him filling me up. Doug and Willie are small but go like mad, giving fantastic orgasms. The others are so-so.

They all love my nipples which show through any sweater and are really big when cold and aroused. I think it's because I've never worn a bra – since my boobs are soft and smallish.

I've never had any more thrush trouble since 90 per cent of my sex is with this lot, which is good, as I am very vagina oriented. Ever since I was a tiny tot I've loved something in it. I keep it clean now and uncovered (long dress usually) and get all tense after about 12 hours without sex.

Now everybody would like this life. We often fuck casually when listening to records, watching TV or just doing the chores. Tillie and Jean prefer the rooms when they go together but often join in on the living room couch or carpet when asked – for our rule is, never unreasonably refuse anyone in need.

Three of the men seem very homo at times and heterosexual at others, but my favourite three don't seem interested in the same sex scene.

I don't think more than a tiny proportion of the population – and then perhaps only for girls between 14 and 24 – could enjoy this commune scene. But for me, at the moment, with this hungry appetite, it's the greatest, the safest and the happiest. I'm sure I'll meet some fellow and really communicate in words and sounds – then sex will be the second thing in my life (after music). But until now it's never really got off the ground and my body scores every time after the words wear off. But I'm changing and each intellectual encounter gets stronger and I think I'll go off and marry by the time I'm 25 or 30.

I wish there had been something like this for me when I was 16 and wearing myself out with masturbation. All the boys at school were such amateurs and life was one long battle against parents, teachers etc. They don't understand that some folk are just born sexy and others aren't. It's not porno or 'bad' company – probably genes.

Miss C.C.,
Glasgow

We'd like to hear from more commune-dwellers about their lifestyle, pros and cons, so do please write to us. (Editor)

LIBERATED LADY

Reading some letters in *Forum* and also feature articles reminds me how an altered approach to life has changed my whole character and happiness.

At 21, two years ago, I was a very ordinary, very bored, pool typist in Britain's most ordinary town – Glasgow. Then my mother suddenly died and I seriously considered marrying a very ordinary young man – but fortunately did not, for I certainly did not really love him.

Then I read an article in a magazine by Germaine Greer about how girls are taken in by convention in matters of sex, marriage, careers, dress, etc. I was especially thrilled by her story about her gradual discarding of underwear and its commonsense sound.

I don't do things by half measures, so I chucked out my six bras, including an uncomfortable strapless one, a painful wired one and even a sexy black frilly one. At first I still wore a full length underslip but after a week this went too. By this time I had got accustomed to the feel of my 34in breasts bouncing all over the place. They felt stretched and even sore but I persevered stubbornly and it was all worth it when a new boyfriend first slipped his hand inside my blouse and was utterly thrilled to find I wore no bra.

Encouraged, I ventured to wear less robust jerseys and even blouses, in spite of the odd girlfriend or workmate commenting about my nipples showing 'disgustingly'. By this time, after a couple of months braless they rarely retracted completely so that they were much prettier.

I still occasionally wear a cheese-cloth blouse top but now prefer a blouse of stiffer texture because then, by merely leaning forward, I can be as sexy as I wish, letting my partner glimpse my nipples, but by keeping more straight-backed can be as demure as I wish. I now find my boobs are at least 35in and have a distinct monthly cycle of tenderness. (To return to a bra now would be a form of self-torture.) They are never really sore when running or dancing – only temporarily tender if a boyfriend has been particularly carried away.

About two months after the bras went, my pantie-girdles followed, and then I started to feel like a natural human being – especially when my tummy actually became *flatter*!

My panties followed since I went on a long dress spree and one brave day I went nude under my long frock. It was hot and I felt good but very self-conscious. Within a few weeks I had the courage to go to work like this and have rarely worn anything since beneath my skirt.

There were problems, but they were nothing to set against the joy of being nude under my frock when out with a groovy boy (they all seemed more sophisticated now) and the general feeling of freedom.

The biggest problem was jeans and slacks, at first. I had terrors of staining them, but found a paper tissue made a temporary plug. Shortly the fact that I was now more particular about hygiene gave me confidence and with a frock on I only ever needed a tissue if I got very turned on by a man (usually in a situation and at a time when it did not matter anyway!) At first I had to continue using knickers at my period time, but, as my sex life increased till I had to go on the Pill, my periods became less of a sudden flood and more of a nearly painless flow controllable by frequently changed (big) tampons. Now I wear no knickers and have plenty of fresh air and *no smell*!

I was on holiday before I got the courage to wear a mini-skirt again and now I love to, often because if I wear a very short tight one I have full freedom of movement and no problems if the wind blows – yet if I wish to I can bend over instead of bending the knees, or sit low, legs apart, knowing the man concerned can enjoy seeing what he wants of me. In an instant, I can be discreet and conventional again.

I have worn crochetted and flimsy dresses at the odd party (I have very dark pubic hair) but, on the whole, I prefer to be able to turn on or off my display at will.

Before long, I was asked to model by a boyfriend who was a car salesman – for a new car – and the photographer took my name and address and started occasionally offering me jobs (no – he wasn't interested in sex with me, I think he could choose from many and his wife was the prettiest, sexiest thing I've ever seen).

Eventually, I was asked to pose topless, then completely nude. I was terrified but in fact really enjoyed it. I noticed that any time I worked with a real pro model (my photographer often used amateurs) they never wore underwear except, obviously, for bra adverts and the like.

I have always been sexy but was earlier frustrated for lack of the chance to be so with interesting as opposed to randy men. I have now found myself and have no problems meeting the sort of man who appeals – even if now I am considering going to live with one man who has everything, as far as I'm concerned.

There must be the odd person horrified to find I wear no bra and that up my skirt is only pubis, rather than pants – but they have given up registering their disapproval – and approval I don't mind. I can tell anyone it takes a lot of determination to persevere to make the change but, having gone so far, nothing on earth would persuade me to revert to the old way of dress (and life).

Miss D.S.,
Glasgow

SCOTTISH COMFORT
Much has been said in recent issues of *Forum* concerning the female bra, but I only recall one letter mentioning the need for the male to enjoy sexual comfort also.

Before I got married I wore normal cotton underwear and was a typical Y-Front male. My wife however complained at what she called my lack of sexual awareness and resolved to put matters to rights. Unknown to me she bought and put in my wardrobe some nylon and satin underwear consisting of vests, boxer shorts and briefs. At the same time she threw away all my cotton underwear. Initially I protested but as the only alterna- tive was to go out feeling 'naked' I was persuaded to get 'with it'. At the time of the discovery I was unclothed and completely unaroused sexually. I put on the vest and then a pair of shorts

342

and as I walked across the bedroom to get my trousers the movement of my circumcised penis against the smooth underwear gave me an instant erection, much to my wife's amusement and pleasure. Having regard to my obvious excitement she made me change into a very close-fitting pair of briefs, commenting that I might be embarrassed if the same thing happened when I was running to catch the train.

The revelation of the importance of male sexual comfort did not end there. Some months later my wife, instead of hiring a dinner jacket suit for a formal dinner, hired for me Scottish Highland Dress, which I had never previously worn. By this time I had learnt to cope with sudden stimulation at unexpected moments and can only say that the cool free sensation of wearing a kilt properly without underwear was entirely pleasurable.

I have now bought my own kilt which I wear on every possible occasion. There is little doubt that after being trouserless for a few hours one's libido increases immensely. The effect after wearing a kilt for several days is even more marked. Initially, one feels somewhat self-conscious, but eventually an overall sense of self-confidence develops and I cannot but claim pleasure at the stares I get when south of the border knowing full well that the girls are all wanting to know the truth behind the eternal question. Those north of the border know the answer and I have never met a Scotsman yet who has refused to let a girl find out for herself! Initially upon donning a kilt, for several hours or days, one is aware of a near painful sensation as one's testicles drag down the scrotum to unaccustomed low levels, but this serves to heighten sexual awareness and, no doubt as a result of keeping the scrotal area cool, heightens one's sexual capacity many times over.

My wife of course goes braless and I confess immense gratitude to her for revealing to me how men can improve their sexual comfort also. Certainly our sex life had never been as good before I was 'educated'. It would be interesting to know the experience of other readers.

W.I.,
Edinburgh, Scotland

HIGHLAND FLING

Your recent Swedish correspondent should not worry about being unable to provide for her family the chance of a natural sexual development, now she has moved to Britain. Even in Presbyterian Scotland it can be done.

There are dozens of remote lakes where one can camp and swim, fish, sail naked and untroubled in a climate almost as good as Sweden's. We do this with our own four children, our neighbours' two and the odd friend of the children.

Our pattern of living is also different but practical. We bought an old house with a secluded garden and gutted it. By the time our first-born arrived we had knocked down walls and had our own bedroom made. By the time our second child was old enough the pair were moved into a large children's room. The children have never been barred from our bedroom and all four take an interest in our lovemaking, pregnancies, breast-feeding, etc. We made an open plan bath and shower area and since we sleep naked, often walk around the house or even the garden unclothed. The children's room has two double beds and two single and none belongs to anyone. The youngest daughter often prefers to sleep alone but it is not uncommon for the two boys to join the elder daughter of 14 in bed.

Our best friend travels a lot for his work and his three children have lately been coming to stay with us for days or weeks on end, to let their parents travel together.

The first time, pushed for furniture, we dumped a couple of double mattresses on the den floor and left them to it. Since then we notice the older cousins sometimes sleep together, my daughter and their son usually do so.

They never really seem to quarrel and when we go camping insist we take the big old ridge tent for them.

Now our family has always discussed sex along with the weather, the butcher's order and homework, etc, so we know that our 14-year-old blames french letters for not having frequent orgasms. We disagree and are reluctant for her to go on the Pill till she is having a more frequent sex life.

She was, however, very accommodating, helping her young brother with his first penetrations. He in turn however has not been so helpful with his young sister who though only inter-mittently interested in sex, had to bribe him to take time and enter her properly. I think it's marvellous when a family pass on their experience and incest soon dies a natural death as soon as a more interesting external relationship appears in the offing.

I am sure this is a healthy attitude to life and encourage it. I think soon my elder daughter will want her own room and we can provide this in a few weeks with partitioning. I don't see her

344

ever wearing a bra. She has never had any time for sanitary towels and though she seems more interested in long frocks than trousers I doubt if she will spend much of her allowance on knickers or tights. The eldest boy seems to be more interested in sports than girls at the moment but the girl is beginning to bring boys to the door. We will face the next development here when it comes but wonder if she may have to adjust to a not very tolerant world very soon.

Mrs K.F.,
Ayr

I am sure a number of families behave as yours does and most of what you say makes sense.

However, what worries me is your involvement in your children's sexuality. Letting them see you naked and even letting them see you having intercourse is one thing but it is quite another for their sexual interests and activity to be a matter of such interest and comment by yourself. It is also possible that much of their activity may result from suggestions or advice given by yourself.

Children do have a sexual interest in their parents (and vice versa) so the parents must try to liberate the child sexually rather than risking its continuing to cling on to them, which can happen if they excessively excite or inhibit it in the course of rearing. Both practices can and do distort psychosexual development. The child must be allowed some real privacy in its sexual and emotional development otherwise it might never manage to detach itself and thereby later be incapable of either really loving or making love to a member of the opposite sex. In one sense there is no such thing as a 'natural death' to incest.

I do not think the environment you are providing is a 'natural' one. It sounds more like a hot-house for forced development! Persuading or encouraging children to do anything, let alone sex, before they are fully ready can harm them. I don't want to worry you but you have, if I understand you correctly, a daughter of 14 with orgasm difficulties, a 9-year-old daughter who is mainly disinterested in sex, a boy who needs bribing to attempt intercourse with a girl and another (or is it the same one?) who prefers sports – which can be a sign of a retreat from sex.

The dividing line between sex education and unwise encouragement is a fine one. I think you might possibly have gone too far and actually be obtaining too much of a thrill from your children's sexuality, especially that of your daughters, than is really wise. This may be causing you to overtly or covertly encourage them to undertake more activity than they really wish.

The final point is the one you raise in your last sentence. Rearing a child to very different standards of sexual behaviour from others runs the risk of leaving the child exposed to possible rebuff by others. One possible consequence, which may surprise you, is that it will leave the child underconfident in its relationships. Perhaps your daughter has very good reasons for not bringing her boyfriends any further than the front door!

Perhaps everything will work out well, but I would beg you to reconsider your behaviour in the interests of the children, and I would not advise other parents to emulate you. (Consultant)

A GAELIC CHILDHOOD

I came across some back numbers of *Forum* and as a very raw newcomer to London wonder if the artificial upbringing in the cities is responsible for many of the sex problems described.

Although I lead a very full life in this swinging city, I had never left my remote Scottish island till I was 15 – five years ago. The school had only 20 pupils aged from five to 15 and we did a lot as a school group. Most of our parents worked very long hours in the kitchen, on the land (croft) and as an extra at the fishing, so we children spent a lot of time together. We bought our clothes by catalogue and they were never very fashionable although after school we wore our older clothes and often went barefoot in summer. I never had a mini-skirt – only an old after-school skirt which had become too short.

It never occurred to anyone to buy a bra and we never missed them. In the summer holidays, since no one possessed a bikini or trunks, we swam naked and were always quite interested in which girl's boobies were growing and which boy had hair round his cock. Our parents must have known this, but never commented – although they must also have known we experimented with sex. In a farmyard atmosphere we all knew about periods and pregnancy from infancy and all knew that when periods became regular we daren't go all the way in the middle of the month.

We had no contraceptives, but we had no VD either. If you

could only use finger play one day you could have it all in the next week – it was a sign of being grown-up – being a big girl. The older girls of course screwed at any time.

Everyone knew who was in love with whom and pregnancy meant a ritual row with the parents, followed by an engagement ceilah, then a wedding. Houses were scarce and so was land, but children scarcer so pregnancy was really a source of joy. I don't remember anyone under 17 ever getting pregnant.

At 15 we went to secondary school on the mainland if we passed high enough. It was a grim life – the Islanders living in local authority hostels keeping together, often sleeping together and speaking the Gaelic which sadly kept us even more isolated from our classmates who were blasé about television, discos, etc, but led an uptight circumscribed life of discipline for its own sake, especially in things like school uniform, absence of proper sex, and the like.

Living a remoter life, most of us studied more and obtained above-average certificate passes. (This sadly meant going to Glasgow or Edinburgh University, joining the Civil Service, or the forces, so that the upper teenage population of the Islands is very low except during the holidays.)

Now working in the fleshpots (an enormous Civil Service office in London) I have no one to talk my native tongue to and find it easy to mix with the warm and friendly Londoners.

Yet, I wonder if my London workmates are really as liberated as they imagine. They seem to have spent so much of their lives aboard a bus, they've done nothing, read nothing and are only in touch through TV. More than half seem to be virgins when they leave school, and make a very emotional mess of their first affairs.

They get excited about going braless to the office (to me wearing a bra would be like the Chinese binding the feet – absolutely mad!) They spend more on stuff to rub into their already clotted pores than I send home and they wonder why my skin always looks natural. They get excited about going knickerless to a party when I couldn't afford the money to buy knickers in the first place (at home we took them off before scrambling down the rocks, or into the bushes, or having sex play in case we damaged them).

Yet they keep getting pregnant, catching VD, or groaning about aching tits or itchy crotches.

How I love the life here. It's great, but even if I am a 'country cousin' with a funny accent whom the fellows are all anxious to screw, I don't think I've missed anything from my childhood out in the sticks. In fact, I think I've had it better than most of my new friends.

Miss F. McN.,
London

Note: Almost every letter in this book deals with more than one sexual feeling or behaviour pattern. Many cross-references are given; however, the reader who wishes to search out any specific topic should look for it under related subject headings.